Marketing Calculator: Measuring and Managing Return on Marketing Investment

Marketing Calculator: Measuring and Managing Return on Marketing Investment

Guy R. Powell

John Wiley & Sons (Asia) Pte. Ltd.

This publication is designed to provide accurate and authoritative information with regard
to the subject matter covered. It is sold with the understanding that the Publisher is not
engaged in rendering professional services. If professional advice or other expert assistance
is required, the services of a competent professional person should be sought.

Other Wiley Editorial Offices

John Wiley & Sons, Inc., 111 River Street, Hoboken, NJ 07030, USA
John Wiley & Sons Ltd., The Atrium, Southern Gate,
Chichester, West Sussex PO19 BSQ, United Kingdom
John Wiley & Sons (Canada) Ltd., 5353 Dundas Street West, Suite 400, Toronto, Ontario
     M9B 6H8, Canada
John Wiley & Sons Australia Ltd., 42 McDougall Street, Milton, Queensland 4064, Australia
Wiley-VCH, Boschstrasse 12, D-69469 Weinheim, Germany

Library of Congress Cataloging-in-Publication Data

ISBN 978-0-470-82395-8

Typeset in 11/12 point, ITC Garamond by Superskill Graphics Pte. Ltd.
Printed in Singapore by Markono Print Media Pte. Ltd.
10 9 8 7 6 5 4 3 2 1

DEDICATION

To my wife, Karen, for putting up with me.

To Robert, Collin, and Kristin.

To the children of the United Methodist Children's Home. The mission of the United Methodist Children's Home is to serve the needs of children and their families in crisis. Ten percent of the royalties derived from the sale of this book will be contributed to this worthy charity. If you would like to learn more about the United Methodist Children's Home, please contact it directly at 500 S. Columbia Drive, Decatur, GA 30030, or www.umchildrenshome.org.

CONTENTS

ACKNOWLEDGMENTS

My greatest thanks and appreciation go out to many marketers who have helped me to write this book. Some of them helped directly—many indirectly. Having trained many, many marketers in workshops around the world, each of their questions and concerns helped me to keep searching for new ways to explain the concepts of marketing effectiveness. The methods I devised for explaining each of these concepts are incorporated into the writing for this book.

Initially, Ken Karakotsios and Jack Koch and, later, Doug Chalmers of DecisionPower, Inc. provided input and insight into some of the advanced concepts concerning the chapter on consumer analyzers. Their new software helps marketers make better decisions in the face of uncertainty. We spent many an hour discussing and emailing different sophisticated marketing concepts.

Darren Choo, Ken Karakotsios, Tim Manns, Donna Peeples, Dominick Popielski, Gurdeep Puri, Aseem Puri, and others helped with the development of the case studies. Roy Young of MarketingProfs and Brian Carroll of InTouch, Inc. provided inspiration and input to complete the book and get it to the publisher. Sami Jajeh and Rory Carlton helped very early on with some of the concepts at a high level and helped me to crystallize them into a logical, presentable outline. Svy Nekrassas provided great feedback and kept the topics very practical. John Riddle provided valuable editing of the initial draft and helped to improve the writing in a number of areas. David Radin, Harry Crytzer, Karl Hellman, Greg Thompson, and Katie Kuppelweiser were kind enough to provide key feedback on specific topics in the book. Their input was very valuable in tightening up some of the explanations of certain concepts.

Sajan Koch, Claire Koch, and Ramesh Sundararajan of InsightAsia helped with gaining valuable input from the Asia-Pacific region for the book and in the development of its marketing plan.

Lastly, thanks go to Laura Gallagher. She spent a lot of time helping with the editing of the copy to make sure I got the text clear and grammatical. I still don't know if I will ever understand all of the English grammar rules that have plagued me since second grade.

PREFACE

The concepts in this book have been honed through countless marketing-effectiveness workshops, presentations, and consulting projects, both in the U.S. and other countries. These concepts have been presented at many symposia, conferences, and expositions. Most importantly, they have been used to drive increased marketing return on investment (ROI) for many organizations— organizations of many different types and sizes, in many different types of marketing environments. There have been very few, if any, industries not involved in one of these sessions. These materials reflect both the input and the results of those training sessions.

Four key concepts have been presented for the first time in written form in this book:
- The marketing-effectiveness framework
- The marketing-effectiveness continuum
- Last-touch attribution
- The marketing-accountability framework

They build on other strategic and tactical marketing concepts that you are, or should be, familiar with. If you can internalize these four concepts and implement them within your organization, they will help you to prove and improve your marketing effectiveness and ROI.

Many of the concerns a marketer has with marketing effectiveness surround the never-ending battle for truth, justice, and the right versus left brain. Those of us that are left-brained don't have any trouble with analytics. We love numbers. Those of us that are right-brained love abstract thought and concepts.[1] We're creative and express things in nonnumeric terms. However, successful marketers must have synapses firing on both sides of their brains. Marketers must not only develop creative ways to communicate with their customers, but now they must also analyze their results in order to measure what they've done, compare them against plan, determine what worked and what didn't, and then iterate for the next round of improvement. Marketers must combine both creativity and analytics. This book will help them do just that.

Those marketers delivering both creativity and analytics will be highly successful and will uncover many latent nuggets of gold.

They will see revenue, profit, and market share grow faster than the competition. They will build a competitive advantage that will be hard to beat. The C-suite will finally consider marketing as a critical investment in the path of corporate success. It will no longer be an expense to hide amongst the other overheads. Bonuses will grow. Your marketing will finally be recognized for the tangible success it brings to the organization. It will be on the critical path to success.

But the first step to improving your marketing effectiveness, especially for the more creative, is getting started. Think of it as the next level of creativity. Think of it as bringing creativity to analytics. JUST GET STARTED!

ENDNOTE

1. Funderstanding, "Right Brain vs. Left Brain," http://www.funderstanding.com/right_left_brain.cfm.

SECTION 1
WHAT IS MARKETING EFFECTIVENESS?

1

INTRODUCTION TO MARKETING EFFECTIVENESS

What truly drives competitive advantage in today's world? How does your company stay ahead when your nearest competitor can simply copy your product's features, and put an improved version on the market a few months after your launch? If it's true that a company has two, and only two, basic functions—innovation and marketing[1]—and innovation can only provide a fleeting advantage, then it is up to marketers to deliver a competitive advantage through improved marketing.

- There are certainly **product differentiators**—Microsoft was able to win the operating system and desktop productivity wars with a superior product, great marketing, and "stick-to-itiveness." When the Microsoft juggernaut comes to your category, watch out or you will be lying by the wayside.
- There are **messaging and creative differentiators**—Witness the success of the Aflac Duck, which catapulted the

company from an annual pre-duck growth rate of 12 percent to a post-duck growth rate of 28 percent in the first year and 29 percent in the second.[2]

- You can **monopolize the messaging medium**—Most of the available baseball, football, and basketball stadium-naming opportunities are gone. The purchase of rights to a sports stadium, such as AT&T Park in San Francisco,[3] allows that company a messaging channel that cannot easily be duplicated by their competitors. That's why these opportunities are so hot—as are product placements in movies, music videos, and electronic games.

- There are **pricing differentiators**—Wal-Mart has built one of the world's largest companies by putting all of their promotional dollars, their economies of scale, and their enormous purchasing power directly into lower prices.

- There are **channel differentiators**—Companies can be more successful selling through one channel than another. Amazon.com has the online book category locked up, though they are no longer limited exclusively to books. Barnes & Noble is catching up online, but has also been able to maintain its position in the bricks and mortar channel.

But can your marketing effectiveness also drive incremental profit, market share, and revenue increases? Can the way you manage, measure, and execute the business of marketing also lead to continuously improving corporate results?

Your ad agency gets paid the big bucks to come up with those incredibly creative, ingenious, and novel commercials. Their "out-of-the-box" thinking can really pay off in the overcrowded and cluttered advertising space—creating increased awareness, brand equity, and imagery scores envied by the rest of the category. But it is possible that you can achieve even greater returns by properly timing (or flighting) and coordinating your media across all appropriate media channels, while simultaneously focusing on pricing, product, and channel initiatives.

Can you drive even greater returns by understanding the future? With a detailed knowledge of how consumers will respond to competitive, channel, exogenous, and other consumer actions, can you minimize risk and optimize your marketing across a set of expected scenarios?

This book will enable you to frame your thinking about marketing and marketing effectiveness. It will show you that marketers need to optimize their actions on a number of different levels. In an ideal world, with perfect information, in which the entire company marches to very specific orders from "on high," it might be possible to achieve some unsurpassable level of marketing performance. We "mere mortals," however, must work in an imperfect world, with imperfect information, and with managerial imperfections—yet still deliver extraordinary results.

Companies optimizing the way they execute their marketing typically see several percentage points in increased market share. That's what this book is about. It's about a methodology and framework that will allow you to manage the business of marketing to deliver the next level in marketing effectiveness—even in the face of imperfect information and an imperfect organization.

Improved marketing effectiveness is not just a tactical advantage: it is also a strategic advantage. How do we know this? In this world where there is little difference between competitive offerings, how can one vendor grow market share while others lose share? If one competitor is able to grow share by managing the business of marketing better than the competition, then they have delivered a strategic advantage in the marketplace. This is the power of getting it right, not only in the design and execution but also in the follow-on measurement and management. We can turn improved marketing tactics—based on a science of improved marketing effectiveness—into an engine that drives growth in revenue, profit, share, and stock value.

This book explains how smart marketers drive continuous improvement in their operations in order to beat shareholder expectations and grow their stock prices faster than the rest. By executing marketing activities with a given strategy more effectively than the competition, marketers can deliver higher revenue for the same dollar invested, more profit, higher growth, and greater market share—and at a lower level of risk.

This book is applicable to all businesses and organizations—whether small, medium, or large; whether manufacturer, channel, or service provider; whether business to consumer, business-to-business, ingredient brands, original equipment manufacturer (OEM), or cause marketer/political entity—this book provides insight into how to drive more revenue, profit, growth, and share for the same marketing dollar.

Results can be spectacular. My own experience has proven that the application of these concepts can deliver multiple share points for a consumer package goods company and US$100–120 million in incremental revenue opportunities for a quick-serve restaurant chain without any increase in the marketing budget. I've attached a series of case studies illustrating similar gains across a number of industries and continents. You can finally find the 50 percent of your marketing that isn't working.

ISSUES AND OBJECTIONS

Many issues concern marketers when it comes to improving marketing effectiveness. Having spoken with thousands of marketers, I've summarized most of them into just a handful:
- "Is there a way to establish a direct cause and effect link between marketing and revenue?"
- "How do I overcome the lack of available data?"
- "Is there a way to implement a test program to determine marketing effectiveness?"
- "How can I use analytical rigor to help grow the business?"
- "How can I evaluate the ROI of past programs and project the ROI for future programs?"
- "How can I predict the success of, and optimize the launch of, a new brand or product?"
- "How do I juggle marketing investments between longer-term brand building and shorter-term, direct-response marketing?"
- "Are there any tricks to collecting accurate tracking data from the sales force?"
- "How do I allocate spending between local versus national initiatives?"
- "Will I need to change my strategy in order to implement improved marketing effectiveness?"
- "Is there a way to develop consistent success metrics across the globe?"

These are all valid issues representing real concerns that marketers have about improving marketing effectiveness. This book is designed to help marketers to understand the answers to each of these questions and to develop an approach to building an infrastructure of continued learning and improvement. When asked how to eat an elephant, the smart answer is "one bite at a time." Improved marketing effectiveness, and its many nuances, can lead to great learning and an improved organizational infrastructure. Just get started: one bite at a time.

Probably the biggest and most frequently voiced objections are:
- "We can't afford the data. We would rather spend that money on more marketing."
- "We can't get the data. Our retailers are afraid they will be revealing trade secrets to us."
- "Using a more analytical approach in marketing is too radical. We believe only great creative[4] can produce great results."

Yes, it is true that improved marketing effectiveness takes money, time, and effort. "There ain't no such thing as a free lunch."[5] But the payoff can be big: higher revenue, bigger budgets, more responsibility, and larger bonuses.

After completing an exhaustive, US$5 million analysis of their marketing, Yahoo! reallocated US$40 million toward clearly defined marketing tactics. "If you got US$40 million on a blunt instrument, what can you get on an instrument that's really well defined or at least better defined?"[6] asked Jeannie Bunker, Yahoo! Vice President, Marketing Execution and Customer Analytics.

Brand advertising and marketing effectiveness

Why do marketers spend money on brand advertising, as opposed to direct-response marketing? Why spend money on marketing activities that aren't expected to deliver direct and immediate results, especially when the vice president of sales, the CFO, and the CEO want results and "want them now!"?[7] Why take precious budget money and spend it on things that may deliver results, but not this month, this quarter, or even this year?

There are many reasons why we spend money on brand marketing. Some of the reasons include:
- **To generate long-term revenue**—though short-term revenue is also generated. Marketing must not only help deliver sales this period, they need to set up the company for success next period, and the one after that.

- **To improve the response to direct marketing**—over what you would achieve without the brand-advertising support. Brand marketing typically will directly improve the results of direct marketing. Increase the value of the brand and the response from direct marketing efforts improve. Integrated marketing campaigns build on this concept, in which the investments in each of the individual media channels are intended to support each other to deliver better results than those obtained by advertising in one channel alone.

- **To be able to charge higher prices**—Consumers and businesses buy not just on price, but also on value. They need to be convinced that they are getting some additional value for one "equal" product versus another. For consumer marketers, how can Nike, for example, charge US$129 for a pair of sport shoes, when you can buy an equivalent pair of imported knock-offs for US$29? In the consumer's case, there is some extrinsic value in the Nike brand that allows the company to successfully charge an additional US$100 over an imported knock-off. For business-to-business (B2B) marketers, a similar phenomenon exists, although the reasons may be different in terms of how employee decision makers evaluate risk and job security versus the functionality and cost of ownership of a product or solution. For example, for years IBM was a safe bet because "you can't get fired buying IBM."

- **To be able to gain access to specific channels of distribution**—This applies more to smaller manufacturers, but could also apply to larger manufacturers that may be perceived to be dropping a brand. Unless the distribution channel is convinced that the manufacturer will help them drive "pull" (i.e., consumers will be motivated to pull the product off their shelves), the channel will tend toward not carrying the product. If the manufacturer isn't going to support and invest in the product, why should the channel?

- **Because all other things are equal**—When the products and prices are equal in a highly contested category, brand advertising should increase the likelihood your product will be chosen.

ALIGNING MARKETING EFFECTIVENESS WITH BRAND STRATEGY

How does improved marketing effectiveness support your brand value? Marketing effectiveness is defined as making marginal improvements to the marketing mix. But what if those changes seem to indicate major shifts in one, or all, of the 4Ps[8] (Price, Place, Product, and Promotion), response to changes in the 3Cs (Consumer, Channel, and Competition),[9] or changes in exogenous factors (the 1E)? Should we make that change? By definition, the improvement of marketing effectiveness based on a model cannot, and should not, require a change in the strategy—that is, in the strategic position of the company or the brand. It should only require minor changes in the 4Ps or 3Cs in the context of that strategy. If, however, the model seems to indicate that the product has potentially been incorrectly positioned, then further analysis should be undertaken. The strategic position can change, especially when that change is supported by proper data-based analysis. Improved marketing effectiveness should not lead to major changes in the 4Ps, but only minor changes. For example, consider the following:

- **Price**—A temporary price change can be considered as a tactical change; e.g., buy one get one (BOGO) free is essentially 50 percent off, but, for most brands, a permanent change of 50 percent would probably be considered a strategic change in position. For example, what would happen to Godiva Chocolatier's strategic position if they permanently dropped their price by 50 percent?
- **Place**—Adding incremental new channel and shelf space, or moving from the food and drug channel into convenience stores, can be in alignment with the strategy. Entering a whole new type of channel, on the other hand, may be considered a strategic change. For example, would Rolls-Royce change their strategic position if their cars were offered in Wal-Mart?
- **Product**—Adding new attributes to a product can be considered a simple competitive initiative or a competitive response, but doesn't necessarily change the strategic position of the product or brand. These attributes could be additional scents, flavorings, or software features. For example, The Coca-Cola Company's offering of Cherry Coke might be more strategic than their later offering of Diet Cherry Coke.

- **Promotion**—Changing the flighting or media spend levels would normally be considered a tactical change, but to stop advertising altogether for a heavily supported brand would be considered a strategic change. For example, if The Coca-Cola Company stopped supporting the Olympics, wouldn't that be considered a significant, strategic, board-level decision?[10]

Now consider a similar differentiation along the 3Cs dimensions:

- **Consumer**—Improved segmentation, based on lifestyles as opposed to demographics, would be a tactical improvement to drive incremental sales of electronic video games to teens and the X-generation. However, targeting these games to seniors in the "greatest generation" might be considered a strategic change. Responding to a consumer boycott of a specific brand or series of brands, such as French wines, could be considered either tactical or strategic, depending on the type of action taken.
- **Channel**—Developing a channel certification program that increases the number of certified value-added resellers would be considered a tactical change in the channel. Conversely, providing your software for download directly from your website might be considered a strategic change, designed to undercut and short-circuit your current channel partners.
- **Competition**—Responding to a temporary competitive price cut could be considered tactical, whereas permanently setting your pricing 20 percent lower than the competition might be considered more strategic.

There is a continuum of changes that can be made in any of the 4P or 3C dimensions: some more tactical in nature, some more strategic. As the analytics surrounding improved marketing effectiveness become more sophisticated, marketers can begin to make improved tactical and, sometimes, improved strategic decisions.

Marketing effectiveness: The new marketing imperative for the 21st century

In general, marketing has not been effective at driving consistent positive results. During the heyday of the late 1990s, spending exorbitant amounts of money on different marketing schemes was *de rigueur*. Millions were laid out to get those infamous 30 second spots at the Super Bowl. Now, of course, many of those companies have disappeared altogether.

The tech boom busted and many marketers were out of a job. September 11, 2001 put the U.S., and parts of the global economy, into a tailspin. Now, in order to keep our jobs, marketers have to prove our worth. We have to become more creative and deliver programs that can drive more revenue and profit at the same cost and we have to prove that they are better than any previous program.

Many statistics reveal the following:
- Thousands of products are launched and quickly fail.
- Most sales promotions lose money.
- Most advertising investments are wasted: "Half of my advertising is wasted; I just don't know which half."—John Wannamacher's famous quote.[11]

Management has even begun to lambaste marketers. The quote that probably goes to the crux of the situation comes from David Packard of Hewlett-Packard: "Marketing is too important to be left to the marketing department." Top management—the team responsible for the bottom line—is too gun-shy to leave the future of a campaign in the hands of a marketing team.

> **More money is wasted in marketing than in any other human endeavor (other than government, of course).**
>
> **Al Ries and Jack Trout,** *The 22 Immutable Laws of Marketing*[12]

How could the CEO and founder of one of the most successful technology companies in the world make a statement like this, if marketing had been doing the job it was supposed to be doing? Is this the plight of marketers? In all but a few companies, marketing has done a bad job at selling its results back to the rest of the company. Are their results really that bad?

Marketing spends most, if not all, of its time understanding the requirements and language of the company's external consumers, but little time understanding the needs and requirements of its internal consumers—the CEO, the CFO, and the other executives in the C-suite.[13] Understanding, measuring, and communicating the results of your marketing in terms that your internal consumers can understand is critical to increasing corporate results and lengthening your tenure.

How can marketers be satisfied with an average tenure for a CMO of only 23 months?[14] For those of us who are numbers-challenged, 23 months is the average. This means that many of the CMOs are in their positions for even less than 23 months—significantly less! And, to add insult to injury, this number is on the decline.

In order for marketers to stem the tide of shrinking tenures, we need to not only start delivering, but also to prove and improve the results of our marketing efforts.

THE US$1,000,000 QUESTION

How will you respond when the CEO comes to your office and says, "I want to give you an extra US$1 million for your budget?" Or, more importantly, how will you respond when the CEO asks, "Where should we cut US$1 million? Tell me why we shouldn't take it out of the marketing budget."

This book was written to help marketers answer this simple yet critical question. This question becomes even more important when it is put in the context of the shareholder. What would the shareholders rather have
1. increasing profits with flat revenue or;
2. increasing profits and increasing revenue?

The only department in the company that can deliver both increased revenue and increased profit is marketing, which I am defining here to include the personal selling—or sales—

function. In the accounting department, purchasing a cash management system can only drive costs lower. In manufacturing, installing a new, faster machine can increase capacity and lower manufacturing costs. Neither of these investments can drive increasing revenue. Only investments in marketing can do that—yet for many companies marketing budgets are the first to be cut and the last to get incremental investments. Clearly, marketing has not done its job at promoting its own effectiveness to those that count—the CEO, the CFO, and the rest of the C-suite. An inability to measure results is no longer an acceptable excuse. "I can't get the data" has to be removed from our vocabularies. We need to replace it with "this is our success metric and here is how we are going to measure it."

We need to answer the above question with a response such as, "If you cut the marketing budget by US$1 million, we will see a decline in revenue of US$6 million over the next four months." If we're able to answer this simple question in this fashion, the CEO will go looking somewhere else for that infamous US$1 million.

WHAT IS MARKETING EFFECTIVENESS?

The purpose of marketing effectiveness is to optimize *marketing spend* for the *short and long term* in support of, and in alignment with, the *brand strategy* by building a *market model* using *valid and objective marketing metrics and analytics.*

- **Marketing spend**—This includes all consumer-facing investments made to drive incremental revenue and profit. Kotler defines these as direct marketing, public relations, channel promotions, advertising, and personal selling.[15] But they must also include customer service and support, as well as marketing to the social network.
- **Short and long term**—Marketing has to make the right decisions to drive incremental short-term results, such as revenue, profit, cash flow, or share, and to put the company into a position to reap long-term results.
- **Brand strategy**—Actions to drive incremental marketing effectiveness must never change the strategic position of the company, product, or brand. If the results of the analysis indicate that a change in brand strategy may be called for, then this is now well past the confines of the definition of

improved marketing effectiveness. It doesn't denigrate the need for strategic change; it just means that the discussion and analytics must proceed to the next level of complexity.

- **Market model**—Having a model of what works and what doesn't, and by how much, allows marketers to make the right marketing decisions. By developing marketing plans that spend in the right areas, in the right amounts, and at the right time, marketers can deliver extraordinary results.

- **Valid and objective marketing metrics and analytics**—Models of consumer response to marketing stimuli must be based on the right data, the right metrics, and the right analytics. "The evidence tells the story," states Grissom from the popular television series, *CSI: Crime Scene Investigation.* If there is any hint of unsound analysis of the evidence, Grissom's conclusions will be thrown out of court. For marketers, the decision process will be stymied and marketers might as well go back to making marketing decisions based solely on gut feel.

CALCULATING ROMI

Marketing effectiveness based on sophisticated measurement, metrics, and analytics had its origins in direct mail. Direct mail marketing professionals would code individual pieces, test different color combinations, alter the call-to-action, and modify other creative elements to drive incremental response rates. They were able to gauge the cost of the creative development, the metrics, and the production costs against the expected response rates, the cost of the offer, and the net revenue generated. This led to the ability to calculate ROI (return on investment), or ROMI (return on marketing investment), based on incremental revenue and contribution margin. Those companies with lifetime revenue streams, such as banks and insurance providers, were even able to calculate marketing effectiveness based on net present values of the incremental cash flows generated. The study of marketing effectiveness was born.

Sample ROMI Calculation:
Creative development and production cost of 100,000 direct marketing pieces: US$100,000
Expected response rate: 1.5%
Expected purchase rate by respondents: 33%
Expected average net revenue (net of shipping and handling): US$1,495
Expected average contribution margin percentage (of revenue): 25%
Total expected revenue: US$740,000
Total expected contribution margin: US$185,000
ROMI (revenue-based): US$7.4 (=US$740,000/US$100,000)
That is, for every dollar invested, 7.4 dollars of incremental revenue were generated and directly attributable to this program.
ROMI (contribution margin-based) = 1.85
(= ROMI revenue-based/100 * 25%)
That is, for every dollar invested, 1.85 cents of incremental profit were generated and directly attributable to this program.
ROI = 85%
(= ROMI contribution margin-based–1.00 * 100)
That is, for every dollar invested, 85 cents of incremental profit were generated and directly attributable to this program.

Marketing effectiveness has two primary components: optimization of the consumer-facing actions (direct marketing, public relations, channel promotions, advertising, personal selling, and customer support and service) and the organization of the infrastructure to support the optimization of these actions. This book will focus primarily on the optimization of the consumer-facing marketing actions. A future book will discuss the optimization of the infrastructure.

THE ROI OF MARKETING ROI

Focusing on marketing ROI and metrics can yield big payoffs:
- Reduction of inefficient spending
- Reallocation of marketing spending to improved tactics

- Shortened marketing process times
- Growth in the top line
- Increased profit
- Marketing professionals who focus on marketing metrics and accountability earn more than those who don't

Reducing inefficient spending by reallocating the budget can have enormous implications. Internally, some groups, departments, and managers will lose influence, responsibility, personnel, and decision-making authority. Others will gain. Externally, agencies will lose spending by their clients—leading to lower commissions and potentially fewer personnel. The political battle for and against improved marketing effectiveness will have just begun.

Cutting marketing process time through improved workflow can also produce many benefits. The company can become more responsive to competitive threats. It can become more aggressive in the marketplace and overall costs can be reduced. I've seen savings of up to US$10 million in hard costs simply through the improved management of marketing assets in large automotive and financial organizations. Other soft costs, such as those saved through improved productivity, are also reduced. Marketing value is increased, including value generated through improved brand consistency or accelerated response to competitive actions.

Of course, growth and profit can be accelerated. *And, we can get paid bigger bonuses.*

Finally, marketers will be able to determine the value and effectiveness of brand marketing, as well as direct marketing.

MARKETING EFFECTIVENESS: THE NEW STRATEGIC ADVANTAGE

Often, when we think of strategic advantage we think of product differentiation, or the development of a differentiated brand value for a particular consumer segment, or many other combinations of real or perceived differentiation in the minds of the consumer. But, in many industries, very little differentiation is possible. For instance, what is the intrinsic difference between the ways that Verizon offers cellular service versus AT&T Mobility?

Both offer their services through company-branded retail outlets. Both advertise with similar messages. One has the fewest lost connections. The other has the biggest network. Although one may have a short-term advantage through exclusive deals with new cell phone models, does one or the other really have better coverage? Does one have a better product or service? Are there really significant differences in their pricing plans? Is customer service from one provider significantly different than the other? Can any of the 4Ps not be almost exactly duplicated by the other provider? Can the consumer really tell any difference?

Indeed, many industries face these same types of challenges. There is no underlying opportunity for the manufacturers to differentiate themselves, and yet each must continue to beat and exceed analyst expectations. Many have begun to do this through process automation, improved consumer service, and improvement in other areas. The last opportunity for them to make substantial improvements is now in their marketing operations and processes. The delivery of persuasive, effective communications into the marketplace can be optimized and enhanced in significant ways to drive increasing revenue, profit, cash flow, growth, and share at lower cost and risk.

Whether a company has a significant, perceived differentiation in the marketplace or not, it can develop a strategic advantage in the way it executes its marketing. In cases where there is little left to differentiate, strategic advantage can still be gained by doing one thing better than the competition.[16] It doesn't matter whether the company is a Fortune 100 consumer-packaged-goods (CPG) provider, a mid-tier OEM components provider, or a small business, as in each case it may have competitive advantage in its own category. But, in order to stay alive, it must continuously find new ways to deliver strategic advantage. The improvement of marketing effectiveness is that new strategic advantage.

Marketing effectiveness and marketing objectives

There are many objectives for marketing, but in particular they must include:

- The development, nurturing, and enhancement of the strategic positioning of the company's brands, products, and/or services in the eyes of their consumers.

- The development, nurturing, and enhancement of creative concepts to reflect the strategic positioning of the company's brands, products, and/or services in the eyes of their consumers.
- The expeditious definition and execution of marketing communication processes to meet and exceed corporate revenue and profit goals for the short and long term at low risk and least cost.

Marketing effectiveness is centered on the pursuit of these objectives—emphasizing the results and risk side of the equation. It includes the development and continuous improvement of the related infrastructure to support the pursuit of these goals, but it doesn't typically include the effective development of marketing strategy and creative concepts, although it could. For the purposes of this book, however, the effective development of the marketing infrastructure, as well as the effective development of the strategy and creative concepts, will not be discussed. Rather, this book concerns itself with the efficiency, effectiveness, and continuous improvement of the execution of the strategy and creative concepts in the marketplace.

MARKETING EFFECTIVENESS: A CHAPTER-BY-CHAPTER OVERVIEW

Marketing effectiveness has many facets. Use this overview to quickly find topics that would help further your understanding of marketing.

SECTION 1—WHAT IS MARKETING EFFECTIVENESS?

CHAPTER 1—INTRODUCTION TO MARKETING EFFECTIVENESS

Chapter 1 introduces the concept of the marketing-effectiveness framework. Each of the components of this framework are discussed. Many of these concepts may be familiar to most marketers, but they are presented here in the context of how to prove and improve marketing effectiveness. Once this framework has been explained, it is used throughout the book as a basis to get across the other marketing-effectiveness concepts. This section be a comprehensive review of key marketing concepts and will be a valuable foundation for all marketers.

SECTION 2—THE MARKETING-EFFECTIVENESS FRAMEWORK™

Marketing effectiveness can be improved in many ways. For example, it can be improved not only with a better strategy but also with better creative and tactics. In order to deliver increased marketing effectiveness, marketers must act in the marketplace, measure results, and then use the proper tools to analyze them. With the proper measurement and analysis of results, marketers can easily improve their strategy, creative, and tactics. The Marketing-Effectiveness Framework was developed to help marketers put structure around the ways they gather market data, analyze that data, and then improve strategic, creative, and tactical decisions.

For any marketing concept to deliver improved results, it must have the consumer at the center. Marketers can then develop their strategy, creative, and tactical activities to their advantage. Unfortunately, there are also other influences acting in the marketplace: there are other competitors, with their own strategy, creative, and tactics; the distribution channel; and exogenous factors, such as the weather, interest rates, and seasonality. Against these influences, consumers make decisions and respond. The Marketing-Effectiveness Framework describes the interaction of these influences on consumer response so that marketers can target improved results measurement and analysis to deliver improved marketing performance.

The following four chapters describe the Marketing-Effectiveness Framework, starting with a model of your own actions in the marketplace. The next chapter looks at how factors outside your control can be modeled, which is followed by a chapter on the modeling of consumer response. This section ends with a description of the marketing-accountability framework demonstrating how marketers should structure the way they capture data.

CHAPTER 2—STRATEGY, CREATIVE, AND EXECUTION: WHAT YOU DO IN THE MARKETPLACE

A marketer's actions are geared around three dimensions: strategy, creative, and execution. In order to understand marketing effectiveness, we need to understand where the levers of improved marketing effectiveness are located. Each of these dimensions influences the ability of marketers to prove and improve their marketing effectiveness.

CHAPTER 3—PLANNING AROUND WHAT YOU CAN'T CONTROL: THE COMPETITION, THE CONSUMER, THE CHANNEL AND EXOGENOUS FACTORS

Marketing effectiveness is driven not only by our actions, but by those of the competition, the consumer, and the channel, plus other exogenous factors that are outside of our control and our competitors' control. By understanding the impact of past influences, we can determine what their effect was on our marketing effectiveness. Looking to the future, we can use this information to develop scenarios that improve the ROI of marketing activities.

CHAPTER 4—THE CONSUMER: THE MOST IMPORTANT COMPONENT IN ANY MARKETING–ORIENTED FRAMEWORK

Only with a clear understanding of how consumers respond to market stimuli can we build an effective model of our marketing actions. A consumer-centric model, whether for business-to-business or consumer markets, is a must in order to fully understand the short- and long-term impact of marketing actions. Four dimensions of consumer response behavior are discussed, including consumer response to advertising information, consumer choice at both the brand and channel levels, and consumer purchase and consumption behavior.

CHAPTER 5—A FRAMEWORK FOR CAPTURING MARKETING-EFFECTIVENESS DATA THE MARKETING-ACCOUNTABILITY FRAMEWORK

In order to improve marketing effectiveness, marketers must capture data from many sources. The marketing-accountability framework provides architecture to help marketers structure the capture of that data and prioritize it so that they can progress along the marketing-effectiveness continuum.

SECTION 3—THE MARKETING-EFFECTIVENESS CONTINUUM

The marketing-effectiveness continuum covers many concepts critical to improving marketing effectiveness. It discusses how marketers can move from one level to the next in managing a complex organization to improve their performance. By taking small, defined steps, the organization can clear the path to measurable improvements. Lastly, the company can set short-, medium-, and long-term goals to understand how to achieve these advancements with a given level of investment in the organizational infrastructure.

Each of the chapters in the marketing continuum includes a cameo, based on real companies, to bring to life some of the challenges and insight that can be gained from each level of the continuum.

Presented at the end of each chapter are actual case studies from many different industries from around the world—each utilizing different analytic techniques. Because of the confidential nature of client relationships, the numbers, countries, categories, brands, and attributes have been disguised in some fashion to make certain that any presented information would not reveal any valuable, confidential knowledge about the categories and brands. In addition, data sources for some of the information have not been provided because they might inadvertently reveal the exact brand or brands discussed. However, data sources are standard sources in the industry, including Nielsen, TNS, IRI, Millward Brown, and many others.

Each of these case studies should be read and understood to uncover insights and methodologies that might help you in analyzing your own brands and categories. None of the numbers presented convey actual results from specific projects in the described markets. Currencies are expressed in U.S. dollars for the U.S. and in local currencies for other countries, or converted to U.S. dollars when the country is also disguised.

CHAPTER 6—INTRODUCING THE MARKETING-EFFECTIVENESS CONTINUUM

The marketing-effectiveness continuum helps marketers to set goals and determine concrete steps in order to continuously improve their marketing effectiveness. The five primary steps (activity trackers, campaign measurers, mix modelers, consumer analyzers, and brand optimizers) are introduced and explained. Organizational implications are also introduced.

CHAPTER 7—ACTIVITY TRACKERS
One of the key components of improving marketing effectiveness is to track all marketing activities taking place within the category. These include marketing's activities, as well as those of the sales and service functions. As the company gets more sophisticated in its marketing analytics, the activities of the competition, the channel, and, potentially, the suppliers must also be tracked.

CHAPTER 8—CAMPAIGN MEASURERS
Campaign measurers often use last-touch attribution to determine the impact of their marketing. This method can be very effective, especially for business-to-business marketers, to determine what works and what doesn't, and by how much. Here, marketers learn how this level of measuring marketing effectiveness can be used to support the management of complex organizations.

CHAPTER 9—MIX MODELERS
Mix modelers can determine the effectiveness of their marketing across the entire mix. With the right data, marketers can measure the effectiveness of most, if not all, of their marketing activities. Armed with this information, marketers can start to spend more on the right things and less on the wrong things.

CHAPTER 10—CONSUMER ANALYZERS
Consumer analyzers look to the future in order to develop scenarios and project the effectiveness of their marketing actions, given the expected actions of the competition, the channel, changes in the consumer base, and exogenous factors. At this level, marketers can make the best tactical decisions to launch new products, respond to competitive action, and understand how exogenous factors can influence the future of the market.

CHAPTER 11—BRAND OPTIMIZERS
At all prior levels in the marketing-effectiveness continuum, marketers are optimizing their marketing investments to drive increased revenue, profit, or market share. Brand optimizers

correlate the impact of their marketing activities against the value of the brand as it is expressed in changes in the value of the stock. This leads to the optimization of decisions for the long term and can help to determine the value of a brand to support mergers and acquisitions.

SECTION 4—THE MARKETING-EFFECTIVENESS CULTURE

Building a culture of continuous improvement in marketing requires a change in culture. Just as Total Quality Management and Six Sigma[17] processes improved the quality of output and reduced costs in operations, building a marketing-effectiveness culture can do the same for the marketing function. All marketers, including marketing managers, will find this section important in helping them to design their organization and determine compensation schemes.

CHAPTER 12—IT'S TIME TO JUST GET STARTED!

Achieving improved marketing effectiveness is not just about making a once only change in the analysis of marketing results. It is a continuous process, requiring training and organizational change to support continuous improvement. Regardless of the amount of data a company collects, there is always more data and analysis that can be done. Yet this must be tempered against the associated cost, potential benefits, and the risk.

CHAPTER 13—CONCLUSION: PUT MARKETING ON THE CRITICAL PATH TO SUCCESS

Marketing should no longer be considered an expense, but must be a considered an investment in the future of the company. It must be part of the critical path to corporate success. In so doing, companies can be more successful than the competition, and grow faster. Marketing effectiveness is a strategic advantage that can be continually improved to stay ahead of the competition.

Not only does improved marketing effectiveness have benefits for the company, it has benefits for the marketer. Those marketers who can prove the effectiveness of their marketing will earn more, and their careers will advance faster, than those who can't.

ENDNOTES

1. "A business has two, and only two, basic functions: marketing and innovation." Peter Drucker, author and management consultant.

2. Linda Kaplan Thaler, Robin Koval, and Delia Marshall, *Bang! Getting Your Message Heard in a Noisy World,* (New York: Doubleday, 2003).

3. And this may change again as soon as this book is published.

4. The word "creative" is often used throughout the book as a noun. Although traditionally used as an adjective, many marketers are now using it as a noun to describe the creative concept, the creative solution, or the creative result. For example Aflac's "duck" campaign represents great creative.

5. Robert A. Heinlein, *The Moon is a Harsh Mistress.* (New York: Orb Books, 1997).

6. Jeannie Bunker, Vice President, Marketing Execution and Customer Analytics, quoted in Scott van Camp, "Top Technology Brands are the Leading Early Adopters of MPM," *ChannelAdvisor,* May 19, 2005, http://www.channeladvisornews.com/story.cfm?item=18 (accessed January 27, 2008).

7. Roy A. Young, Allen M. Weiss, and David W. Stewart, *Marketing Champions: Practical Strategies for Improving Marketing's Power, Influence, and Business Impact.* (Hoboken, NJ, and John Wiley & Sons, 2006).

8. Philip Kotler and Kevin Lane Keller, *Marketing Management,* 12thed., (New Jersey: Prentice Hall, 2006).

9. Lawson Abinanti, Messages that Matter, "The 3C's of Successful Positioning - Part III: Get your channel involved in positioning. It's good for both of you," http://www.messagesthatmatter.com/columns/3Cs_of_Positioning_Part_III.pdf.

10. Yes, it would.

11. Rex Briggs and Greg Stuart, *What Sticks: Why Most Advertising Fails and How to Guarantee Yours Succeeds,* (Chicago: Kaplan, 2006).

12. Al Ries and Jack Trout, *The 22 Immutable Laws of Marketing: Violate Them at Your Own Risk!,* (New York: Harper Business, 1994).

13. The C-suite is made up of all the C-level executives in the company. These include the CEO (chief executive officer), COO (chief operating officer), CFO (chief financial officer), CMO (chief marketing officer), CIO (chief information officer), and others. This can also include titles such as, the president, senior vice presidents, and vice presidents acting as key executives in the organization.

14. Kate Macarthur, "No Respect From CEOs, Short-Term Thinking Depress Tenure," *AdAge.com*, June 19, 2006, http://www. accessmylibrary.com/coms2 (accessed January 27, 2008).

15. Kotler, op. cit.

16. Patrick Barwise and Sean Meehan, *Simply Better: Winning and Keeping Customers by Delivering What Matters Most*, (Boston: Harvard Business School Press, 2004).

17. Total Quality Management and Six Sigma define how quality management must be implemented throughout the entire manufacturing process. Manufacturers must monitor quality, and look for deviations in that quality, in order to deliver consistent quality of output. Six Sigma was originally developed by Motorola, the winner of the 1988 Malcolm Baldrige National Quality Award of the National Institute of Standards and Technology.

SECTION 2
THE MARKETING-EFFECTIVENESS FRAMEWORK™

STRATEGY, CREATIVE, AND EXECUTION: WHAT YOU DO IN THE MARKETPLACE

THE MARKETING-EFFECTIVENESS FRAMEWORK™

The Marketing-Effectiveness Framework™—also known as the Return on Marketing Investment, or ROMI, framework—provides a systematic approach that marketers can use to understand their marketplaces, the consequences of their own activities, and the activities of their competitors, in order to determine the relative effectiveness of different marketing investments. They can now understand the impact of the levers for improved return on investment (ROI) when developing their marketing plans.

By understanding the relative impact and effectiveness of marketing programs, executives can optimize their marketing investments to grow revenue at a lower cost, and with lower risk. Often considered an expense, marketing can now be seen as an investment—returns must be measured, proved, and improved. Marketing metrics and results measurement are key factors in determining which marketing activities should be undertaken and to what extent.

Recent surveys show that chief marketing officers (CMOs) view the measurement of marketing effectiveness as one of the most significant concerns in driving their businesses. The Marketing-Effectiveness Framework was developed so that marketing executives could evaluate their activities in a way that not only supports their key strategic objectives, but also allows them to squeeze maximum value out of every invested marketing dollar. The framework employs critical marketing metrics and a data-driven approach, while keeping the consumer at the center of the marketing efforts. No longer must there be a conflict between improving marketing metrics and maintaining consumer proximity.

The Marketing-Effectiveness Framework helps senior marketing executives to determine how best to invest marketing dollars. It helps to provide an objective answer to the question, "Why should we spend an extra million dollars on marketing? Why not invest it in operations to save costs or in product development to generate new capabilities and products? And, how can we feel confident when we make that investment that we will reap the expected benefit?"

The Marketing-Effectiveness Framework provides these answers and helps marketers to improve their effectiveness through a clearer understanding of their investment options and a metrics-based model of their effectiveness. The results are no less than astounding. Marketers can justify their budgets in good and bad economic times, defend them when the budget axe comes swinging, and earn higher salaries and bonuses throughout their careers.

The Marketing-Effectiveness Framework operates in two dimensions, which, when taken together, map the organization's marketing ROI and the effectiveness of its program investments in developing and managing the company's strategy, creative, and execution. It provides a path for moving along both dimensions simultaneously, in order to improve performance in achieving corporate goals.

The first dimension describes a model of the organization's marketing activities, and those of its competitors. Along this dimension are the various actions that a company can take to "get the word out"—to stand out amongst the clutter, to deliver superior value, and to meet evolving consumer needs.

The second dimension is that of the consumer, because successful marketing depends on a comprehensive understanding of the consumer. For this reason, the Marketing-Effectiveness Framework looks at awareness and brand equity, the purchase funnel, segmentation, product and channel choice, and consumer shopping and consumption behavior.

Marketers who can build a combined model in these many dimensions—that is, of themselves, their competition, and their consumers—will be able to leverage their marketing investments to deliver the most revenue and profit for their companies.

In many categories market data is limited or nonexistent, yet building even a partial model of your market based on the limited available data can lead to significantly improved results. For example, even a model of just your advertising activities (i.e., one that does not explicitly take the consumer or competition into account) can often help to improve the impact of the mix of advertising media employed. Not only will the return on marketing investment be improved, but also the model may uncover insight into the types of data that need to be collected in order to take it to the next level of value. Each of the case studies at the end of Chapter 8 operates at this level.

COMPANIES AND COMPETITORS

The Marketing-Effectiveness Framework designates three key elements that make up the hierarchy of key levers of a company and its market: strategy, creative, and execution (Figure 2.1).

STRATEGY

Models of business and marketing strategy abound; the most familiar are:

- The "4Ps" (product, price, place, and promotion)[1]
- The "Five Forces" model developed by Porter[2]
- The models defined by Moore in *Crossing the Chasm*[3] and *Inside the Tornado*[4]

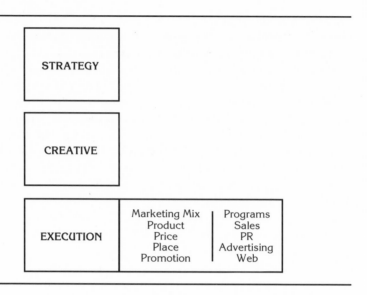

Figure 2.1: Marketing-effectiveness hierarchy within the Marketing-Effectiveness Framework™

This book will not explore these strategic models in depth; it is not written to help marketers to develop a strategy, but to explore how the chosen strategy impacts marketing effectiveness in the marketplace.

Strategy is not something that changes on a day-to-day basis; it generally follows these tenets:

- Strategy charts a course for a longer period. Just don't give up too early.
- Strategy should be sustained and built upon over a number of years. Look at the big picture.
- Strategy should be reviewed and, if necessary, adjusted on occasion, but in general should remain relatively constant. Keep a constant watch and observe.

If this is not the case, rapid and frequent changes in strategy may indicate that the company doesn't really have a strategy at all, or that what has been identified as strategy is in fact merely the quarterly or annual planning cycle.

In the context of the Marketing-Effectiveness Framework, the difference between strategy and execution is one of degree.

Incremental changes in one or more of the 4Ps can be considered simply an execution level change; whereas significant, long-term changes in any of the 4Ps would be considered a strategic-level change.

For example, the launch of a new product is, on the surface, considered a strategic decision. Significantly, changing the level of advertising, in combination with a significant price increase, could also be considered strategic. That is, in the eyes of the consumer, the position of the product in the category has changed. On the other hand, minor price promotions, such as "buy one get one free" (BOGO), are more tactical in nature. However, the move from never having offered a BOGO promotion to offering a first BOGO might be considered strategic if the product or brand image may be detrimentally affected by the perceived "cheapening" or "discounting" of the brand.

Hypothetically, you could imagine that if you ran the same marketing campaign in the context of a good strategy, you would get better results than if you ran the same campaign in the context of a bad strategy. This means that having a well-defined and effective strategy is one way in which you could improve your marketing effectiveness. So, strategy belongs at the top of the Marketing-Effectiveness Framework.

Creative

Good creative is critical to improving marketing effectiveness, and reflects the company or brand strategy in a message that the target consumer can comprehend, identify with, and be influenced by to take the desired action. Developing great creative concepts is at the top end of delivering marketing ROI, but the developments of a crisp subject line and call-to-action are also critical. Even the marketing implementation can be creative. I've watched the "Oprah Giveaway" of 276 Pontiac G5[5] cars many times, and each time I am astounded at the originality and bravado that went into that one marketing activity. If you are fortunate enough to find a good creative team, do whatever it takes to keep them on board!

While good creative should always work better than poor creative, great creative can change an industry. Think about any number of national campaigns that have had such a significant impact on the market. That's why great agencies are worth every cent they're paid. The best agencies can capture the essence of their client's strategy with a concept that quickly gains attention, develops interest, delivers desire, and, finally, leads to action.

The Aflac Duck is one of the best ongoing examples of great creative. People of all ages now recognize the quacking advertising icon. With this extraordinarily creative advertising campaign, the Kaplan Thaler Group, Ltd[6] took a conservative insurance company and put it on the map—literally turning Aflac into a household word. More importantly, though, it drove significant increases in marketing ROI. In the two "post-duck" years, sales growth reached 28 percent and 29 percent per year, compared with the "pre-duck" growth rate of only 12 percent— without any change in marketing investment! This incredibly aggressive and creative concept delivered extraordinary results. And, of course, everyone is trying to repeat the concept with the next great duck idea.

Great creative concepts don't come along every day. But the success of most creative can be significantly improved through proper copy and concept testing. Seemingly minor changes in creative can deliver greatly improved results in the marketplace.

After a campaign, ad response models can be built—allowing measurement of the impact of the specific creative concept. Being able to measure the response enables us to determine the value of the creative. In this way, the value of creative efforts can be compared from one campaign to the next. And, over time, with ongoing measurement, the level of saturation or wear-out of a particular campaign can be determined—signaling when to phase in new creative, or how to adjust spending and placement.

Although there may be exceptions—great marketplace successes that began with great creative and then were followed by strategy—all in all, first comes the strategy, and then comes the creative. Once your strategy has been properly defined and elucidated, creative follows. With both of these in hand you can now begin to plan your execution in order to deliver the best results possible at least cost and risk.

EXECUTION

Ninety percent, if not more, of the activities undertaken in marketing have to do with tactics and execution. Once the strategy has been set and the creative chosen, then the programs must be executed. If we are spending a disproportionate amount of time on strategy, then we probably don't have a strategy. We simply have a bunch of disjointed tactics masquerading as strategy. Creative, the top-level concept expressing the unique selling proposition of the brand in the marketplace, on the other hand, follows the strategy. This also shouldn't necessarily change that often.

Once the creative concept has been developed, we can go off and execute against that concept. We develop the flighting plan, we buy media, and we transform the creative into an integrated marketing campaign. We execute to deliver an effective marketing mix—defined by the 4Ps, 3Cs, and 1E—in alignment with the strategy that uses the creative concepts provided.

If genius is 10 percent inspiration and 90 percent perspiration, then once the genius in strategy and creative has been determined, marketers must spend 90 percent of their time perspiring over tactics and execution. If we can execute marketing programs well, we can continue to notch up results. But effective execution of a single marketing activity is not enough. Each marketing program is executed in the context of all other programs, competitive actions, and exogenous changes, and by the marketing infrastructure.

Marketers must get the mix of activities just right—spending just the right amount at the right time for the right activity in each area of the marketing mix in order to maximize returns.

Execution can be broken down into two areas: marketing mix and program execution. Improvement in each of these areas can help marketers produce and maintain superior results.

EXECUTION AND THE MARKETING MIX

At the execution level of the Marketing-Effectiveness Framework, we now consider its two main areas: marketing mix and program execution. For most marketing departments, one of the greatest opportunities for improvement is to properly orchestrate the marketing mix. An effective analysis of the marketing mix can reveal how much revenue or profit can be realized by every incremental dollar spent in each marketing channel. Although they aren't exactly the same, optimizing the marketing mix and optimizing integrated marketing campaigns go hand in hand.

Integrated marketing campaigns use multiple marketing media, such as TV, newspaper, and outdoor, to deliver a marketing message into the marketplace. They rely on synergies between media, diminishing returns, and other marketing media mechanics to improve results. The case studies at the end of Chapter 9 illustrate how four companies were able to improve their marketing mix using marketing–mix modeling.

Such analysis—for example, using a marketing-mix model—not only identifies which marketing programs deliver higher marketing effectiveness, but can also reveal the return for each of these investments in the context of raising or lowering prices, increasing or decreasing the level or type of distribution, or the addition or subtraction of product features. Accurate models of the marketing mix, built on valid metrics and analytics, are critical to achieving superior marketing results. The results of a proper marketing-mix analysis can lead to the optimization of the marketing mix along each of the 4Ps.

Too frequently, marketers confine their thinking to the pigeonhole of simple integrated marketing campaigns without considering all of the elements that touch the consumer. In many business-to-business companies, where the sale is converted through an inside or outside sales force, the personal selling function—the optimal balance between investing in sales versus investing in marketing—is not often sought. Instead, the personal selling function is considered separately from the marketing media components. The coordinated interaction that can be achieved between these two vital corporate functions is simply ignored. Because the sales team converts the order and registers the revenue, they often receive the benefit of the doubt in any analysis. Their proximity to the customer is hard to ignore. The sales team may acknowledge that marketing played a role in developing the lead or shortening the sales cycle, but determining the significance of each marketing activity, in combination with the personal selling function, is generally not undertaken.

The value of marketing, however, is undisputed. Just ask any sales team whether the investment in marketing should be cut down to zero. The answer will always be a resounding "no!" The question is then, "How much do we invest in marketing versus sales?"

Organizations with strong personal selling functions look to the marketing department to generate leads. The way for marketers to optimize their marketing is to accurately attribute the value of each lead source. Did the lead come from the direct mail program? Or was it the seven previous impressions of the print advertising, combined with the prior year's trade-show attendance, that prepared the prospect to finally respond when he or she answered the cold call from the sales team? Marketing-mix analysis can help marketers to determine the specific "lift" accorded to each marketing channel versus all others, even, and especially, as they run concurrently in the marketplace.

The gains can be significant when the true impact of each of the elements of the 4Ps is understood. With a more effective marketing mix, the corporate top and bottom lines can be easily grown.

While strategy determines the 4Ps in the strategic, long-term context, the marketing mix involves all elements of the 4Ps at an incremental level; that is, at the margin. While significant changes in the 4Ps must be considered strategic, marginal, incremental changes to the 4Ps—within the marketing mix at the execution level—can deliver greatly improved results while supporting and driving the strategy. For example:

- **Product**—Minor product feature changes can be included in a marketing-mix analysis. Examples of such incremental features might include the introduction of a salad menu in a quick-serve restaurant, a larger hard drive on a personal computer in the high-technology industry, or improved consumer satisfaction levels in a service business.

- **Price**—When considering price, it is important to deal consistently with either the absolute price or the relative price in the marketplace, including all channel-promoted prices, such as BOGO, "25 percent off if purchased before," or "6 months same as cash." It is always necessary to use the "sell-through" price or "point of sale" (POS) price—the price to the consumer, rather than the "sell-in" price—the price to the channel. Price is what consumers exchange for the value they receive from the consumption of the product or service. In most industries, price is nonzero. But there are industries where price is actually zero, such as television viewing and credit card usage. In fact, the price can even be perceived as negative in some industries. In particular, credit card users receive an apparent benefit—negative price—in the form of frequent flyer miles or other promotions for every dollar charged on many of their credit cards.

- **Place**—The distribution channel has a number of facets that come into play in improving the marketing mix. For fast-moving consumer goods, for example, distribution variables include the number of stores, placement (e.g., which aisle and shelf), availability, and display (e.g., end-cap) within the store. For business-to-business markets, distribution includes the type of channel employed, such as the Internet, sales agents, value-added resellers, or system integrators.
- **Promotion**—Marketing-mix analyses include both mass media activities that are intended to generate brand awareness, such as TV advertising and PR, and direct-response marketing activities, such as direct mail, coupons, e-mail, and online advertising. Many analyses also consider the specific creative campaign, providing the ability to determine which creative delivered the best results.

Marketing-mix models also allow the marketer to determine potential synergies between marketing channels. For example, can the print advertising campaign achieve a higher impact when run concurrently with TV advertising? If so, how can we plan the individual marketing channel programs and flighting to take advantage of these synergistic effects? Additionally, marketing-mix models provide the determination of the halo and cannibalization effects between products or brands. For example, does an advertisement promoting the BMW Z4 Roadster that delivers consumers into the showroom positively or negatively affect sales of the BMW 3 Series or the 5 Series? Does it deliver halo or cannibalization? Does the effect vary by region?

EXECUTION AT THE PROGRAM LEVEL

The second main area of execution within the Marketing-Effectiveness Framework is program execution. Once the proper marketing mix has been determined and the budgets allocated, the marketing team then optimizes each program for the best results possible. Optimizing specific programs leads to the next level of payoff in terms of return on marketing investment. It applies to all media channels that "touch" the consumer: sales, TV advertising, the Internet, e-mail marketing, direct marketing, radio, PR, outdoor, and so on. It also includes any in-store or in-channel activities, such as display, feature, and BOGO.

Optimization and improvement can apply both in isolation and in synergy with other elements. In isolation from other marketing channels, each of the activities is critical for achieving optimal marketing results and needs to be itself optimized. For example:

- Landing pages for pay-per-click campaigns
- Calls-to-action for direct mail campaigns
- Flighting for TV advertising
- The hiring and training of sales personnel

From a synergy perspective, the timing, messaging, and design for each of the elements in each of the marketing channels can be coordinated to deliver the greatest impact. In the automotive industry, print campaigns that overlap with TV campaigns can deliver significantly higher results. Coordinating the messaging, design, and timing between the various media through integrated marketing campaigns will, in most cases, deliver superior results compared with when the activity is executed in isolation.

ORGANIZATIONAL CONSIDERATIONS

Assuming that managers are managing the execution of each of the marketing-mix elements, how should decisions be made regarding the optimization of the allocation of the marketing budget across each of the media channels?

For example, the VP of sales is making decisions to improve his slice of the pie—spending appropriate amounts on training and travel, demanding a certain call volume, and pushing for improved close rates. But, if Internet advertising is driving higher incremental sales, shouldn't the Internet advertising manager be accorded more of the sales and marketing budget pie? If budget decisions need to be made according to the best results per media channel, then shouldn't there be a separate function within the organization—untainted by political motives—to support this critical decision making? Indeed, the top consumer packaged goods (CPG) companies are doing just that: setting up a modeling and analytics function to support these types of decisions. The goal of this function is to build highly accurate models based on valid and objective data gained from the marketplace. Marketing budget allocations are no longer made based on gut feel.

ENDNOTES

1. Philip Kotler and Kevin Lane Keller, *Marketing Management,* 12th ed., (New Jersey: Prentice Hall, 2006).

2. Michael E. Porter, *Competitive Advantage: Creating and Sustaining Superior Performance,* (New York: Free Press, 1998).

3. Geoffrey A. Moore, *Crossing the Chasm,* rev. ed., (New York: HarperCollins, 2002).

4. Geoffrey A. Moore, *Inside the Tornado: Marketing Strategies from Silicon Valley's Cutting Edge,* (New York: HarperCollins, 1995).

5. Claire Atkinson and Jean Halliday, "Madison+Vine: Pontiac gets major mileage out of $8 million 'Oprah' deal; Giveaway a PR victory, leads to follow-up shows," *Advertising Age,* September, 2004.

6. Linda Kaplan Thaler, Robin Koval, and Delia Marshall, *Bang! Getting Your Message Heard in a Noisy World,* (New York: Doubleday, 2003).

3

PLANNING AROUND WHAT YOU CAN'T CONTROL: THE COMPETITION, THE CONSUMER, THE CHANNEL, AND EXOGENOUS FACTORS

No company operates in a vacuum. Besides the competition, the consumer, and the channel, there are numerous factors that are, for the most part, beyond our control—from government regulations and interest rates, to the weather, strikes, boycotts, and seasonality.

When planning and measuring the effectiveness of marketing programs, the impact of the competition, the consumer, and the channel (the 3Cs), and exogenous factors and their influence, must be understood and controlled. How do they impact marketing investments? Can the risk associated with them be mitigated? Are there changes in exogenous factors that can provide a competitive advantage?

THE COMPETITION

All players in the category have a similar model by which they operate. Competition can be fierce, and everyone must always be at the top of their game. Some of the players are better at it than others, but the rules and framework by which they operate are the same.

They also operate by the three key marketing-effectiveness dimensions already described: strategy, creative, and execution. Their actions are revealed in how the 4Ps are presented to the marketplace.

Competitors can take strategic actions, make creative changes, or simply execute their marketing plans. Strategic changes can also take place when new entrants introduce new technologies or concepts that redefine the category. Consumers define categories by the selection they have in their consideration set when choosing a product. When new entrants introduce new products or solutions, categories can change. Similarly, competitors can exit a category—potentially affecting the definition of the category. When this happens, strategies must be re-evaluated and elements of the marketing plan's execution must be revisited.

The marketers that have a better understanding of their Marketing-Effectiveness Framework than their competition will deliver better results in the marketplace.

An understanding of the company and the competitive aspects of their Marketing-Effectiveness Framework must be played in context of the understanding of the response behavior of the consumer.

THE CONSUMER

Consumer response behavior is one of the largest influences of marketing effectiveness. Ways to understand how consumers respond to competitive offerings and competitive media, and go shopping, are described in the next chapter. There are, however, other consumer factors outside of consumer response behavior that add an important different dimension to marketing effectiveness.

In this chapter, I consider how improving marketing effectiveness must also include an understanding of the consumer base, not related to their response behavior. These include the ways in which changes in the consumer base affect how effective our marketing will be. Consumer segments change by growing or declining. Consumers purchase products—either competing solutions or ours—and are then temporarily, or permanently, out of the market. For example, most consumers will only ever purchase one life insurance policy. They will, however, purchase a house or new car every 5-6 years. Once purchased, they are out of the market until they get ready to purchase a new house or car 5-6 years later. In fast-moving consumer goods (FMCG) they can be taken out of the market through competitive offers to load the pantry prior to your new product launch.

Also, short-term changes to consumer behavior must be taken into account. These can include boycotts of French wine or of American branded products in the Middle East.

THE DISTRIBUTION CHANNEL

The distribution channel plays a critical role in the marketplace in almost every industry. Marketers have unique opportunities to improve their effectiveness by both understanding the types of available channel partners, and their influences on how and where consumers want to purchase, and taking advantage of them.

For business-to-business companies, large customers may want to buy directly from the manufacturer, believing that in this way they can develop the most leverage against the manufacturer in terms of service or price. Moderate-sized business customers may want to purchase through a channel partner that can integrate a number of manufacturers' products into a complete solution where the channel takes on the challenges of service across the solution set. Smaller customers may not be able to purchase from the manufacturer directly because the manufacturer may not be willing or able to be where the consumer is located, or may not want to take on the burdens of collection or the cost of many small transactions.

Distribution channels, however, bring on their own complexities in terms of taking control of the price the consumer pays, the message the consumer receives at the point of purchase, the location on the shelf, and even the information about the purchase provided back to the manufacturer. Just as manufacturers act at the strategic, creative, and execution levels, so do distribution channels.

Wal-Mart sent tsunamis—not just ripples—back to the manufacturers when they decided to no longer provide store-level transactional information to the manufacturers through the traditional syndicated data sources (Nielsen and IRI). Instead, they replaced it with Retail Link. Only a few years later did they make some of the transactional information available, with many limitations, which made it more difficult for many consumer packaged good (CPG) manufacturers to understand the direct impact their marketing was having with their consumers through this trade partner.

Although the channel is not directly under the control of the manufacturer, the manufacturer does have some control over how the channel offers their products and services to the consumer through various marketing development funds or cooperative marketing arrangements. With many business-to-business channels, special incentive funds can be offered. In consumer distribution channels, higher discounts can be provided to increase shelf-space and share of shelf, and to improve shelf placement. Displays can be funded to provide in-store banners, end-caps and other point-of-purchase marketing promotions to drive incremental sales volume.

Lastly, specific trends in the distribution channel can impact revenue. As one trade partner adds stores and locations, sales through that partner will grow. As others decline, sales through that partner will decline. Companies that are themselves the channel typically report sales growth using the term "same store sales." This represents the growth in revenue for stores that were in operation throughout the reporting period typically one year.

EXOGENOUS FACTORS

Exogenous factors affect the overall market, but may also affect certain competitors differently. For example, higher gas prices may affect sales of gas-guzzling SUVs more than smaller SUVs with hybrid engines.

On the other hand, some exogenous factors affect all companies in a category, such as the weather's effect on soda or beer consumption. Although each competitor may be affected differently, the entire category is affected to some degree. Thus, the effect of exogenous factors may need to be considered at both the category and the individual segment, competitor, and product levels.

With exogenous factors "controlled for,"[1] marketers can now determine how well their marketing activities are driving incremental revenue in good times and bad. Just as everyone wants to receive kudos for good marketing programs delivering exceptional results in good times, no one wants to take the fall for good programs that don't fare well in bad times. With the exogenous factors controlled for, the value of the marketing program can stand on its own. It is either good or bad, regardless of the influence of the external factor.

This can apply especially to economic factors in just about every industry. Some exogenous factors may be more important than others in specific categories:

• Weather (both temperature and precipitation) in the beer industry
• Seasonality, especially the holiday shopping season in the retail sector, which often more than doubles during the Christmas shopping season
• Holiday sales in the automotive industry. Just about every major holiday leads to increased sales ranging from 25 percent to over 100 percent for some holidays, such as Christmas, Halloween, and President's Day.

For example, an analysis of the annual statements (2001-04) of Federated Department Stores—owner of the Macy's brand, which is the largest operator of department stores in the U.S.—shows that average monthly store revenues hover at just over US$3 million, but in December, during the holiday season, they peak at just under US$6 million.

In the long term, the impact of certain exogenous factors can be mitigated. For example, lobbying efforts may result in the relaxation of certain government regulations. Advertising with a mitigating message may reduce the impact of factors that would otherwise be damaging to a company's reputation or sales. For example, advertising can be used to mitigate the impact of a boycott as illustrated in Case study 12 (Agent-based modeling and simulation: Carbonated soft drinks in North Africa).

For the most part, exogenous factors are independent of marketing activities, and change little over the analysis period. But, if these mitigating marketing activities take place during the analysis time frame, they need to be controlled for in the analysis of marketing effectiveness.

ENDNOTE

1. "Controlled for" is a term used in testing and many other statistical analyses. When designing and executing a rigorous in-market test, there are many variables that may influence the results and jeopardize the veracity of the test. For example, if there are different influences during the weekend versus the rest of the week, these would be "controlled for" by making certain that the test period spans full weeks. The Glossary of Statistical Terms from "SticiGui: Statistics Tools for Internet and Classroom Instruction with a Graphical User Interface," by Philip B. Stark of the Department of Statistics, University of California, Berkeley, (http://www.stat.berkeley.edu/~stark/SticiGui/Text/gloss.htm (accessed March 18, 2008)) provides the following:

   Control for a variable

   To control for a variable is to try to separate its effect from the treatment effect, so it will not confound with the treatment. There are many methods that try to control for variables. Some are based on matching individuals between treatment and control; others use assumptions about the nature of the effects of the variables to try to model the effect mathematically, for example, using regression.

4

THE CONSUMER: THE MOST IMPORTANT COMPONENT IN ANY MARKETING-ORIENTED FRAMEWORK

THE CONSUMER

In any given category, every competitor operates according to similar rules. Each develops marketing strategies, creative concepts and tactics in the context of their individual capabilities and constraints. Each operates to deliver profits to the bottom line and revenue growth to the top line. Exogenous factors impact each of the competitors—some differently, some similarly. But at the center of the market is the consumer: "The consumer is king." The consumer is the one who has the final control over the success of any campaign. Within the category, the consumer responds to each of the competitors and exogenous factors in a unique way.

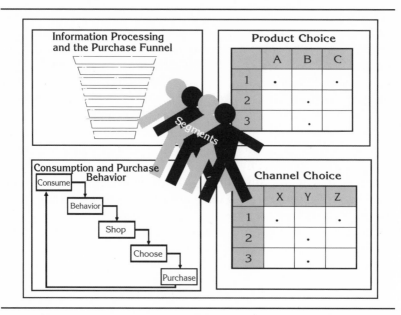

Figure 4.1: Consumer-response model

If consumers are at the heart of the market, so too are they at the heart of improved marketing effectiveness. There are many consumer models; one that I've found to be most effective is described below and shown in Figure 4.1. It has five key components, each of which must be considered in light of the complexities of a given category. These components are:
- Segmentation
- Information processing and the purchase funnel
- Product choice
- Channel choice
- Consumption and purchase behavior

SEGMENTATION

Improved segmentation is one of the key methods used to drive incremental marketing effectiveness at the consumer level. Segmentation involves clustering consumers with similar characteristics into manageable, identifiable groups. There are many books written on segmentation. This book does not describe how to improve segmentation, but to reiterate that segmentation is a key dimension to improving marketing effectiveness. In an ideal world, where marketing communications had no cost, we would target each prospective consumer individually—at a time when they are ready to be targeted, with the right, personalized message in the right medium. On the other hand, the consumer base could be viewed as a single segment in the category. Treating all prospective consumers in the same fashion may allow us to be successful in the marketplace, but we may be able to be more effective with our marketing by trying to uncover a certain number of common characteristics among groups of our prospective consumers.

Given that marketing communications activities have some cost—and different costs in different media—it is typically more effective to aggregate prospective consumers into groups or segments. This grouping can be done for many reasons. Typical rationales for segmentation include:
- Purchasing/renting a direct mail list
- Improving and targeting the message and concept
- Adjusting the pricing
- Adjusting the product offering or feature set
- Choosing a distribution channel

Depending on the type of business question to be answered, types of segmentation include:
- Attitudinal
- Behavioral
- Need-states or benefits-based
- Demographic/firmographic[1]/geographic
- Psychographic/lifestyles
- Loyalty

Improved segmentation can lead to:
- Improved customer satisfaction
- Cost savings and higher operational efficiencies
- Improved response to marketing activities

Case study 2 (Direct marketing and CRM: Mobile telecommunications company in Asia) illustrates how a telecom provider in Asia-Pacific was able to uncover a number of marketing opportunities by segmenting its fixed-line business along a number of behavioral and demographic dimensions.

Through this improved segmentation, the company was able to reduce churn and improve the success of its up-selling and cross-selling activities.

Somewhere between a segment of one and a segment for every consumer is a correct, or optimal, number of segments. There are tools that can help to determine the optimal number of segments (e.g., latent class segmentation).[2]

However, segmentation doesn't come without its drawbacks. Many problems with segmentation arise when trying to apply a segmentation scheme to solving an unrelated problem—using attitudinal segmentation to determine a choice model, or trying to purchase a direct mail list with only partial or incomplete information, for example. Given that we know exactly what the characteristics of our ideal consumer segments are, we often can't go to the "list store" and buy a differentiated list based on our desired segmentation criteria. Instead, we're typically offered a list where we can target recipients based on a few selected characteristics (often called "selects") that only approximate our desired segmentation criteria. With this approximated segmentation we now have to determine or modify our targeted messages, offers, and other components of our marketing program. This leads to inaccuracies, overlap, and some loss of effectiveness in our targeting. The segmentation process must be flexible enough to operate within these constraints. We need to be able to purchase targeted mass media or a direct marketing list. That list should allow us to segment it with the highest probability of matching our segments in the way we need them covered to drive the best results from our marketing messages and offers.

Further drawbacks include comments from (nonmarketing) managers, such as, "We just did a segmentation, why do we need another one?" Often more than one segmentation method is required: each to answer a specific marketing or business question. It is the business question that determines the type of segmentation scheme and the methodology required.

Lastly, we need to think about how we collect data. We often capture data, such as transaction and order history, name, address, phone number, or even marketing source coding, but we don't capture demographics, psychographics, purchasing process, or other key information that would allow us to market to our consumers and prospects more effectively. Part of the segmentation process may dictate how we need to collect consumer data in the future to drive even more value out of the segmentation process. For example, to deliver a successful social networking strategy, we might want to profile existing customers by potential markers for being an influencer or an advocate. Once these markers are known, customers with a higher propensity of being an influencer can be identified and targeted with specific messages to support their desire and ability to "influence" other prospective customers in their networks.

INFORMATION PROCESSING AND THE PURCHASE FUNNEL

Consumers process the information delivered to them from competitors, the channel, influencers, and other consumers in the marketplace. Based on that information, they form a "mental model"—an image of the brand or product in their minds. They become aware of the product, add the brand to their consideration set, and build brand equity. Based on their particular needs and preferences, consumers will value one brand over another. Originally developed by McKinsey & Company, the purchase funnel models how consumers process information about brands, regardless of the source. With this understanding of consumer information processing, marketers can direct specific messages in specific media to drive the preferences for one brand over another. A sample purchase funnel is shown in Figure 4.2. Your purchase funnel may be different or have different steps, but in general it will follow this flow.

Lastly, the purchase funnel model can be tempered by the consumer experience of that product. Feedback loops can be established. For example, a negative customer service experience may take a particular brand wholly out of the consumer's consideration set. It may take years to overcome this negative brand equity, or it may take a similar negative experience with a competitive brand—or a convincing message that the brand has changed—to lead the consumer toward placing the brand back into the consideration set.

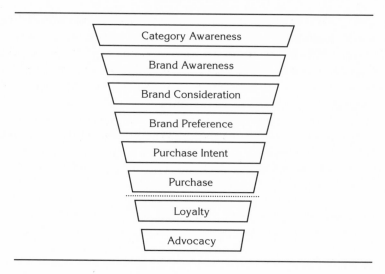

Figure 4.2: The purchase funnel

Operating in parallel with the purchase funnel is the sales funnel. The sales funnel is what the manufacturer observes as the consumer traverses the purchase funnel. This sales funnel process is especially important for business-to-business marketers who incorporate personal selling as they meet with customers, provide product information, answer questions and concerns, deliver proposals, run product tests, and, finally, win the business. For more information on this topic see *Marketing ROI* by James Lenskold[3] or *The Loyalty Effect* by Fredrick F. Reichheld and Thomas Teal.[4]

The purchase funnel concept was developed to provide an understanding of how consumers move from nonawareness, through awareness to purchase consideration and, finally, to purchase. There are many forms of the purchase funnel concept: Figure 4.2 shows a generalized version. Manufacturers can tailor the description of the purchase funnel to fit their markets and improve their understanding of how and why consumers move from one level in the funnel to the next. The levels can be adjusted and others can be added. As shown above, you may also find it useful to add post-purchase steps of "loyalty" and "advocacy" to the funnel.

- **Category awareness**—Most consumers are aware of most categories. However, as new products are developed, and new technologies become available, consumers must be made aware that the particular category exists. For example, Apple's iPod put the music player category on the map. A further refinement to category awareness could be category consideration. If the products offered in the category are not needed, then the consumer may be aware of the category but may never purchase in the category. For example, senior citizens are aware of music players, but may simply not see the need for them.

- **Brand awareness**—Once consumers are aware of the category, they must learn that a particular company provides a product or solution within the category. Category and brand awareness are often accomplished through the mass media, but they can also take place through direct marketing, the distribution channel, and advocacy—word-of-mouth and social networking.
- **Brand consideration**—Consumers, who are aware of the category, and the various brands within it, must now begin to consider which brands they might purchase; the brand enters the consumer's consideration set.
- **Brand preference**—Consumers who are considering a particular set of products generate preference for one brand over another. The levels of brand awareness through brand preference are often referred to as "upper funnel" components of the purchase funnel.
- **Purchase intent**—Once there is consideration and preference for a brand, the consumer develops an intention to purchase the product. The consumer visits the desired channel with the intention of making a purchase in the chosen category. Purchase intent can then be further influenced either through the channel or through direct marketing means. For consumer products, having the product on display (e.g., at the end cap) by the trade partner can influence purchase. For large ticket items, the channel may have a commission-carrying sales person on staff to influence the purchase decision. For business-to-business products, purchase intent can be strongly influenced by the channel sales person at the point of purchase.
- **Purchase**—The consumer actually chooses the product, places it into the shopping cart, and purchases the product in the preferred channel at some price. Purchase intent and purchase are together often referred to as the "lower funnel."

- **Loyalty**—Once purchased, the product experience must be satisfying enough that the consumer will become a repeat and loyal purchaser. High post-sale customer satisfaction can lead to high loyalty and the willingness to continue purchasing from the brand. Loyalty programs specifically targeting this level in the purchase funnel include, for example, frequent flyer programs from the airlines and frequent buyer programs from mass retailers.
- **Advocacy**—There is no better result for a product than to have consumers advocate its value to others. This is often described as the "holy grail" of marketing—positive word-of-mouth. But are there ways for a company to increase the willingness of its consumers to advocate the product? A whole new field of social networking, word-of-mouth, and viral marketing is being developed to help marketers take advantage of the mechanics of advocacy marketing.

Through persuasive marketing communications, manufacturers can target consumers at specific stages in the purchase funnel, and speed their progress toward purchase. A marketing program intended to increase brand awareness attempts to put more consumers into the top of the purchase funnel; increased brand awareness at the top of the funnel tends to increase the volume of consumers traversing all subsequent levels in the funnel. For example, analysis may determine that for every percentage increase in brand awareness, a 1.5 percent increase in purchases will take place at some point in the future.

Analysis of the marketplace using the purchase funnel concept can reveal the presence of bottlenecks in moving consumers from one level to the next. If brand awareness is high, but purchase is not occurring, improving a program targeted at consumers further down in the purchase funnel may be necessary to help move prospective consumers past the purchase funnel bottleneck.

Information about the brands and the category is generated through five broad types of communications, each with a corresponding persuasive value:

- **What we say**—Includes our advertising in all its forms, including both brand advertising and direct marketing. It is typically positive in its persuasive value, but can be negative in some segments. For example, the Miller Brewing Company "Catfight"[5] ads were generally received positively, although some women's groups protested against them. The level of consumer response is also influenced by the media habits of the consumer. If they don't overlap with our media schedule, the consumer may never hear what we have to say. Understanding media mechanics can help marketers to take advantage of how consumers receive and perceive media through different media channels.[6]

- **What the competition says**—Direct, comparative advertising is less frequent, but it can still be found, particularly in certain categories. The "cola wars" are a prime example— where in the mid 1970s Pepsi issued the Pepsi Challenge against Coca-Cola. A second example is the beer wars between Anheuser-Busch and the Miller Brewing Co., where direct side-by-side comparisons were made between these popular brands. This advertising method was also popularized by Procter & Gamble, whose advertising compared their brands against "Brand X." Business-to-business advertising often provides a feature-by-feature, side-by-side comparison between multiple named or unnamed brands.

  Another effect of competitive advertising is that it delivers increased category awareness and involvement, thus "raising all boats" in the competitive set. It may be that, in the short term, competitive advertising takes market share from other competitors, but in the medium term all competitors' sales increase because of the overall increased category awareness and consideration.

- **What the channel says**—Channel communications may or may not be completely aligned with your messaging, but are often very compelling because they take place at a point close to the purchase. The effect from channel messages is normally positive, but can be negative if the channel perceives that it can make more money by switching the consumer from your brand to a competitive brand. Brands suffer further when the channel provides their own private label products, with similar packaging and messaging, on the shelf directly next to the leading brand or brands.

- **What outside experts say (analysts, paid endorsers, legislators, opinion leaders)**—Typically driven by your PR efforts, these messages can be very powerful. However, the message delivered by experts may often differ from the message the brand would like to see. It, too, can be either positive or negative. And, it can be expressed in comparison with the competition: further diluting the effectiveness of the desired message. Nevertheless, this component can be very credible and persuasive, simply because it is delivered by someone other than "us." It is delivered by someone perceived as independent and trustworthy. Michael Jordan's work as a paid Nike endorser is a great example of a paid endorser being able to positively influence the Nike brand and many other products in his endorsement portfolio.

In the pharmaceuticals category, endorsers may also include doctors and healthcare professionals. Doctors themselves look to experts in their fields to help them make the right prescription recommendations for their patients.

- **What consumers say (and see other consumers do)**—Consumer-to-consumer communications, or word-of-mouth and consumer observation of other consumers, are often the most persuasive—yet least characterized and leveraged—of all communications elements. Messages can be either positive or negative. They can have a low frequency or a high frequency verging on the virulent. Communications can be between members of a segment or can cross segment barriers. The message can be delivered in two ways:
  - o **Unprompted**—Brand recommendations are made and passively received from unprompted communications by a consumer. One example would be a shopper approaching another shopper, exhorting, "Don't choose that brand. This is the one you want. I use it, and it's the best."
  - o **Prompted**—This describes a consumer proactively gathering information and opinions from friends and associates. For example, while searching for a new automotive insurance provider, consumers may ask their friends and colleagues what insurance they use and how their experience has been.

Each of these communications types can have different impacts on how the consumer is influenced in terms of timing, persuasive value, and cumulative effect.

PRODUCT CHOICE MODEL/
CHANNEL CHOICE MODEL

Choice is determined by the valuation by the consumer of the net utility that a particular product provides along three dimensions. Those products with the highest net utility have the highest probability of being chosen at the point of purchase. The three dimensions are:

- **The utility of the product attributes**—Products and channels have perceived attributes that satisfy a particular need. Through the satisfaction of that need, products deliver value and utility to the consumer.

  Products and channels both have real, intrinsic attributes—such as taste, color, and speed, or, in the case of a channel, location, convenience, and service. Attributes, as well as the perceptions of those attributes, may change over time as the company and its competitors optimize their offerings with new features and capabilities to meet new consumer needs.

- **The disutility of price**[7]—Price represents the exchange of value a consumer makes in return for the perceived value a particular product may provide. Although usually negative, there are products and categories where a higher price imparts a higher utility. This can be the case in both wine and jewelry.

- **The utility of the brand**—Brand value is one product attribute that is developed through the processing of information, as described above in the discussion on the purchase funnel. It is the emotional response one brand delivers over another. It also delivers a value against which a consumer will pay a certain price. Every message received about a brand, or even the category, can add to or detract from the value of the brand. In addition, the perceived value of the brand in the mind of the consumer can decay if engagement with the brand ceases or slows. For example, if the consumer never again sees an ad or an endorsement for Nike, will they be more or less willing to pay a premium for Nike branded products?

The brand value can be defined as one single element or it can be made up of a combination of extrinsic or emotional attributes. These can include features based on lifestyle or personality characteristics: "I look cool drinking this brand of cola," or "This product makes me feel secure." The perceived value of extrinsic attributes may change over time as a result of changing fashions, trends and marketing messages communicated by the brands into the marketplace. For example, Michelin's messaging about the safety of their tires is designed to increase the perception among parents of the safety that their tires provide in protecting a parent's most valuable asset—their children.

Products				Preferences by Segment		
	A	B	C		1	2	3
Sweetness	8	6	5	Sweetness	8	6	5
Healthy	8	5	5	Healthy	3	5	5
Price	5	3	1	Price	5	3	1

Figure 4.3: Product choice modeling attribute levels (left) and segment preferences by attribute (right). A score of 10 represents the highest relative preference, 1 the lowest.

Figure 4.3 shows the attribute levels three products A, B, and C have across intrinsic, extrinsic, and price attributes in the category. For example, product A has a level of 8 for the "sweetness" intrinsic attribute, a level of 8 for the "healthy" extrinsic attribute, and a level of 5 for "price." It also shows the relative preference levels segments 1, 2, and 3 have for these attributes. In this example, segment 1 has a very high relative preference (8) for "sweetness" while it has a low relative preference (3) for the "healthy" attribute and a medium relative preference for "price."

For each of these product attributes, consumers in different segments have different preferences. Based on the relative weighting of the preferences and attribute levels—i.e., the utility of the intrinsic attributes combined with the utility of the extrinsic attributes and weighted against the disutility of price— one consumer segment is more likely to choose one product over another. The most probable choice will be the choice that has the highest combined utility. The consumer will choose a channel in a similar fashion. In the case of new products, where distribution may not yet be ubiquitous, the choice of channel may be influenced by the consumer's perception of where the product might be available.

As mentioned above, perceptions concerning specific attribute values may change over time, and that change can be influenced by competitors in the category. When the consumer becomes educated through marketing messages, the relative perceptions of attribute values can change. In the 1990s, Volvo Cars built its advertising campaign on the value of safety and security, thus elevating the value of the safety and security attributes in the minds of its target consumers. Case study 14 (Agent-based modeling and simulation: Unsweetened tea in Japan) illustrates how modeling the choice process plays a key role in the development of an agent-based model. With the understanding of intrinsic and extrinsic preferences, an agent-based model can be built to improve how new products can be successfully launched.

CONSUMPTION AND PURCHASE BEHAVIOR

The consumer must also consume and purchase the product. Understanding the consumption and purchase process can also help the marketer to improve their results. As shown in Figure 4.4, consumers consume products, and then they go shopping. While shopping, they choose a product and purchase it. Once purchased, they now have "stock" in the pantry from which they can repeat the consumption process. Factors driving purchase and consumption include:

- **Pantry loading (stocking)**—Consumption can only occur if the product is in stock in the consumer's pantry. For consumable products, if they are not in stock, or stock is low, in the pantry, the consumer must go shopping. In other cases e.g., if there is an overabundance in the pantry consumption can increase. Marketers can influence pantry levels, by offering "buy one get one free" (BOGO) and other promotions. Marketing activities that cause pantry loading may be done prior to a new competitive launch, to clear the way for a new product launch, or simply to increase the revenue numbers for the period.

- **The shopping trip**—The purchase during the shopping trip may be made as part of a consumer's regular shopping trip to the store or during a special trip specifically taken to make the purchase. In addition, the product may be purchased in combination with other products in order to fulfill a specific need: for example, chips and salsa along with soda. The regular shopping trip can be further influenced by a prepared grocery list. Consumers that shop based on a prepared grocery list would be influenced differently than those consumers purchasing on impulse.

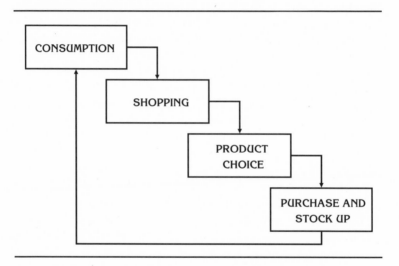

Figure 4.4: The consumption and purchase process

- **Purchase decision process**—Purchasing decisions may be made individually or by committee; the latter is particularly common in business-to-business markets, although family units can also affect how purchases are made—especially for big-ticket items, such as homes or furniture. In the consumer white goods sector, for example, marketers must target both the husband and wife with appropriate messages in order to increase success. In business-to-business—for example the sale of high-end software—marketers must provide specific messages for the C-level executive, the champion, and specific influencers when promoting enterprise level purchases.

- **The budget**—For big-ticket items for the consumer and business-to-business markets, the purchase decision is often made in consideration of a limited budget. A budget may allow the purchase this period or it may delay it to a future period as the purchaser saves over multiple periods in order to afford the purchase. In business-to-business markets, specific budgets are set aside in order to make a specific capital outlay. If there isn't a specific line-item in the budget, the marketer may find it advantageous to target specific messages during the customer's budget planning process as they approach their new fiscal period.
- **Task-based purchasing**—Purchases may be made during regular shopping trips, or they can be task-based; that is, the need for the product may be driven by some compelling event. For example, an upcoming wedding will drive consumers to buy a wedding gown or rent a tuxedo. An upcoming birthday party may influence the purchase of cake-decorating supplies. McDonald's has found that targeting messages immediately before and after the lunch period provides greater response than any other time period in the day.[8]
- **New product search**—New products are often not immediately available in every channel, and this may cause a consumer to actively go out and seek a new product at a specific channel known, or assumed, to carry it. Marketers can help the consumer in this case by making certain the messaging includes the names of outlets where the newly launched product can be found.
- **Initial like/repeat like**—For new products, especially in foods and beverage, there is the added factor of how well the product is liked the first time it is tried versus the next time and the time after that. Initial like is often influenced by the perception of the particular attribute promoted in the marketing and other literature, and by how well it meets or exceeds expectations generated through the advertising. Marketers can make certain their messaging reinforces these perceptions.
- **Consumption rate**—Consumption, which drives purchase, may be continuous at some relatively predefined rate—as it is for detergents—or it may take place only once or infrequently—as is the case for many durables and investment products. It may also take place on impulse. Alternatively, the

product or service may be purchased once but consumed, paid for, and renewed regularly—as in telecommunications. Or, the product may be consumed more voraciously or inefficiently depending on the quantities on hand in the pantry. For example, can extremely large packages of cotton swabs, containing 300 or more, cause consumers to inefficiently consume them because they perceive them to be in overabundance?

- **Inertia**—Often while shopping, consumers don't make a concerted decision for each and every purchase. In many categories, many purchases are simply made based on inertia. In this case, switching costs away from the preferred brand is weighed against both the effort of having to consider the features, preferences, prices, and brand value of a competitive offering, and the risk of purchasing a potentially unknown or uncertain set of attributes. Marketers must often advertise heavily or provide steep discounts to induce consumers to engage in that first trial use of their new product.
- **Product availability**—Of course, the particular product or product variant must be available in the channel when the consumer wishes to purchase it. Otherwise, a purchase in the category may not take place, or a purchase will be made for the next best available item.

Sequential purchase process

Another aspect of choice that is tightly coupled with the purchase process is called the sequential purchase process. In consumer packaged goods (CPG)—also known as fast-moving consumer goods (FMCG)—such as soap, hand cream, and detergent, the choice is made at the store, in front of the shelf where all the available brands are shown. In other industries, such as automotive insurance and jewelry, all the choices are not available at one time. Consumers begin to evaluate one brand and make a decision based on that evaluation to either purchase that brand or make no purchase. They then move on to evaluate the next brand at a later date and make a choice to purchase that next brand or to make no purchase. The purchase and choice process takes place over a longer period of time. Once a purchase is made, no other searching is done and those brands not evaluated may never enter the consideration set for a full evaluation.

Sequential purchasing behavior is changing, though, as the Internet now provides the opportunity for consumers to gather information across many choices before visiting the agency, jewelry store, or car dealer to negotiate the purchase.

BRINGING IT ALL TOGETHER

Because consumers are at the center of our marketplaces, they must be at the center of the Marketing-Effectiveness Framework. Consumers respond to many influences. Understanding their behavior and response to these influences can lead to significantly enhanced ROI.

By analyzing competitive activities, exogenous factors, and consumer behavior within a single cohesive framework, marketers can identify low-cost and low-risk factors that have the greatest leverage in the marketplace. With this framework, a more optimal mix can be determined, which leads to the desired results, given the constraints under which the company is operating (e.g., capacity, budget, profit, and revenue growth goals).

Because the consumer decision-making process changes little over time, models built on a consumer-centric framework can be very robust, even in dynamic markets.

For marketers, a comprehensive framework for modeling the market and simulating consumer behavior can help execute marketing programs to deliver better results. The Marketing-Effectiveness Framework provides a systematic approach for marketers to understand their marketplaces and the consequences of their activities, and those of their competitors, in determining the relative efficiencies of different incremental marketing investments.

The consumer-centric, Marketing-Effectiveness Framework (Figure 4.5) can help marketers structure their measurement and management to improve marketing results at all levels of strategy, creative, and execution. It shows how modeling the consumer response must take into account not only our marketing but also that of our competitors. With better marketing answers and greater marketing effectiveness, executives can improve their return on marketing investment, help the company to outperform the competition, and improve their careers.

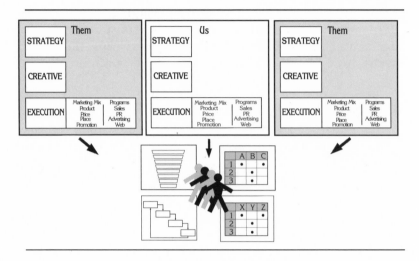

Figure 4.5: Consumer-centric, Marketing-Effectiveness Framework

Accurately projected results based on this framework help manufacturers to make better marketing decisions. There are many techniques that can be used to support the marketer as he or she embarks on improved analytics to drive increased marketing effectiveness. The selection of the best modeling technique can be influenced by:

- Data availability, granularity, timeliness, and periodicity
- The dynamics in the marketplace, including expected competitive, consumer, and channel behavior, and exogenous factors

Analytical modeling techniques that function very well in certain markets may not be appropriate in others. In some markets, simple tracking tools may be used to help determine the effectiveness of particular marketing activities. In others, it may be possible to build more sophisticated statistical models. In yet others, highly sophisticated analytical techniques may be required to evaluate a range of possible actions across a set of potential competitive actions and scenarios. By using the proper analytical techniques in the right markets, improved results can be delivered and risk can be reduced.

ENDNOTES

1. Just as demographics describe specific traits of consumers and consumer segments, firmographics describe similar traits for companies. Typical firmographic traits include company size (measured in revenue or employees), location, or vertical industry.

2. Latent class segmentation is a statistical method to analyze consumer attributes to determine clusters of consumers that can be grouped together. It provides a measure of optimal segmentation yielding an optimal number of clusters.

3. James D. Lenskold, *Marketing ROI: The Path to Campaign, Customer, and Corporate Profitability.* (New York: McGraw-Hill, 2003).

4. Frederick F. Reichheld and Thomas Teal, *The Loyalty Effect: The Hidden Force Behind Growth, Profits, and Lasting Value.* (Boston: Harvard Business School Press, 2001).

5. Michael McCarthy, "Miller Lite's 'Catfight' ad angers some viewers," *USA TODAY,* http://www.usatoday.com/money/advertising/2003-01-14-beer_x.htm, (accessed January 15th, 2003). The Catfight ads, originally aired in 2003, showed two women coming to blows arguing over whether Miller Lite beer was "great tasting" or "less filling."

6. Rex Briggs and Greg Stuart, *What Sticks: Why Most Advertising Fails and How to Guarantee Yours Succeeds,* (Chicago: Kaplan, 2006).

7. Utility is a term often used in the study of economics and represents the positive value or benefit a consumer receives when purchasing and consuming a product. That product provides benefit through the fulfillment of consumer needs both physical (intrinsic) and emotional (extrinsic). A consumer exchanges money for this value by paying an agreed price. The payment of money represents a loss in utility of the consumer. It is a negative utility or disutility.

8. Briggs and Stuart, op.cit.

5

A Framework for Capturing Marketing-Effectiveness Data: the Marketing-Accountability Framework

The marketing-accountability framework

The marketing-accountability framework is made up of measurements and metrics. Those measurements are based on both the things that affect the market—the independent variables—and things that result from those effects—the dependent variables. Changes in the independent variables cause consumers to change their behavior and their response. We can measure dependent variables to observe the impact of those responses. These observations are known as the success metrics.

In order to build a successful marketing-effectiveness culture, we need to gather information in both dimensions.

The marketing-accountability framework also needs to be flexible as the sophistication of the marketing-effectiveness culture grows and changes. As the business questions become more complex, the data required to support them may need to become more detailed, more accurate or more current.

These components of the marketing-accountability framework—the 4P3C1E framework—and the success metrics should be tracked over time; that is, at regular time periods in equal ways, so that trends can be monitored and relied on as accurate inputs into the chosen analysis. Each of the case studies described in chapters 8, 9, and 10 lists the required data and how it fits into the 4P3C1E framework.

THE 4P3C1E FRAMEWORK

The 4Ps, 3Cs, and 1E have been touched on numerous times previously. Now, we need to put them into a framework to use as we progress up the marketing-effectiveness continuum.

4Ps

When applying the 4P approach to tracking activities, activity trackers must look at tracking changes made by their company along these four dimensions:

- **Price**—Price represents what the consumer of the product paid at the point of purchase. It must include the changes made in price per channel, and per customer group or segment, and whether they were temporary, such as a buy one, get one (BOGO) free or other short-term discount, or permanent.
- **Product**—Product includes the new products and brands offered, and the changes made to those products, including added or removed features and new packaging. It also includes post-sale product attributes, such as changes in the customer service level, average hold times, contract lengths, and warranty stipulations.
- **Place**—Place defines the channel where the product is offered for sale to the consumer. It must include specific details in the channel, such as the amount and location of shelf space and in-store promotion for consumer markets, and the levels of authorization and training provided or required for business markets.

- **Promotion**—Most marketers begin with the promotion P when tracking activities. This is often the component of the 4Ps most under the control of the marketer. In many instances, the product feature set, pricing, and even the distribution channel are outside of the purview of many marketers. While the addition of new channels or changes in pricing are often step-functions, promotional activities can be one-time events, or repeated events as the marketing plan unfolds. In order to track promotion P activities, marketers must track the number of impressions purchased, the number of e-mails distributed, or the number of clicks-through purchased or delivered for a given campaign. They must also track when these events took place and how much they cost, including, in some cases, the incremental personnel costs associated specifically with that marketing program. If, for example, a specific program requires two temporary employees to execute the post event follow-up, then these costs must be associated with this particular marketing event.

  Promotion P activities that take place in the channel must also be tracked. Advertising implemented by the channel can deliver incremental revenues for the product. For example, The Coca-Cola Company must track the advertising done by their bottlers. Channel companies, such as retailers and restaurants, must track manufacturer advertising to the end-consumer in addition to tracking their own advertising. This primarily applies to manufacturer advertising that would lead to higher visits to their stores or restaurants, and higher purchases of their products. For example, traffic and purchase volume will increase in the stores of the Liquor Control Board of Ontario (LCBO) when any of their suppliers advertise their products. When Stolichnaya Vodka advertises their brand, sales volume for the LCBO goes up across the entire vodka category. In order to accurately model the influences on sales volume and store traffic, the LCBO must include advertising by all of their suppliers.

3Cs

The 3Cs are made up of the competition, the channel, and the consumer.[1] I have chosen to define the 3Cs as follows:

- **Competition**—Once the 4Ps of your own marketing mix are tracked, similar information for the competition—their own 4Ps—is necessary to understand the impact competitive marketing may have on your sales.

- **Consumers**—This should include specific changes in the consumer set. Segment sizes can grow, or their attributes may change. For example, in the Internet-access business, the growth rate of the number of consumers with broadband access needs to be included. If broadband access is a key enabler for the uptake of your product, such as online gaming, then this is a key attribute to track in order to determine and model your marketing effectiveness; or, it could be determined by the growth in the Hispanic segment with a certain household income. On the business-to-business side, this could include the number of businesses belonging to your installed base or your competitors' installed base.
- **Channel**—Although this is partially covered in Place in the 4Ps, this typically includes the makeup and growth of a particular channel. For consumers selling through a particular trade partner, this could include the growth rate of the number of stores of that channel partner. It could also include the mix of stores of a certain quality or type, such as mall stores versus strip stores versus stand-alone stores.

1E

Exogenous factors can be key influences on marketing effectiveness. Seasonality and holidays are key factors for both business-to-business and consumer marketers, but so are interest rates, weather, and major events, such as the SARS outbreak in China, Hurricane Katrina, or the September 11 attacks in the United States. For the TV entertainment industry, exogenous factors could include the news events of the day. These exogenous factors are not necessarily predictable, but by looking in the past we can see the ways in which they impacted the success of our marketing. Looking into the future, we know that, generally, there will be some exogenous influences on our revenues that are outside of our control. There are six dimensions[2] of exogenous factors. These are described below and classified based on the types of time series they represent:

- **Predictable events, such as holidays, seasonality, time-of-day, and day-of-week**—Marketers routinely take advantage of these exogenous factors. Father's Day sales and Mother's Day sales represent just a few of the many actions consumer marketers use to drive increased revenue. In the summer, marketers are going to provide more shelf-space for sunscreen than they will during the winter. In Asia, marketers must account for the fact that each country is affected differently by religious holidays depending on the makeup of each of the key religions—Christianity, Islam, Hinduism, and so on.

- **Random (stochastic) events, such as the news or the weather**—When it is raining, umbrella inventories will be moved next to the checkout. As news events come about—each with different levels of interest for your target segment—they may impact the viewership of your TV programs or your advertising on those programs when the news is aired in your time slot.
- **Discontinuous or one-time events, such as regulations, strikes, or boycotts**—Marketers cannot, in the short term, change the regulatory environment. They have to market within the restrictions of the current regulations. Longer term, however, marketers can act to change the regulations. Similarly, if a strike or a boycott affects demand in the category, marketers must take this into account when planning, and developing their tactics.
- **Economic factors**—Interest rates, gas prices, and the economy can impact the effect of marketers' actions in the marketplace. Taking these into account can help marketers improve their effectiveness.
- **Components and technology**—External technology changes can also impact your sales. For example, the increase of digital cameras affects film, and the increased use of Internet video is due to the growth of broadband Internet access. Sales of new PCs are enhanced when a new version of Microsoft Windows is launched.
- **Other**—Many trackable or measurable factors that are not included in the above categories still impact revenue. However, they are outside of the control of the marketer.

SUCCESS METRICS

Success metrics are the consumer response variables that we want to measure in the marketplace because they are good indicators of the impact of our marketing on our target consumer base. They should not be confused with input metrics, such as marketing dollars spent, impressions purchased, or share of voice delivered. Success metrics are outputs that we are expecting to change through the application of marketing activities in the marketplace.

Success metrics fall into several broad categories:
- **Financial success metrics**—Financial success metrics are those that we can get out of our internal financial systems, or based on the internal financial systems of our trade partners. These include:
  - o **Revenue**—the dollar, or currency-weighted, value of the units purchased at the shipment or point-of-sale POS/level
  - o **Unit volume**—the number of units, or equivalent units, purchased at the shipment or point-of-sale (POS) level
  - o **Contribution margin**—the incremental profit margin generated for each incremental unit sold
- **Survey-based purchase funnel metrics**—Purchase funnel metrics are interim metrics that can be measured through surveys and tracking studies. They represent the opinion of the consumer or consumer's memory about what was going on in his or her mind. These measures are softer than the financial success metrics because of the way in which they are measured in the marketplace. Here are four examples:
  - o **Purchase intent**—Purchase intent measures the relative likelihood that a target consumer would purchase a product at some point in the future.
  - o **Brand awareness**—Brand awareness can be measured based on whether a particular brand is mentioned as a participant in a category (unaided) or selected from a list and recognized as a brand participating in a category (aided).
  - o **Brand equity**—Brand equity can be measured in the way consumers prefer one brand over another, or how willing they would be to associate with one brand over another.

- o **Net promoter score**—This score, developed by Reichheld,[3] measures the willingness of a consumer to recommend a brand or product to a friend or colleague.
- **Directly measured interim metrics** are indicators of consumer response in the market. As the indications of consumer engagement with the brand, they can be directly measured in several ways:
  - o **Leads of a certain quality**—Leads represent the names of prospective customers that have registered their names or the name of their companies with a supplier. They can have varying quality hot, warm, or cold, or different levels. Their quality can be gauged based on their needs, their available budget, the time frame they need to make a decision, and other factors.
  - o **Hits, clicks, visits to, or downloads from a Web site**—Web sites can track the number of hits, clicks, visits, and other actions taking place. These can be tracked against different marketing activities in order to gauge consumer response to these activities. There are many other actions that can be tracked, such as webinar registrations, votes, and submitted articles—each representing some level of engagement the Web visitor has with the Web site and the brand.
  - o **Qualified trade show booth attendees, calls to an 800 number, store visits**—Similarly to Web visits, visits to a trade show booth and calls to an 800 number represent actions that can be measured and tracked to report some level of engagement with the brand. Each measures indirectly the level of engagement and depth in the purchase funnel for each consumer.
- **Indirect interim metrics** are metrics that provide insight into the marketplace, but that aren't necessarily directly measurable. These include adstocks used in a marketing-mix model and deduced preferences for brand attributes in an agent-based model. These metrics are indirect because they result from the development of the model. Adstocks are determined as part of a marketing-mix model and provide the best fit to deliver the required results. In an agent-based model—depending on the availability of the data—certain

preferences are deduced as part of the calibration of the model. Each of these metrics can provide invaluable insight into the way that the market functions.

- **Calculated metrics** are made based on several metrics and calculated based on a formula:

  o **Market share**—This includes the market share for any of the competitors in a particular category. It can be measured either in unit volume or dollar volume. In the consumer packaged goods (CPG) sector market share data can be based on syndicated data sources, such as Nielsen or IRI, based on volumes sold through the channel. Or, for high-tech, they can be based on reported shipments made to industry analysts, such as Forrester or IDC.

  o **Share of wallet**—Share of wallet may not be directly measurable, but information about it can be gained through primary market research. It represents the share of purchases the customer makes of your products versus those of the competition.

  o **Customer Lifetime Value (CLV)**—CLV, which is usually measured in margin (although a similar measure of customer lifetime revenue could be used), determines the value of the customer over the span of time that he or she remains a customer. It estimates the sum of monthly service payments as well as margin generated from probable up-sell and cross-sell opportunities over that lifespan.

  o **Loyalty**—Loyalty measures the level of ongoing engagement a consumer may have with the brand after the initial purchase.

By monitoring various success metrics, marketers can measure the health of their brand, the likelihood of future purchases in both the short and long term, and many other critical behaviors of their target consumers. In response to their marketing activities, competitive activities, and other elements in the 4P3C1E framework, these metrics can be used to determine the effectiveness of their marketing.

Each of these success metrics can also be components of a "marketing dashboard"[4] in order to monitor the short-term success of various marketing activities and project the long-term health of a brand.

ENDNOTES

1. Lawson Abinanti, Messages that Matter, "The 3C's of Successful Positioning - Part III: Get your channel involved in positioning. It's good for both of you," http://www.messagesthatmatter. com/columns/3Cs_of_Positioning_Part_III.pdf, (accessed January 27, 2008).

2. David Williamson, Peter Cooke, Wyn Jenkins, and Keith Michael Moreton, *Strategic Management and Business Analysis,* (Oxford: Butterworth-Heinemann, 2003). PEST is a classification scheme that can be used for classifying exogenous factors into Political/ legal, Economic, Sociocultural, Technological, and Environmental. Other acronyms, including STEP, STEEP, PESTEL, PESTLE, or LEPEST, also describe different frameworks for evaluating exogenous factors.

3. Fred Reichheld, *The Ultimate Question: Driving Good Profits and True Growth,* (Boston: Harvard Business School Press, 2006).

4. A "marketing dashboard" is made up of graphs and charts showing the status of key performance indicators in marketing. It helps marketers to monitor and manage ongoing activities, review the results of past activities, and project the results of planned marketing activities. For a great book on the subject please see: Patrick LaPointe, *Marketing by the Dashboard Light* (New York: Association of National Advertisers, 2005).

SECTION 3
THE MARKETING-EFFECTIVENESS CONTINUUM

6

Introducing the Marketing-Effectiveness Continuum

How do you improve what you are doing today? What can you do to make your marketing activities more effective? How do you—or should you even—move up to the next level of sophistication in your marketing effectiveness?

Just as you can't eat an elephant all in one bite, you can't implement the entire Marketing-Effectiveness Framework all in one bite.

Improving marketing effectiveness can seem like a daunting task. There are many internal and external obstacles to be overcome, including:

- Reliable data, which can help drive better marketing decisions, is perceived to be expensive and/or difficult to come by.
- Never seeming to have enough in the budget or time in the day to pay for both the data and a systematic mechanism to analyze it.

- Senior marketing executives who find it difficult to sacrifice hard-earned budget dollars on data and analytics; they would rather take that money and spend it on lead generation or brand development, not "waste" money on measurement and analysis.
- Marketers and their agencies who often resist being measured by business and financial results, as opposed to less meaningful interim measures such as call volume, reach and frequency, lead volume, or other simple indirect methods.

Yet CEOs are demanding improved, measurable, and verifiable results from their marketing departments and, more importantly, their marketing investments. They want results. They not only want to build a brand that resonates with consumers over the long-term, but also expect marketing to drive short-term consumption and purchase of the company's products and services. Marketing must be as accountable as the sales department for making the numbers this month, this quarter, and this year.

The marketing-effectiveness continuum helps marketing executives to benchmark their organization's current level of accountability, and to understand and develop a plan to deliver improved marketing effectiveness and return on marketing investment (ROMI) in the short and long term.

It can help them to:
- Gauge their current marketing effectiveness
- Develop strategies that drive improved return on marketing investment
- Evaluate and determine actions that are necessary today, so that they can continue to enhance marketing return on investment (ROI) in the future

As marketers move their organizations up the marketing-effectiveness continuum, the results delivered from their ability to gauge the effectiveness of their decisions will allow them to move from making more tactically oriented decisions to making more strategically oriented decisions. Its *raison d'être* is to benchmark progress and develop plans to move to the next level along the continuum.

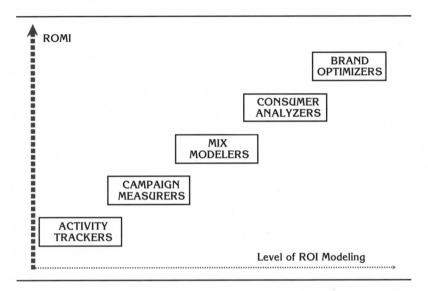

Figure 6.1:   The marketing-effectiveness continuum

Once a company has benchmarked their current level on the marketing-effectiveness continuum, they can use the Marketing-Effectiveness Framework to map a course for improved marketing ROI. By using the marketing-effectiveness continuum, marketers can make superior decisions about the definition of marketing programs, the allocation of marketing resources, and the response to competitive initiatives, which should lead to improved results at lower cost and risk.

The marketing-effectiveness continuum (Figure 6.1) classifies an organization's marketing effectiveness into five broad levels:
- Activity trackers
- Campaign measurers
- Mix modelers
- Consumer analyzers
- Brand optimizers.

Activity trackers—The activity tracker classification represents the first step to improving marketing effectiveness. Having now trained thousands of marketers, it has become obvious that many marketers—probably over 90 percent of them—have difficulty tracking their activities and attaching costs to them. Until this can be done, marketers simply can't make any progress to develop a clear picture of what works and what doesn't. Being able to track activities over time, and assign costs to them in a systematic manner, is a critical first step to improved marketing effectiveness.

Looking into the future, activity trackers must also be able to have a plan of what is going to happen and how they are going to spend their company's hard won marketing investments. Regardless of whether they are going to change—and of course they will—activity trackers must be able to have in one location an activity plan, including the associated budget detailing what they are going to do in the marketplace to drive increased revenue, profit, and share.

This is more of an infrastructure capability, but once activities can be tracked and costs applied, marketers can then finally take their first steps along the

> **“ You can't manage what you don't measure. ”**

marketing-effectiveness continuum. Tracked activities include all of their media activities, such as:

- **For advertising**—gross rating point cost (GRP)[1] and cost per impression or cost per thousand (CPM)
- **For a Web site**—the number of hits, clicks-through, or impressions purchased
- **For a direct mail program**—the drop size and the cost per unit dropped.

The key criterion for an organization to be an activity tracker is that marketers focus on activities alone—before tying those, activities to revenue, margin, or some other result. Even the largest of organizations have entire divisions, product lines, or regions that are operating completely blind. Becoming an activity tracker can seem daunting, because now clear and concise information across all segments, products, categories, channels, and media must be tracked to show what was spent and how it was spent.

I've seen major, globally recognizable brands with whole divisions not tracking their activities in any meaningful and concise fashion. Here are a few examples of marketers that have yet to become activity trackers:

- Consider the business-to-business (B2B) division of a consumer paper products manufacturer. The consumer side of the business uses sophisticated modeling to determine its marketing effectiveness. On the other hand, the business-to-business side of the company may simply track its marketing effectiveness through the level of quota attainment of its sales force. If the sales force makes quota, the marketing must have worked. Marketing dollars are simply spent without any tracking or quantifiable goal.

- The marketing team for a B2B software company responsible for promoting a Web-based service offering spends simply based on gut feel. Instinctively, integrated marketing campaigns are supposed to work better than other single media activities, but B2B marketers may believe there is no way of knowing. Nor is there any way of knowing the extent of their superiority. The mix is simply a guess or SWAG.[2] In these cases, quite often, marketing activities are simply justified by the fact that they can tie one sale—anecdotally, of course—to the marketing campaign. It's often stated that the margin from that one large customer will cover the entire cost of the program, and then some. The other unmeasured benefits therefore must have delivered other value, making the program very "effective." It took 12 person-weeks to reconstruct the elements of their past marketing activities over the prior 18 months.

- Or, for an initial attempt at instituting a marketing-effectiveness culture, an Asian-based international airline instituted a marketing-approval process requiring an estimate of the expected ROI of the marketing activity. The marketing team was required to make reasonable guesses of what they thought the results might be. If they sound "reasonable" then they get approved. If not, the requests are returned asking for more detail. Worse still, there is no follow-up to even take a stab at determining whether there was any corresponding up-tick in sales or not. The approved marketing activities weren't tracked in any meaningful way in order to learn from past successes.

- Consider the case of the Caribbean division of a white goods manufacturer. In the larger countries outside of the U.S., marketing activities are tracked on an ad hoc basis and some analytics are done to tie revenue to marketing. The smaller countries, such as those in the Caribbean, choose their activities based on the apparent success in the other, larger regions. The assumption was that if they were successful in the large countries, they will be successful in the small countries. Anecdotal calculations are made, or a simple lift calculation surrounding the period of the activity may be undertaken. But exactly what actions were taken and their measured impact was never tracked.

- An Asian-based, high-tech company selling long-term services contracts primarily to Global 500 companies markets their services mostly through relationship-building, such as golf outings and wine tasting, and informational events, such as seminars and technology summits. Event success was based on exit surveys measuring the participants' enjoyment of the event. The automated tracking of event attendees was not undertaken and post-event marketing to the attendees was not possible.

Even large organizations, that should know better, have trouble tracking their activities, especially concerning their future marketing plans. In large complex organizations, many different agencies and departments have media plans and activities spanning many products and brands, media channels, and categories, which makes it extraordinarily difficult to aggregate their planned activities into one place. Smaller companies have difficulties tracking key metrics in their media-buying function, other than through their budgeting and expense-tracking process. Small and regional country sales and marketing teams, such as those in the Caribbean example above, may only track the marketing activities that appeared to have been successful—purposely ignoring those that appeared to have failed.

These are just a few of the early attempts, or nonattempts, at instituting marketing effectiveness. For these companies, their next big challenge is to start tracking *all* of their marketing activities. Once this is done, they will have a baseline of data with which they can take their marketing analytics to the next level.

Becoming an activity tracker requires the systematic tracking of activities in the past, and the planning of activities looking into the future. This is a simple test: your company or marketing department is an activity tracker if it can produce both a report that shows associated dollars for all activities having taken place over the last three years, and a plan of the upcoming activities and associated dollars over the next 12 months.

Campaign measurers—Campaign measurers can directly measure the results of the majority of their direct-response marketing activities. They can link either revenue, contribution margin, or discounted cash flows to the cost of marketing activities in order to calculate ROMI—also known as marketing efficiency or advertising efficiency. Or, they can link indirect results, such as leads generated or the incremental purchase intent or brand awareness developed. The effort required to take this step can be significant for an organization depending on many factors including: the maturity of the brand, product, or division; business-to-business versus consumer market; the availability of data; or the channel structure, to name a few. But doing so generates valuable insight into which marketing programs are truly delivering ROI. For example, the quality of a particular program can be compared against a hurdle rate to determine if the planned program will deliver the right level of results for a given level of investment and program risk. With this information, budgets can be allocated and marketers can begin to hone their activities.

LAST-TOUCH ATTRIBUTION

Quite often campaign measurers use "last-touch attribution." Last-touch attribution generally ignores the impact of all other prior or simultaneous touches. If a prospect receives three newsletters, sees an advertisement on television, but finally purchases through the 800-number using an offer code provided on a direct mail piece, for most companies, the full weight of the purchase is attributed to that single direct mail piece. But what is the incremental lift from the television advertising and the prior newsletters? Last-touch attribution is a highly valuable method to determine the effectiveness of direct response campaigns. It does, however, ignore all other touches received by the customer. Synergies are ignored, along with the incremental value of the brand, in determining ROI. Nevertheless, it is a valid method for direct-response marketing managers to use to improve the marketing effectiveness of their particular media channels.

Case studies are provided in Chapter 8 to show how other marketers use campaign measuring to improve their marketing effectiveness and execute their marketing strategy. The cases are:
- Case study 1—A/B testing: Plumbing services in North America
- Case study 2—Direct marketing and CRM: Mobile telecommunications company in Asia
- Case study 3—Last-touch attribution: Dental equipment supplier in North America
- Case study 4—Loyalty marketing: International hotel chain based in Asia
- Case study 5—Rebate redemption: Gas utility in North America
- Case study 6—Direct measurement: Enterprise software in the Asia-Pacific

Mix modelers—Mix modelers develop sophisticated models of their markets and calculate marketing efficiencies across their entire marketing mix—the 4Ps. Marketing-mix modeling that uses statistical regression analysis is the most common method, although more advanced system dynamics or other methods can be used. Statistical regression analysis develops the best-fit correlations between independent variables (i.e., your marketing inputs) and dependent variables, such as revenue or unit volume. System dynamics is a tool that defines relationships between different levels in the purchase funnel to develop a model of the market. With these types of modeling tools, marketers can now develop effective models to deliver increased revenue and margin—based on modeled marketing efficiencies—across the entire marketing mix. This includes both brand and direct-response advertising. Additionally, marketers can utilize marketing-mix modeling to measure complex market dynamics such as:
- Advertising saturation, diminishing returns, and breakthrough
- Synergy between marketing media
- Halo and cannibalization
- Baseline revenue calculation

The most interesting aspect of becoming a mix modeler is the realization that the measurements of the direct results of campaign measurers are now—from a marketing-mix perspective—incorrect! Marketers intuitively knew this, but were, until now, unable to differentiate the conclusions from these results. The group most profoundly affected by this conclusion is often the sales force. They now need to admit that the marketing efforts do provide incremental benefit to them, and the marketers now have proof!

ATTRIBUTION IN A COMPLEX MARKETING MIX

Let's assume that the response rate on a direct mail piece was 1.5 percent, if it was dropped when no other concurrent marketing was taking place. Let's take that same piece and drop it while a branding campaign was running concurrently on television. The response rate in this case is measured to be 1.7 percent. Who should get the attribution for the incremental 0.2 percent response? The answer is—both! The branding campaign on television delivered a 0.2 percent lift over and above what would have been expected had there been no television advertising. On the other hand, the direct mail manager made the right choices as to the execution of the direct mail piece, timing it properly in coordination with the TV branding campaign. (This has important organizational implications, which will be discussed later in this book).

From a mix perspective, the attributions to each of the marketing media elements can now be properly assigned. In our example above, 1.5 percent was attributed to the direct mail campaign and 0.2 percent was attributed to the TV campaign. This is especially important in complex media environments where multiple campaign concepts and media activities are running concurrently. With this result, the true incremental impact for each marketing element can now be determined and properly attributed. Each organizational unit can receive the deserved credit for the effectiveness of their media execution.

Case studies are provided in Chapter 9 to show how other marketers use insights gathered from understanding their marketing mix to improve their overall marketing effectiveness and allocate marketing investments between media. The cases are:

- Case study 7—Marketing-mix modeling: Regional restaurant chain in North America
- Case study 8—Marketing-mix modeling: Kids' snacks in the United Kingdom
- Case study 9—Marketing-mix modeling: Mobile telephone service provider in Asia
- Case study 10—Marketing-mix modeling: Premium lager beer in Europe

Consumer Analyzers—Consumer analyzers use their knowledge of consumer response behavior to deliver further insight into marketing effectiveness, including the incremental value of the brand. By combining data from their major competitors in the category with a greater understanding of the consumer, consumer analyzers can start to answer tactical and strategic questions. What emerges is a model of consumer behavior that can allow the simulation of the future with great accuracy. With this level of modeling and simulation, tactical and near-strategic decisions can be made with confidence. Even more remarkably, marketers can utilize simulation methods to answer more challenging questions, including:

- What is the best marketing mix to launch a new product into a new or existing category?
- What are the diffusion dynamics in the market?
- What are the implications of social networking?
- What is the ROI and expected response to nontraditional media?
- How can we avoid a price war?

Case studies are provided in Chapter 10 to show how consumer brand marketers use insights gathered from understanding their competitive environment to make critical decisions and minimize their risk when operating in highly dynamic markets. With this information, they are able to optimize their marketing mix when launching a new product and prepare for eventual competitive responses to their actions.

- Case study 11—Agent-based modeling and simulation: Consumer packaged goods in North America
- Case study 12—Agent-based modeling and simulation: Carbonated soft drinks in North Africa
- Case study 13—System dynamics: Fast-moving consumer goods in India
- Case study 14—Agent-based modeling and simulation: Unsweetened tea in Japan

Brand Optimizers—Brand optimizers reach the pinnacle in understanding marketing ROI and effectiveness: they can evaluate not only how a specific program or mix of programs helps to determine increased revenue, profit, or share, but they can also evaluate the impact marketing activities have on the share price. With this information, the particular brand can be valued with the purpose of making a strategic decision of whether a brand should be bought, sold, merged, or totally realigned. And, the particular marketing investment can be valued to understand which brands should be receiving further investment across the portfolio of brands.

Climbing the marketing-effectiveness continuum

Moving up the continuum is not just about executing programs more competently. It is the implementation of structural changes in the marketing organization to look for opportunities to improve the data-gathering process, the measurement and metrics processes, and the analytics function—with the goal of squeezing more results out of every marketing program investment.

Making consistent, repeatable small steps to improve the infrastructure is critical to long-term success. It's not enough to improve measurement in one quarter and forget about it in subsequent quarters. The small increments of organizational change must be real, long-lasting, and independent of personnel. They must be systematic and preferably supported by technology, organizational infrastructure, and training.

There are two dimensions to marketing effectiveness. One has to do with improving the management of the *business of marketing*—i.e., making the internal process flow smoothly and getting the right people and technology in place to support that process.

The other dimension has to do with managing marketing investments. Where other departments in the company invest in plant and machinery, marketers invest in communications in the marketplace—getting their message out to the most prospects, at the least cost, as persuasively as possible.

Marketing must optimize this investment although, in some cases, improvements must come in small measured steps, with the end-result of major improvements for the company as a whole. In other cases, companies can make giant leaps in their effectiveness if they are able to marshal their teams to make significant changes in the way they think about their marketing activities and what it takes to drive more revenue in a measurable, consistent fashion. Often, however, a company can't simply move all at once from where it is today to where it wants to be. Many small and consistent steps allow continuous improvement, without the cost and risk of significant organizational and political disruption. The marketing-effectiveness continuum helps companies to benchmark their current effectiveness, determine weaknesses that can be corrected in the short term, and allow them to plan where they can be in the long term.

ENDNOTES

1. Gross rating point (GRP)—A unit of measurement of audience size. It is used to measure the exposure to one or more programs or commercials, without regard to multiple exposures of the same advertising to individuals. One GRP = 1% of TV households. (Nielsen Media, Glossary of Media Terms, http://www.nielsenmedia.com/glossary/terms/G/G.html, (accessed January—27, 2008). If there are 110 million households in the U.S., then 1 GRP represents 1.1 million households.

2. SWAG is an acronym for Scientific Wild Ass Guess.

7

ACTIVITY TRACKERS

ACTIVITY TRACKER CAMEO

This story is about Lisa, who was recently asked to present the effectiveness of her Web marketing at a business marketing conference. It is her first big public presentation, so she wants to get it right.

Lisa works for Tempered Chemicals—one of the leading providers of the industrial components that are made into plastic items, from high-end tools to automotive parts. She is the marketer for these products. The company has been providing marketing materials and technical collateral to support the sales force, but she was recently given expanded latitude—under a large umbrella of skepticism—to update their Web presence and to develop and execute a Web-based marketing plan. She was even given a US$50,000 budget to support this new Web marketing channel for the first year.

She decided to make the site very educational, but also used half of her budget to do pay-per-click (PPC) advertising.

She was asked to provide the measurements that she made to gauge success. She thought about it and felt she had a great story. But as she prepared, she realized that she was only able to go so far. As part of the preparation process, she improved her analysis methods and added to her analytical rigor as she continued to enhance the Web marketing program.

Lisa realized that her first objective was to develop and qualify good leads off of the Web site. Her goal was to have a Web survey filled out for each lead. If the Web survey was filled out then it became the primary qualification process for definition of a lead.

She had some initial success here.

She realized that she could go further: that her success was not simply the number of leads generated, but it was the number of leads generated of a certain quality. Because the sales cycles could last 2–3 years, and could often represent an enormous investment in sales resources, it really mattered that the leads she generated were well received by the sales team.

Lisa knew it didn't matter that she could tie revenue to a lead. One lead could be worth US$500,000; another could be worth US$50 million. And, they only needed to convert four or five leads on an annual basis in order to make their revenue plan. In that situation, much of the typical Web-oriented marketing-effectiveness material she found wasn't applicable to her business model. With only a few good leads— each potentially worth an amount differing by orders of magnitude—it didn't matter whether she could tie revenue to any particular media type or not. It just mattered that she developed leads at a high and consistent quality.

Point #1: The measurement has to fit the business problem. Sometimes revenue, or profit, is not the right success metric to determine marketing effectiveness.

Lisa knew that she could do better, which in this case meant to determine where in the purchase funnel each lead was located in order to show how she was able to feed and support the sales pipeline. She also knew that no other competitor was anywhere near as active on the Web as she was in her product market space. The competition was smaller and based outside the country, and she wasn't sure where they were getting their leads from, although she assumed that it was probably from the big, biennial chemicals trade show.

Her competitors spent so much on that trade show, and it happened only once every other year. Through the Web, on the other hand, she was able to generate more leads throughout the year at a fraction of the cost.

Point #2: Upper-funnel metrics, such as cost per lead and lead quality, are better measures of success than trying to match leads to far-off revenue recognition.

As far as she was concerned, cost per qualified lead was king, so she needed to make sure that the qualification of a lead was as clear and impartial as possible. She knew that she could double her ad spending, but first she had to show that the investment in Web leads was paying off better than the results from the biennial trade show. Metrics and analytics must be made part of the culture. Through her success, she was able to show not only a few of the sales team, but, more importantly, the division president and even a few of the engineers, that tracking and measuring "marketing stuff" would actually work: that they could improve their business through the tracking and measurement of the right things.

Lisa also realized that the customer analysis they had done to identify on a worldwide basis all potential users of their new chemical was woefully inadequate. Twenty of the 34 highly qualified leads that they received off the Web weren't even listed. That fact alone will be very pertinent for the upcoming presentation at the conference.

Point #3: Costs of the refined lead qualification report should also be included in the cost per lead equation.

Overall, the marketing and sales function had significantly more data than they thought. The sales force automation system was a treasure trove of good information. Lisa was able to utilize this valuable sales funnel information to her advantage.

The interesting thing about this job—and she had only been in it for about a year—was that she was showing all of the older, 15–20-year tenured veterans what a little simple guerilla marketing could do. She knew that none of them would lose their job, but she also knew that she was already getting the eye of the division president.

Point #4: ROMI helps the career.

Lisa dreamed about working at a bank where a good friend of hers worked, where they knew down to the penny the amount of revenue each marketing activity brought in. In industrial marketing, though, that just isn't possible. Lisa knows that it will be great presenting this at the conference. Maybe she can meet up with some other folks in a comparable industry with similar marketing challenges. When she gets back, she is going to ask the president about getting a raise and a promotion.

Point #5: Not every company can climb to the top of the continuum.

Lisa's company can't climb very high in the marketing-effectiveness continuum. It simply doesn't make sense for some types of companies to strive for that. This was hard for her to swallow, but it became one of those great business stories that would make for an interesting presentation at the Business Marketing Conference. She did climb the continuum in one measure, though. She went from being a nonmeasurer to being a top-level activity tracker. They made a lot of progress, and it wasn't that difficult. She was also able to make some advancement toward becoming a campaign measurer as she began to tie leads and lead quality to their marketing campaign.

ACTIVITY TRACKERS

In order to move up to the next level of sophistication, marketers must be able to effectively track their activities. It is the foundation for all other levels in the marketing-effectiveness continuum. If marketers aren't measuring their activities, they will find it very difficult, if not impossible, to improve their marketing effectiveness. Some of the characteristics of marketers not acting as activity trackers include:

- Budgeting and marketing spend are determined primarily based on cost, with little expectation of a measurable outcome. Spending within budget is their primary objective.
- There is no methodical connection between marketing activity and success. Anecdotal evidence for the success of a campaign may be noted. Little or no consistent measures of success metrics are in place to measure the success of a marketing program. Any measurement is typically limited to tracking of costs relating to marketing inputs.
- There is little to no investment in the tracking of marketing activities, interim success metrics, or outcomes.

In order to become an activity tracker, marketers must track all marketing activities. They must track costs, manpower, and impressions purchased in the marketplace over time. Impressions can include cost per thousand (CPM), clicks, hits, or gross rating points (GRPs).

Activity trackers may, of course, have good insight into their consumers and customers, but they are unable to use that information as it applies to measuring their marketing effectiveness. They may try to deliver rudimentary measurements but they "just don't have time" to go back and evaluate the results in a consistent and systematic fashion.

Once you can track activities, you can begin to measure the effectiveness of your marketing. All of the other levels in the marketing-effectiveness continuum rely on a marketer's ability to track activities in order to deliver reliable and accurate measures of their marketing effectiveness.

THE ACTIVITY TRACKER TEST

Based on anecdotal evidence and research across thousands of companies, I estimate that about one-third of all the companies in existence today can't track their marketing activities in a systematic and complete manner. These companies can be very small businesses, sole proprietorships, divisions of multibillion dollar companies or sophisticated multibillion dollar companies.

To be activity trackers, marketers must pass the following test: they must deliver a spreadsheet or other application of all of their marketing activities going into the past 2–3 years within 30 minutes, and have a plan of marketing activities looking into the future for the next 12 months. The 30-minute time limit is a key part of this test, because it means that the marketing activities and plans are tracked in a consistent fashion and are readily available. I would imagine that most marketers—if given a longer time period such as two weeks—could recreate their marketing activities and plans if so challenged.

Activity trackers, track with varying levels of sophistication. At the lowest level, they track simply their own marketing activities—the promotions P. This may or may not include their own activities of their sales force, such as the number of calls, visits, or proposals submitted. At the next level, marketers need to track details of the other 3Ps—product changes, price changes, and place (distribution) changes. Whether these are under the control of the marketer depends on the particular analysis method, but tracking the 4Ps is a critical component to providing the required data to improve marketing effectiveness. At the highest level, marketers need to track the same 4Ps of the competition. Lastly, information on the channel and the consumer—as well as exogenous factors—round out the information-gathering requirements of the most sophisticated marketers.

However, just because you're not tracking at all levels of the 4P3C1E framework doesn't mean that you can't improve your marketing effectiveness. Even capturing valuable information at the lowest levels of just your key marketing promotional activities can yield valuable insights into improving your marketing effectiveness.

CHALLENGES FACING ACTIVITY TRACKERS

The activity tracker classification applies to all types of companies: business-to-business companies, consumer companies, industrial and original equipment manufacturers (OEMs), as well as channel companies and other organizations. Activity trackers are often limited in their ability to move up the marketing continuum for many reasons. The following discussion addresses some of these challenges by type of company, but tracking activities is the first step and the foundation in the process to deliver improved marketing effectiveness.

INDUSTRIAL AND OEM COMPANIES

Industrial and OEM companies provide unbranded components and products that are completely integrated into the product of another company. They usually have a sales team calling on their customers' engineers or purchasing agents. Marketing activities include those done by the sales team—i.e., personal selling, such as the number of calls, the number of visits, and the number of proposals submitted. They also include activities from the marketing department, such as the number of leads generated and the number of attendees to their booth at a trade show.

There are a number of well-known exceptions in which industrial marketers market directly to the end consumer. Probably the most well-known exception is Intel, with its "Intel Inside" campaign driving the value to the consumer of having their microprocessor product—as opposed to AMD—in a PC or laptop. These types of brands are called ingredient brands, where the end product—the PC or laptop—has a higher perceived value to the consumer because of the mix of branded ingredients in making the finished product. Because ingredient brands spend significantly to drive brand awareness at the consumer level, they often measure interim outcomes and, in some cases, can track direct outcomes. Other ingredient brands include Dolby Laboratories, Stainmaster Carpet, and Teflon.

In most cases, for industrial and OEM marketers, the primary marketing emphasis is to support the "belly to belly" sales effort of the sales force. Products are sold to either purchasing agents or engineers, who make the purchase choice based on relatively clearly defined needs. The number of potential customers for the product or service may also be limited—making many of the traditional marketing functions obsolete. If, for example, there are just a handful of automotive customers, then they are all probably already aware of the brand, and the company is already being included in the purchase process through a request for proposal, or RFP.

Although difficult to achieve, key activities to track include the numbers, types, and quality of the activities of the sales team. This can include the number of sales calls made, the number of personal visits done, and the number of proposals submitted. Any marketing activities must also be tracked in a similar way.

BUSINESS-TO-BUSINESS COMPANIES

Business-to-business companies, which sell products or services that are consumed by businesses, are also often classified as activity trackers. Their products can either be consumables, such as office supplies, or nonconsumables, such as software and services, or plant and equipment.

Small business-to-business companies find it especially hard to move beyond the level of an activity tracker because of their limited set of customers and prospects. As in the case of industrial and OEM marketers, they are typically very sales-centric, and marketing is seen only as a support function.

Often surprising to consumer marketers who routinely operate with a high level of marketing measurement sophistication, is that they, too, may have large business-to-business divisions in their companies that can only track activities. A good example of this might be Kimberly-Clark, which sells tissue under the Kleenex and Scott brands, but also provides tissue and other paper products in a business-to-business environment to restaurants, hospitals, and other businesses.

Business-to-business marketers can improve their marketing effectiveness in a similar way to industrial and OEM marketers by tracking sales activities. In addition, they need to begin to track their own marketing promotional activities, such as direct mail, trade show participation, and other marketing impressions generated in the marketplace.

CONSUMER COMPANIES

Consumer companies can typically move past the activity tracker level to higher levels in the marketing-effectiveness continuum. Consumer companies at this level in the marketing-effectiveness continuum are often limited by their ability to obtain accurate point-of-sale (POS) data from their distribution channels. Even in these cases, many consumer companies can still obtain sufficient data to become either a campaign measurer or mix modeler. If the consumer company sells directly to the consumer—either through the Web, their restaurant, their store, or their catalog— they typically have the wherewithal to develop key metrics to tie incremental revenue to marketing activities.

Exceptions might include the international operations in smaller companies, or smaller consumer companies that haven't reached a critical mass to be able to afford the cost of campaign-measurer level metrics.

If data isn't available, consumer marketers may find it necessary to develop creative ways to sample their outlets in order to obtain some level of accurate and timely POS data at a reasonable cost.

When the cost of the POS data and associated analytics is prohibitive, consumer marketers may be able to consider running A/B tests, pre- and post-tests, or other market tests and surveys to develop measurements that are both meaningful and actionable. These are powerful capabilities, and they can help marketers significantly improve their marketing effectiveness, especially at the program level.

Surprisingly, many large consumer companies cannot pass the activity tracker test. Because of their size and complexity, accurate tracking of their marketing activities across all of the media is rarely housed in one centralized location or data warehouse. They may be engaging in sophisticated research and analytics on their consumers, their competition, and their channel, but their ability to quickly put their hands on their past actions and future plans is missing.

CHANNEL COMPANIES

Channel companies come in many forms. They can be wholesalers, retailers, or sales agents. They offer value in many ways by providing, for example, location, credit, consumer access, bundling, and assortment across many competitors, as well as unique marketing opportunities. Many of these companies have enormous opportunities to improve their marketing effectiveness by investing in this critical function. For channels with large internal sales forces, they usually measure their personal selling function very accurately. The impact of their other P, promotion marketing, is often not measured.

For many major channel brands, the channel relies on the manufacturer to help them make marketing investment decisions related to the promotion of the manufacturer's products. And, because many of these marketing activities are directly and almost wholly funded by the manufacturer through co-op marketing dollars or market development funds, their reliance on the manufacturer to choose the right marketing vehicle is very high. Also, accurate models built by the manufacturers must include any spending in the channel, whether funded by the manufacturer or undertaken by the channel of their own volition.

One of the exceptions to this rule is the large retailer that can develop sophisticated metrics surrounding the optimization of their offerings in order to increase the value of the shopping basket, as well as their own marketing activities. For many retailers, what is often missing is the measurement of the impact of the channel's own marketing toward driving incremental channel sales. Tracking these activities in light of the marketing activities of the manufacturer can help retailers to determine the marketing effectiveness of the channel's own marketing activities.

Lastly, some investment in the channel is often made by the manufacturer to support their position within the channel partner itself. Even though the overall value of the particular marketing activity may not be entirely crucial to increased sales, some of the investment is made to garner better shelf placement or some other advantage not afforded to a manufacturer that doesn't spend marketing dollars in the channel.

OTHER COMPANIES AND ORGANIZATIONS—POLITICAL, CHARITIES, NGOS, GOVERNMENT, BUSINESS-TO-GOVERNMENT

Government organizations are typically very lax in their desire or ability to measure results. Either bureaucrats can't afford to find out the effectiveness of their marketing, or they market so infrequently, and with such internal resistance, that measuring its effectiveness may seem counterproductive. Worse yet, the political consequences of a failed marketing investment may be catastrophic. Often it seems they would rather not know.

Also, the goal of advertising may not always be to lead to a sale, such as in the case of cause marketing. The goal may be to reduce the occurrence of teen pregnancy, teen smoking, or to increase military recruiting. The cause may be sufficiently nebulous as to require a creative definition of success metrics. In these cases, in order to measure the campaign effectiveness they must have some sampling capabilities in place to see whether their advertising made a difference. For example, how does a city know whether its campaign to increase carpooling is actually working? Or, how does a state development corporation know that its efforts are delivering the incremental growth of new foreign businesses into the state?

Charities, political organizations, and non-governmental organizations (NGOs) reflect the same kind of criteria as businesses, in terms of where they reside on the marketing-effectiveness continuum. Charities and NGOs may even be less capable than businesses of measuring tangible results because they have significantly more complex decision-making structures, which make it extremely difficult to allocate funding to measurement. Quite often, all consequential decisions are made by the board or the trustees, as opposed to having a single CEO as the decision maker. For example, at the San Diego Zoo and Wild Animal Park—where there is both real revenue generated through gate receipts and a desire to support a cause, such as endangered species preservation—it can be very difficult to garner the internal political wherewithal to spend precious dollars on metrics when those dollars are expected to be spent supporting the cause—endangered species preservation.

Business–to-government marketers can also have great difficulty in tracking activities. This is especially true for large military sales. Winning the contract may take huge amounts of business development in terms of pre-sales expense, demonstrations, and lobbying. Then, once the contract has been won, ongoing marketing must continue to maintain the contract and keep it in the governmental procurement budget. A good example of this could be selling tank turrets to the army. The initial awareness for some new capability may be done through trade fairs, secret demonstrations, and other means. These activities must be supported through lobbying efforts to make certain that funding can be set aside for a major purchase. Then, after the purchase is contracted, contract funding must be continued over multiple election cycles and economic downturns, risking that the contract may be canceled or cut midstream. The various activities associated with both a sale of this nature and the post-sale "selling" function are numerous, with many nuances, and provide specific difficulties in measuring that are often not seen in business.

TRACKING ACTIVITIES

Tracking activities can fall into a number of categories. To be able to track all activities impingent on the marketplace, marketers must consider not only their marketing, but also customer service, inside sales, and outside sales. These can be mapped into the 4P3C1E framework as follows:

- **Customer service** represents a component of the product P. Marketers have the option of trading off customer satisfaction and service levels with investments in marketing. This post-sale expectation of service is certainly critical to long-term viability, but still represents a product attribute that a customer purchases.
- **Inside and outside sales** represent both a marketing promotion P and a product P. The Web site acts similarly to the sales team by answering questions, providing feedback, and delivering information. In many cases, the Web site can also take orders—just like the sales team. This function represents the promotion P. The sales team can increase purchase intent at the point of purchase through their sales skills.

On the other hand, some customers would rather purchase a number of products over the Web, as opposed to through a salesperson. If they add value to the sale, through pre-and post-sale handholding, then they represent a component of the product P. For example, CDW offers PC products only over the phone. Many of these can also be purchased from Amazon.com or other Web-only providers. These same products can also be purchased from a face-to-face salesperson from a local PC reseller. In this example, the value of the sales channel becomes a key attribute in what gets purchased, and how it gets purchased. This can take place in both the B2B and consumer-marketing environments. For example, Kmart offers virtually no sales help in their stores, whereas Best Buy differentiates itself through its highly trained sales staff, and yet both stores have many similar electronic products.

As the activity tracker gets more and more sophisticated, he or she will get better and better at capturing all activities across the 4P3C1E framework. These activities must be captured as a time series, and this can provide some difficulties. Some data is available hourly or daily, including Web clicks, downloads, and registrations, while other kinds of date are available weekly, such as TV GRPs and still others are available monthly, such as print media data. Some marketing activities are executed on an ad hoc basis, and those simply need to be captured with the date, time, and creative components, if necessary, of execution.

Manual sales efforts are more difficult to track. For example, the number of cold calls, the number of face-to-face sales calls, and the number of proposals submitted, and other similar efforts, are less prone to be tracked. Additionally, many sales individuals resist heavily the tracking of their activities.

GETTING STARTED AS AN ACTIVITY TRACKER

This section outlines some specific steps marketers can take to become an activity tracker. As mentioned previously, many marketers don't track any of their marketing activities. Of the remainder, most of them track only some of their key marketing activities. So, for most marketers, beginning to track specific activities is a big, yet valuable, step toward starting on the path of improved marketing effectiveness.

The four steps to becoming an activity tracker are:
1. Tracking past activities or reconstructing the past
2. Planning future activities
3. Determining your success metric or metrics
4. Iterating this process to deliver continuous improvement

In terms of tracking past activities and planning future activities, I've found the 4P3C1E framework ideal in helping marketers to take this first valuable step in improving marketing effectiveness.

1. TRACKING PAST ACTIVITIES OR RECONSTRUCTING THE PAST

For those of you who aren't currently tracking marketing activities, one option is to begin to reconstruct the past. If you are already tracking current and past marketing activities, then the question for you is the completeness of that tracking. The method below follows the 4P3C1E approach and covers the 4Ps for your company and your competitors, and changes in the consumer base and the channel, the 3Cs, and exogenous factors—1E.

To start, just tracking or reconstructing your promotional activities, such as advertising, direct mail, e-mail, and Web clicks, can deliver many valuable marketing insights. Reconstructing all of the components listed below can be achieved through successive iterations. Initially, though, make certain that all of the key influences in the market, in your opinion, are included as early on as possible.

Your activities—Looking into the past, we need to be able to quickly recount what our marketing activities were, and their associated costs and creative concept. Costs include all creative, production, and execution costs. If applicable, these should also include variable personnel costs. For each activity, you should be tracking the basic information of the program, for example:

- How many direct mail pieces were dropped? How many e-mails were distributed? How many Web clicks were purchased? How many GRPs were executed and what was their flighting?
- What was the call to action, if any? Was there some type of promotional offer? For example, "purchase before the end of the month and get 15 percent off." Was it supporting one particular product variant, and which one? Was it offered in only one channel or across all channels?
- What was the creative concept of the promotional activity?
- How often did the price paid by the end-user at the point-of-sale change and to what levels?
- Did the offered product features change? Did the service level change?
- Were any new channel partners added? Did they add more outlets? Were additional salespersons added?

In an ideal world, you would be able to go back and review all marketing activities week by week for the past three years. If, however, you have only one year or less, that can still be a good start. Table 7.1 shows a potential data structure. Including samples of the specific pieces, artwork, and media can be very helpful.

Competitive activities—Activity tracking can be enhanced by collecting similar information for each of your key competitors—keeping track of their promotional activities, their pricing, any product changes and any changes in their channels. Often this type of competitive marketing data can be purchased from third-party syndicated sources, such as Nielsen Media Research, TNS Media Intelligence, and others.

Marketing activity	Sample units of measure	Cost	Wk 1	Wk 2	Wk 3	Wk n
Direct mail	Quantity in address list	US$350,000	0	12,000	24,000	5,000
E-mail	Quantity in list	US$800,000	90,000	75,000	0	15,000
Trade shows	Number of booth visitors	US$1,000,000	0	0	2,000	0
Print advertising	Quantity in subscription	US$3,500,000	28,000	28,000	14,000	28,000
TV	Gross rating points	US$12,000,000	73	65	61	37
Seasonality	Business days per week	N/A	5	5	4	4
Revenue	Dollars	N/A	US$27M	US$28M	US$25M	US$32M

Figure 7.1: Sample marketing activity data structure

Consumer changes—Changes in the targeted consumer population can include target segment size and growth, segment disposable income, and other changes that might enhance or detract from your revenues. This type of data is also often available from third-party sources. For business-to-business marketers, this may also include the number of businesses that have adopted some type of enabling technology relied on by your offering, such as broadband Internet access, or an installed Internet firewall. Or, it could be the number of customers in your and your competitors' installed base that are no longer a prospect for your solution.

Channel activities—Changes in the channel should also be tracked, including the number of stores for each channel partner, any of their own marketing promotions supporting traffic to their stores, as well as anything else that might impact sales of your, and your competitors', products. For business-to-business marketers, this could include the number of authorized resellers or the level of inventory on-hand of your products.

Exogenous changes—Initially, you need to assess the types of exogenous factors that impact sales in your category, such as:
• Are there seasonal effects or holiday effects?

- Does the weather impact sales?
- What about interest rates, employment, economic growth or decline, or stock market growth or decline?

If any of these have an impact on demand, you must also consider them when building your marketing activity data warehouse. Often these data types can be purchased or are available, free of charge, from various sources.

2. PLANNING FUTURE ACTIVITIES

Looking into the future can be more challenging, because of the continued dynamics of competitive actions, consumer trends, or exogenous factors. But, as you build your marketing plans and budgets, you want to build them to yield the most revenue for the least amount of marketing spend. In just about every business, marketing plans change—and change quite often. And so they should. Nevertheless, in order to develop an accurate picture of your future marketing effectiveness, your marketing plans must be written down and evaluated for their expected effectiveness. It should be a rolling process as the months and quarters unfold, and competitors and other factors behave differently than expected. This will allow you to take the first step in determining whether your marketing plan will help the company "make the numbers" by month, by quarter, and for the year. When your plan is combined with the results developed as a campaign measurer described in the next chapter, you will be able to build a forecast of the revenue that will be generated through your marketing efforts—this will also be discussed further in the next chapter.

3. DETERMINING YOUR SUCCESS METRIC OR METRICS

The ultimate success metric for any marketer is the incremental, high-margin revenue generated for every dollar in marketing.

Unfortunately, in many industries, it is often impossible to measure the direct result of marketing against incremental revenue. It could be that the sales cycle is exceedingly long, e.g., years for chemicals or quarters for enterprise software or totally unpredictable, e.g., for automotive collision repair.

In these cases, interim measures of success may be more pertinent to understanding the factors underlying increased marketing effectiveness. Some success metrics that may be helpful include:

- Financial success metrics
  - Revenue
  - Unit volume
  - Contribution margin
- Survey-based purchase funnel metrics
  - Purchase intent
  - Brand awareness
  - Brand equity
- Directly measured interim metrics
  - Leads of a certain quality[1]
  - Clicks to a landing page of a Web site
  - Web content downloads
  - Webinar registrations
  - Qualified trade show booth attendees
  - Calls to an 800-number
  - Market share

Except for the hard financial success metrics, marketers must have good reason to employ interim measures. Ideally, these metrics should be able to provide some type of estimated conversion factors in order to estimate the future value of the associated revenue underlying these metrics. For example, if in the past every new level 1 lead[2] had a 66 percent probability of converting into revenue within 6 months—worth on average US$250,000—then this would be a valid success metric. Or, a good interim metric could be that every incremental 1 percent in purchase intent would translate into 0.75 percent incremental purchases within 6 months. Another good interim metric could be that every 1,000 webinar registrations would translate into 250 level 1 leads, 100 level 2 leads, and 50 level 3 leads.

4. ITERATING THIS PROCESS TO DELIVER CONTINUOUS IMPROVEMENT

In an ideal world, all information across all competitors, channels, and consumers would be available in full detail and immediately on a regular basis, at no cost. In reality, only a certain portion of the data is actually available, often at some relatively high cost. Although your business may require different priorities, marketers can iterate along the following steps to deliver continued improvement in their activity tracking and marketing effectiveness:

1. **Get started**—As obvious a step as this is, it is often the most difficult. Nothing can improve your marketing effectiveness if you don't make a conscious effort to get started.

2. **Direct-response (promotion P) marketing activities**—Begin with your direct-response marketing: for most companies it is the simplest to focus on. Tracking these activities may also begin to help you get to the next level in the marketing-effectiveness continuum.

3. **Add your brand or indirect (promotion P) marketing activities**—Once a specific methodology has been developed in step 2, this third step should be pretty simple.

4. **Add the remaining three Ps (product, price, and place)**—This step is actually easier than it may appear. Most of the changes in these Ps are step changes that happen relatively infrequently. They are, therefore, quite often very easy to track.

5. **Add competitive 4Ps**—Once you are tracking your own activities, now comes the next level of difficulty in tracking. This step is often accomplished through the purchase of syndicated data, although there are often other available sources of this information. If necessary, this step can be accomplished in a progressive fashion by first determining which competitive actions most impact your sales. Is it their price? Their advertising? Their new product introductions? Begin with this, and then add the other less influential Ps to your tracking activities at a later date.

6. **Add customer, channel, and exogenous factors**—Often these types of data are already being collected in some fashion. For channel growth, this data can be easily obtained by simply asking your channel partner for it. For exogenous factors, this data can be found from online sources at minimal to no charge.

Once you start tracking your marketing activities, and using that tracking data to begin to inform your marketing decisions, it becomes like a drug—a good drug—and marketers become happily addicted to making data-based decisions. The more data you have, the more you want. Your C-suite will also want you to have more data when they finally see the marketing department making decisions based on information, as opposed to gut feel. Finally, you will know you are a certified activity tracker when tracking marketing activities becomes a line item in your budget.

Although every company should be spending a portion of their budget on activity tracking, this first step of investing in data is often the most difficult. Not only is there time and effort involved, but there are also costs that must come from somewhere. These costs come out of other budgets, potentially even reducing the number of actual executed marketing activities. Marketers must choose between tracking activities and doing more marketing. This raises the questions:

- What is the ROI of marketing ROI?
- If I were to simply invest in activity tracking, how many marketing activities must I forego in order to be able to afford it?
- Will there be a return on investment larger than the risk associated with the loss of the actual marketing activity?

As a benchmark, I've found that many consumer packaged goods (CPG) companies spend anywhere from 3 percent to 9 percent of their marketing budgets on marketing research, data collection, and analytics. With this investment, they purchase syndicated data, primary research, tracking studies, and industry reports. These companies represent the best marketers in the world in some of the most competitive categories. If they require this level of investment to manage their marketing effectiveness, how can you justify spending nothing, or significantly less than this benchmark level, to improve your marketing effectiveness?

Just get started!

HOW CAN MARKETERS IMPROVE THEIR ACTIVITY TRACKING?

As a marketer, the goal of becoming an activity tracker is to start to manage your marketing investments in a systematic fashion. Once this is done, many types of analyses can be carried out to start to tie success to specific marketing activities. Without the tracking of the underlying activities, marketers are shooting in the dark. Decisions are made by gut feel, and marketers are sacrificing the opportunity to make significant revenue gains without having to increase their budgets.

The following examples and methodologies illustrate different techniques that marketers can use to begin to compare their tracked activities against success, or proxies of success, in the marketplace. The Marketing-Effectiveness Framework provides a structure to develop these success metrics and help you to drive success for the company, regardless of the difficulties that might exist in the corporate structure and culture, in the market or in the channel.

PURCHASE FUNNEL ANALYSIS

As was partially illustrated in the cameo above, a chemical company selling new chemicals through engineers to large consumers may be able to track leads that are created. These can be considered as top-funnel metrics. Interim steps in the purchase funnel can include the percentage and speed with which leads:

- Move to an engineering evaluation
- Move to a design win
- Move into production

The four steps in this industrial marketing environment have associated metrics:

- The number of leads of a certain quality that are generated
- The number of engineering evaluations outstanding
- The number of design wins achieved
- The number of customers in production and, potentially, the share of total customer purchases of your product

For consumer marketers, interim success metrics could include:

- **Brand awareness**—either aided or unaided
- **Brand imagery**—e.g., "This brand is for people like me," or "This brand is good value for the money."
- **Purchase intent**—e.g., "I am extremely likely to purchase this product."
- **Advocacy**—e.g., "I am extremely likely to recommend this product to a friend."

Each of these can be measured through survey techniques, and each represents how successful your marketing has been at moving consumers to deeper levels in the purchase funnel.

These results may also work to help your channel sales team by providing hard data for them to leverage when negotiating cooperative marketing activities with their channel partners.

MAPPING THE SALES AND BUYER'S CYCLE

The sales and marketing processes that make up the sales cycle need to be mapped against the steps in the purchase funnel, or the buyer cycle, in order to see if there are any discrepancies or process bottlenecks. This is critical to allocating resources against activities that will make a difference in the market.

A sample mapping is shown in Table 7.2.[3] If, for example, the company is not being included in the consideration set when the prospective customer acknowledges their pain, then it may be that the company's awareness needs to be improved. If the company is losing at the proposal phase, then it could be that the sales team is not properly trained. Marketing can help to insert activities at each level in the combined buyer's and sales cycle to deliver more prospective customers to the next lower level in the cycle.

DATA

For just about every company, regardless of size, the biggest challenge to improved marketing effectiveness is the collection of accurate, valid and objective marketing data. Even the biggest and brightest marketers, who are managing the most well-recognized brands, will always complain that they don't have enough data.

BUYER'S CYCLE	SALES CYCLE
Unaware of need	Position in category
Compelling event	New prospects
Acknowledge pain	Identify problem
	Qualify and prioritize
	Establish credentials
Define need	Define need
Allocate budget	
Receive proposals	Propose solution
Select vendors	Prove concept
	Beat competition
Choose vendor	Obtain management approval
Award contract	Close contract

Figure 7.2: Matching the buyer's cycle with the sales cycle

Data will always need to be more accurate, timely, and granular. It is important to ask what type of data is currently collected, where it is stored, how often it is collected (its periodicity), how accurate it is and how many resources are currently being invested in its collection in order to determine how a company can become either a successful activity tracker or begin to operate at any of the other levels in the marketing-effectiveness continuum.

Developing a data strategy that includes the acquisition, storage, analysis, and timely dissemination of the data is critical to success in marketing. Developing a data strategy along the guidelines of the marketing-accountability framework is a key building block toward that success.

TOOLS

Tools that can be found at the activity tracker level are often not very different than those at other levels in the marketing-effectiveness continuum. For business-to-business companies and those consumer marketers with a one-to-one relationship with their customers, customer relationship management (CRM) and sales force automation (SFA) systems play an important role in supporting the pre- and post-sale sales and service relationship. CRM systems help manage the ongoing relationship of the company with the customer, which can include the tracking of support or service incidents, as well as up-selling and cross-selling activities. SFA systems primarily help to manage the pre- and post-sales relationship with prospects and customers, and are chiefly used by the sales team to track the status of specific opportunities as they progress through the purchase cycle. Each of these tools can be enhanced to help manage the business of marketing and improve marketing effectiveness. They can help to track and analyze the kinds of marketing, sales, and service contacts that the company has with existing, and prospective, customers.

For all companies, regardless of whether there is a one-to-one relationship or not, marketing tools that support activity trackers can include marketing resource management (MRM) and marketing investment management (MIM) functions. The key functions of these tools must include detailed campaign tracking, planning, and budgeting.

VALUES

Often marketing is not being driven toward accountability. For whatever reason, accountability has never been part of the marketing process DNA. With this value change in the marketing function, activity trackers can start to plan how their activities will support corporate objectives. In many cases, especially for those that have made tentative steps toward tracking activities, it requires a values change across the organization all the way up to the CEO. The CEO must demand that the marketing department starts to produce measurable results. The CFO must provide the rigor around the data, and be willing to invest in systems and data that are helpful in determining accountability.

The CIO must be willing to provide the reports and systems with the right accuracy and timeliness to help marketers deliver reliable results. The CMO must help his team understand the corporate financial objectives, which are made up of revenue targets and expense budgets, and how the marketing function helps to achieve them. The marketing team must begin to realize that some processes do require rigor, which doesn't have to

THE IMPORTANCE OF MANAGING THE BUSINESS OF MARKETING

If the CFO can have highly accurate and sophisticated cash-management systems, why can't the marketer have marketing dashboards and marketing resource management systems? Why is it that the marketing department is often the last to receive any kind of automation to manage the business of marketing? Why is it that the typical tools afforded the marketing department are limited to Microsoft Excel or Microsoft Project? Why is it that the finance function spends a significant amount of money on cash management, when the marketing department doesn't spend anything, relatively, on managing the business of marketing? Certainly cash is important, but, without effective marketing, cash will be harder and harder to come by.

to stifle creativity, and that, yes, with appropriate rigor the marketing team can deliver continuously improving results in line with corporate objectives.

PERSONAL SELLING AND MARKETING EFFECTIVENESS

Is the sales department part of marketing or not?

Now, before we go on, let's discuss one key point which may determine how companies classify themselves, either as activity trackers or campaign measurers, or both. Are the companies in which most marketing, including promotions and personal selling, is made up of a strong sales force, activity trackers or campaign measurers?

If we consider for a moment that the sales team is just another arm of the marketing department, and that it delivers marketing messages, just like the Web or other media channels might, then it might be correct to assume that these companies are campaign measurers. In fact, the definition of a campaign measurer is that most, or all, of a company's direct-marketing spend can be tied directly to results. With very few exceptions, sales-driven companies can absolutely tie their personal-selling activities to revenue. Kotler classifies the sales team as one of the five pillars of marketing, that is, under the 'Personal Selling' pillar.

Contrast this to a company that sells only over the Internet, such as Amazon.com. Amazon.com advertises through the Internet and elsewhere, and takes orders over the Web. Are they considered an activity tracker or a campaign measurer? I would argue that in this case and, in the prior case, these companies should fall into the campaign measurer classification, especially if they have concrete metrics tying marketing and selling activities to incremental results.

On the other hand, in the unlikely case that the sales team is not rigorously tracked, then this company would be classified as an activity tracker.

Other nuances of this question include business models in which the sales team sells only to the channel partner. The sales team doesn't directly influence the total amount that is sold to the end consumer; rather the team enables the channel partner to make the sale. The channel salesperson is compensated based on shipments to the channel, not necessarily sell-through to the end user. Marketing supports the channel partner through both lead generation at the consumer level and channel-support programs at the channel level. A good example of this would be a high-tech hardware company selling through a two-tier distribution model. The high-tech hardware is purchased by the consumer from a reseller that buys it from a wholesaler. If it is the goal to sign up, authorize, and train more resellers to promote the company's products, then the marketing activity success metric may be the number of resellers signed up with the wholesaler. In this case, the salesperson had little to do with the actual sale to the consumer, and yet he or she does get paid and measured based on the level of purchases made by the wholesaler and, potentially, by the success of the wholesaler authorizing additional resellers.

BECOMING AN ACTIVITY TRACKER

Activity tracking is the basis in marketing to building an effective infrastructure that can support its ability to connect the dots between results and activities. With a data infrastructure in place, marketers can easily become a campaign measurer, mix modeler, or consumer analyzer. Activity tracking is the foundation for all the other levels in the marketing-effectiveness continuum. Each of these other levels requires a detailed knowledge over time of the various activities undertaken by the marketing department, and other key influences in the marketplace following the 4P3C1E framework. Now, with the addition of the measurement of success metrics (which we will learn more about in the coming chapters), marketers will be able to evaluate the success of their marketing programs, compare them against each other, and spend more on the good ones and less on the bad ones. Marketers will be able to continuously improve their outcomes and be an integral part of corporate success. They will become part of the critical path to corporate success.

ENDNOTES

1. Brian Carroll, *Lead Generation for the Complex Sale: Boost the Quality and Quantity of Leads to Increase Your ROI*, (New York: McGraw-Hill 2006).

2. See http://www.siriusdecisions.com for a good treatise on the classification of leads by levels.

3. Reproduced from James D. Lenskold, *Marketing ROI: The Path to Campaign, Customer, and Corporate Profitability*, McGraw-Hill, New York. © 2003.

Campaign Measurers

Campaign-measurer cameo

Inventive Software is a mid-tier provider of mission-critical software sold exclusively to businesses. It had grown successfully since its founding, except for this last year. The company's software has unique capabilities, which they have been able to leverage in the marketplace for the number three spot in the industry. The software is mostly sold direct to small- and mid-sized companies, either on a subscription basis or as an outright purchase of a software license.

The company has been marketing in a discontinuous fashion and yet it was easily able to grow at an astounding pace—until now. Because they had grown so fast—except for this dreadful last year—they never had to worry about metrics and marketing effectiveness. Everything seemed to just work. Every trade show they attended delivered a large quantity of leads. They distributed the leads to their reseller community, and the business magically grew. They always congratulated themselves on their ability to successfully and aggressively market to their customer base in order to become the number three provider in the category. Everyone was happy.

Unfortunately, the market soured and they didn't have a clue as to what worked anymore. The VP of Marketing was let go, and they brought in a new VP. Joan was a creative type, having come from an agency. She had sold her marketing agency, but didn't really make that much money out of it. Now, on the corporate side, she had to go back to her roots. She needed to prove that what she was doing was working—and prove it fast. Unfortunately, there was nothing in place to capture, qualify, or track leads. The marketing lead qualification and conversion process was a disaster, to say the least.

The first thing Joan did was implement clear-lead tracking. In parallel with that project, she converted her entire budget over to what she felt would work best and deliver quantifiable results. She turned to direct mail. It wasn't glamorous like the Super Bowl ad she did once, but she knew in her gut that it would work. However, that was a stretch for the rest of the team to believe. The total available market was about 200,000 mid-sized companies. In the past, the company had invested in great trade shows, creative print ads and even some good PR. The sales team wanted to see some big print ads that they could show to their customers because they wanted to be considered a player. The channel wanted the trade shows so that they could be wined and dined on the company's money. And she had to make the big decision to cut everything else off and just do direct mail. Her plan was to get the lead engine working, and once it was working she would then again be able to invest in other marketing vehicles, such as the annual trade show or the big print ads.

Point #1: When nothing works, get started and get started simply. Go back to the basics.

Joan decided to set some realistic goals and map out the entire sales process. She also took stock of all of the leads that were in the hopper—unfortunately, there were nowhere near enough leads to cover the current cost of running the business. Her creative team was really upset when they found out they

*weren't going to be doing any really cool stuff. They were
even afraid that they would only be able to work in black
and white—that four colors would be a thing of the past! This
was going to be as down and dirty as you can get. Worse than
that, she took every lead, and had the team investigate the
status and source of the last 250 leads to see what happened
to them—and that meant reviewing each and every one of
them in excruciating detail. Joan called this the "Benchmark
250 Plan." Some of her team, however, called it the "shifty,
50-50 plan," because they were less than 50 percent certain
that it was going to help.*

Point #2: Get the data. Reconstruct it if you must.

*The team was wrong. With this analysis they were able to
generate a benchmark that allowed them to understand what
they were going to have to beat in order to get more funding
and better creative work, and in order to begin working in
four colors again. The process wasn't without its casualties.
Two of her staff left after two weeks, but Joan wasn't actually
sad to see them go. The company didn't need that type at
this moment. She knew that they were great creative talent,
and that maybe a year from now they would need to replace
them, but not right now. She had a job to do, and that was
to generate revenue, prove that it was working, and right the
ship of lead generation.*

Point #3: Prove that marketing is generating revenue.

*Getting data turned out to be easier than she thought. To get
data, someone in marketing just needed to want it. ROI didn't
have to be just a tool for the CFO. It turned out to be a way
to help Joan get closer to her customers. By measuring what
works—including the taglines—she was able to understand what
messaging is appropriate, and what their true needs were.
Unfortunately, it's never as easy as you want it to be. Joan
wanted to cancel three of the trade shows, but the cancellation
costs were just too high. She wasn't going to waste any money
on them though, and she surely wasn't going to blindly sign
up for them for the following year. Not unless they worked,
and worked better than her Benchmark 250.*

Once they had the Benchmark 250 in place, they now had a hurdle rate with which they could measure their effectiveness and begin to see what would work and what wouldn't.

Point #4: Determine the definition of good. How good is good enough?

Unfortunately, the market got a lot more complicated when the company had to sell software on a subscription basis. The sales team loved it; they felt that most customers would want to purchase software this way because they could take it out of the operating budget, as opposed to the capital budget. The price objection was negated. Of course, Inventive Software's CFO didn't like it on two levels. First, he knew it was just a sham against his fellow CFOs who were trying to control costs. Spending money out of one bucket and not out of the other didn't mean that the money didn't get spent. It just meant that it got hidden and, worse yet, it actually cost the company more.

Of course, he was happy about the increase in profit. Over a three year period the company made 50 percent more money, and the customer still had to sign a three year license agreement. It was all a shell game that worked in Inventive Software's favor. But the problem was that cash—getting paid an upfront lump sum versus receiving small payments over three years—was very expensive, and they needed a way to compare the value of a subscription customer versus a license customer. He knew that net present value (NPV) and customer lifetime value (CLV) were the right methods of measurement, yet he was having trouble predicting the value of the customer after the third year. Worse yet, even though the math made sense, it still meant that the company didn't have the cash to fund their customers' preferred method of purchase. He would have to build the right financial model in order to drive cash into the company during the transition period. He lamented to the CEO, "We had more customers and sold more software, and yet we had significantly less cash."

Point #5: Use the right calculation method.

In the end, the simplest thing to do was to give the marketers a factor to work with to calculate the returns on their marketing investment. He decided the KISS method—keep it simple, stupid—would work best here; although there was a lot of risk to take on, he wanted to keep the calculation methodology as simple as possible.

So, through consultation with the sales and marketing teams, the CFO was able to make some assumptions about the value of a new customer between those that purchased the software outright and those that bought it on a subscription basis. Surprisingly, the subscription-based customers were more valuable by a ratio of nearly 2-to-1.

CAMPAIGN MEASURERS

Campaign measurers and activity trackers differ in their ability to connect the dots between marketing activities and the incremental revenue or success metric generated by those activities. Campaign measurers and activity trackers both focus at the program level, with little ability to look at the entire marketing mix. These companies may have some consumer information, but they lack the ability to bring the consumer information into a complete model of the categories in which they operate. Campaign measurers can measure the results from most, if not all, of their direct-response marketing efforts, but they can't measure any—or they can only measure very little—of their indirect or branding activities.

The distinction between direct-response marketing and indirect, or brand, marketing is crucial because in direct-response marketing a specific consumer action can be measured. With the inclusion of an 800-number, Web landing page, redemption code, or other call-to-action, marketers have the ability to measure an immediate response from their direct-response marketing. Directly related to direct-response marketing is "last-touch attribution." As explained previously, in last-touch attribution the entire weight of the last touch is attributed to that particular marketing activity. For example, if a customer receives three direct mail pieces and eight newsletters, but responds to an e-mail campaign, then the entire weight of the response is attributed to the e-mail campaign—the last touch—even though there was clearly some value delivered by the three direct mail and eight newsletter touches.

Campaign measurers can cover all types of companies, including both business-to-business (B2B) and consumer companies. As discussed previously, companies with strong personal-selling models typically fall into this classification because they measure the impact of their personal-selling activities with some rigor. As long as the company can attribute some direct result to a majority of their marketing and personal-selling activities, they can be classified as campaign measurers.

Companies can deliver complex, and apparently successful, integrated marketing campaigns with both direct and indirect components, yet they may have difficulty determining the right mix of various marketing elements. Decisions about the mix are made more on intuition and less through scientific method and valid metrics. Campaign measurers look at marketing at the activity or program level—as opposed to the mix level, which will be discussed in the next chapter. Because of this, they tend to ignore synergies between marketing activities. Their primary measurement goal is to measure the impact from one single marketing activity.

One of the most critical elements for campaign measurers is the definition of the success metric. This can be an outcomes-based metric, such as revenue, profit, or market share. Alternatively, the success metric can be an interim metric gathered through surveys, such as brand awareness, brand imagery, purchase intent, or share of wallet. Or, the interim metrics can be directly measured through inbound calls or clicks to a Web landing page.

CHALLENGES FACING CAMPAIGN MEASURERS

Campaign measurers face different challenges depending on their type of market. If they are selling through a sales force, then the success metric is often leads of a certain quality. For those selling to the end-consumer, redemption rates and response rates are good indicators of success.

INDUSTRIAL AND OEM COMPANIES

Two key dimensions drive the success of marketing for industrial and original equipment manufacturing (OEM) companies: the number of customers they have, and their share of wallet with each customer. Industrial and

OEM marketers are classified as campaign measurers if they can track the results of their marketing and personal-selling activities along these two dimensions. As discussed previously, by definition the industrial and OEM companies build a supplier's product into their products and then go on to sell them to end-consumers. Industrial and OEM companies can be broken down into two categories: those companies with a handful of potential customers, such as automotive suppliers, and those with many customers. In both cases, the marketing and selling functions must target the decision maker within the industrial or OEM client. These can be, for example, the purchasing agent or buyer in the automotive industry, or the contractor and architect in electrical components, such as home wiring and fixtures. Marketers and the sales team must focus their efforts on these decision makers in order to increase the likelihood that their products will be incorporated into their customer's products.

To expand further on the example mentioned above, an industrial or OEM campaign measurer could be a supplier of lighting and electrical fixtures in the residential and commercial electrical industry. Marketing can help to win new contractors and architects that specify a precise solution, as well as drive increased purchases from existing customers. But the purchase of the home, or the commercial building, is generally not dependent on the brand of electrical cabling or fixtures behind the sheetrock in the wall. The new homeowner is buying the home for different reasons that are significantly more influential.

In the automotive industry, end-consumers aren't going to purchase a car because of the brand of fastener used to connect various components to the body of the car. The purpose of marketing and sales in this case is to make certain that their fastener is used in as many car models as possible, and that their share on each model is as high as possible. With these as success metrics, these industrial suppliers can determine the success of their marketing and selling activities. Interim success metrics might include how many design wins the company has for inclusion of their fastener in the car design.

Industrial and OEM marketers can improve their support of the sales efforts by closely monitoring and measuring:
- The win/loss rates of proposals across all the members of the sales force
- The share of wallet for each customer

- The length of the sales cycle
- The sales stage, such as the engineering design phase, for all key accounts

Ingredient brands are only limited by the available data from determining direct results from their campaigns. If their partners provide point-of-sale (POS) data, or if they survey end-consumers properly, they can also obtain good campaign success metrics.

BUSINESS-TO-BUSINESS COMPANIES

Business-to-business companies are most often classified as campaign measurers. They invest in both direct and indirect marketing, they may have a direct sales force, and they are able to measure their results to their direct marketing activities. For them, the cost of tracking these results has been improved through the implementation of essential sales force automation (SFA) or consumer relationship management (CRM) systems. This can work even for companies selling through a one- or two-step distribution channel.

With proper tracking techniques, in combination with SFA or CRM systems, the cost of tracking a lead from the initial generation to final conversion to a sale can be monitored. Many enterprise software providers are very capable of this end-to-end market source coding or lead tracking.

Interim results—measured in terms of the number of leads generated and their corresponding lead quality—can be tracked and accounted for. If we separate the process of lead generation from the lead nurturing, management, and conversion processes, we can use the number of leads of a certain quality that are generated as a valuable measure of the effectiveness of a specific marketing activity. Many companies use the monikers of hot, warm, or cold leads, but this is now being supplanted by a lead-quality classification based on levels one through five. Level one leads are now sales ready: they rank high, with a defined budget, a clearly defined need, a stated purchase time frame, the right level in the decision authority hierarchy, and other criteria. Level five leads are not sales ready: they must either be nurtured or discarded because they rank very low in sales-readiness criteria. Levels two through four are at various stages: these levels must be defined and agreed upon by both the marketing team and the sales team in order to optimize the management of leads as they progress from the initial lead-generation process, to the leadnurturingprocess and, finally, to the lead-conversion process. Depending on your organization, a post-sale service component can be added, making up the four key stages in the sales lead-management process funnel.

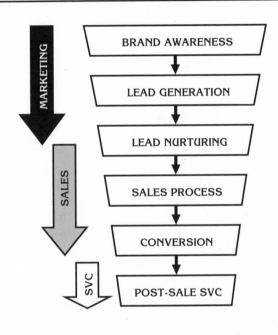

Figure 8.1: Sales lead-processing funnel

Figure 8.1 illustrates the sales leads-processing funnel, mirroring the purchase funnel as seen by the customer. The metrics surrounding this process can lead to a number of important management metrics that can improve the lead generation, qualification, nurturing, and conversion process. For example, all else being equal, if level one leads are not converting, then either the leads are qualified incorrectly or the sales team requires more support and training.

Marketing effectiveness can be measured throughout the purchase cycle, based on the number of leads generated of a certain quality, the speed with which they move from one quality to the next, and the success with which they are converted.

Business-to-business marketers can improve their marketing effectiveness in two ways:

* Analyzing penetration and share across different customer segments
* Developing lead-tracking and lead-qualification mechanisms to determine how leads were generated, and how long each lead takes to convert to the next level in the purchase funnel

CONSUMER COMPANIES

Many mid-size and smaller consumer companies can be classified as campaign measurers, especially those that are selling through a channel. When the channel is unwilling, or unable, to provide POS data or consumer purchase data in a timely and periodic fashion back to their suppliers, it becomes difficult to measure the impact of indirect and, in some cases, direct-marketing activities.

It may also be that the consumer company can obtain POS data from some channel partners, but not others. In this case, they can develop reliable campaign measurements—and possibly marketing-mix models—but not across all channels. The same is true across regions, where data may be available from some countries, but not others. For example, in Spain and other smaller European countries, POS data is only available on a bi-monthly basis. This is too infrequent to generate an accurate statistically based marketing-mix model.

Some of the tools that can be used to measure the response to specific campaigns include direct redemption of coupons and direct responses to specific calls to action, such as 800-numbers, Web landing pages, or A/B testing.[1]

For example, a coupon campaign may have a redemption rate of 0.75 percent, or a direct mail campaign may generate US$200,000 in incremental revenue to up-sell some new capabilities to existing customers.

Alternatively, a consumer credit card company may execute a national advertising campaign by advertising in all markets except for a handful of control cities, such as Austin, Cleveland, and Denver. The company can then compare the difference in lift between the rest of the country and the three control cities. With this difference, the company can track even the direct results of an indirect or branding national TV campaign.

CALCULATING ROMI FOR COUPONS USING LAST-TOUCH ATTRIBUTION

Step one: Calculate the total marketing costs. Assuming the cost of distribution associated with a ten million unit coupon drop was US$4.95 per thousand, the total distribution cost is 10,000,000 * US$4.95 ÷ 1,000 = US$49,500. Assuming the redemption costs of the coupon include a face value of US$1.00, a redemption handling cost of US$0.12, and a redemption rate of 0.75% (a total of 75,000 redeemed coupons) then the redemption costs are 75,000 * (US$1.12) = US$84,000. The total costs of the campaign are US$49,500 + US$84,000 = US$133,500.

Step two: Calculate the total incremental revenue. Assuming the revenue of the product to be US$3.95, the total incremental revenue generated[2] is 75,000 * US$3.95 = US$296,250.

Step three: Calculate the ROMI and ROI factors. The ROMI factor is US$296,250 ÷ US$133,500 = 2.2. Assuming a product contribution margin of 75%, the margin-ROMI = 2.2 * 0.75 = 1.65. The marketing ROI = 65%.

CHANNEL COMPANIES

Although there are many types of channel companies, three primary types are discussed below:

Wholesalers, or distributors, selling to retail, but not to consumers or end-consumers—Marketing done by wholesalers on their own behalf is typically done to win new retailers and resellers. In this case, it resembles the marketing carried out in business-to-business, with a high component of personal selling. Such companies are often limited by their ability to measure the impact of brand activities, but they can see direct and immediate impact to their direct-marketing activities. Here, marketing results can be measured by the number of new resellers or retailers of a certain profile that have signed up to their network. In addition, marketing success metrics may be based on building share of wallet within each of the resellers or retailers. Wholesalers also have similar challenges to industrial and OEM marketers.

Retailers, including restaurants—Marketing done by retailers, restaurateurs, and chains to attract new consumers can be easily measured and tied directly to revenue. They see each and every transaction because they own the POS data, so they can easily measure both the results from specific campaigns and, for larger chains, the results across the mix. In addition to their own advertising, retailers and restaurateurs must also track manufacturers' marketing activities in support of incremental visits to and purchases from the retailer.

Resellers—Resellers, which are defined here as companies selling to businesses, typically have strong personal-selling components to their marketing activities. In this case, they may be limited in their ability to see the results of their brand activities, but should be able to measure their direct marketing activities reasonably well.

OTHER COMPANIES—POLITICAL, CHARITIES, NGOs, GOVERNMENT, BUSINESS-TO-GOVERNMENT

The same comments that applied to activity trackers apply here.

ROMI METHODS FOR CAMPAIGN MEASURERS

Simple metrics can be very effective at helping companies to measure the success of their campaigns. ROMI indices or marketing ROI calculations, such as those shown in the above coupon redemption example, can deliver effective decision support in helping companies to understand the relative results of their marketing efforts. These, combined with an appropriate hurdle rate, can help them to determine the definition of "good enough."

ROMI indices are simple measures. They are used either in the planning process to look forward, or they look into the past by calculating the actual effectiveness of a past marketing activity. They are calculated by dividing the incremental revenue that the program generates by the incremental marketing investment for the program.[3] Variations on ROMI indices can include contribution margin-based indices, asset-growth indices, unit volume, or other outcomes-based success metrics. Marketers can also use interim measures, such as marketing cost per level one lead, or marketing cost per click-through. Calculations using ROI are similar to the contribution-margin ROMI in that they express the incremental contribution margin generated as a percentage of investment. Typically, the CFO or CEO will prefer seeing campaign results expressed as an ROI figure. Marketers, on the other hand, prefer the simplistic ROMI factor, based on revenue, for most of their decision making. Nevertheless, they should be able to convert from one metric to the next as required.

Marketers can also express the ROMI index based on changes at higher levels in the purchase funnel, such as brand awareness, brand consideration, or purchase intent. For example, the cost of an incremental percentage increase in brand awareness per marketing dollar can be valuable in optimizing indirect activities or brand activities.

With ROMI indices calculated across the range of direct-response marketing activities, the marketer can now decide which activities work better than others. With this in hand, the marketer can now begin to adjust the mix of direct-response marketing activities to improve results.

ROMI hurdle rates[4] can be determined to provide the definition of "good enough." By using appropriate hurdle rates, marketers can understand what it takes to deliver marketing activities that will meet, or exceed, corporate goals. Any marketing program that delivers more than the appropriate ROMI hurdle rate should be accepted. Any marketing program that delivers less than the ROMI hurdle rate should be reconsidered or discarded. Separate hurdle rates can be established based on the type of marketing activity. For example, in the case of an Indian bank with a high churn rate—number of customers lost per time period—on its credit card accounts, marketing activities to drive acquisition of new accounts may be more desirable than those that push up-selling and cross-selling in order to maintain a constant or growing level of total accounts. In this case, the ROMI hurdle rates for up-selling, cross-selling, or customer rescue—marketing to existing customers once they have expressed a desire to cancel their account—may need to be set artificially high in order to maintain a constant or growing customer base. This is true even though the return on up-selling and cross-selling may be higher than customer acquisition. Because the bank needs to continuously replenish its credit card accounts, the company must invest proportionately more into acquisition versus retention. For this Indian bank, the hurdle rate for customer acquisition was set lower than the hurdle rate for up-selling and cross-selling.

Campaign measurers can be very sophisticated in tracking the results of their direct-marketing campaigns, but they may be limited by many of the issues outlined above. These limitations will determine whether they are able to measure all of their direct-marketing activities, or only a portion of them. If they can illustrate the value of the data for their channel providers, they may be able to negotiate with those channel partners to begin providing the data.

Sophisticated business-to-business campaign measurers are able to measure the results of their campaigns as their consumers and prospects move through the sales cycle. In categories with long sales cycles, campaign measurers can measure the quality of leads generated, and connect each lead back to a specific marketing activity using, for example, marketing source coding. An SFA system can then be used to evaluate the opportunity value, the probability, and the expected close date in order to calculate some expected value of future revenues from a specific marketing activity and plan.

As the lead progresses through the buyer's cycle, the expected value of both the lead and the entire marketing program can be updated as time passes and more information is gained. This expected value can then be used as a point estimate of the expected future revenue for a particular marketing activity.

Case study 3 (Last-touch attribution: Dental equipment supplier in North America) highlights how the marketers for this company used last-touch attribution combined with market source coding to analyze their marketing effectiveness and improve how they invested their marketing budget across their key marketing media.

Other more-sophisticated campaign measurers may also be able to connect some of their brand activities to revenue. They may be able to measure the synergies of some of their brand campaigns with their direct-response campaigns. These measures might be less rigorous, but they still provide some general results for the incremental, synergistic value of some of their brand marketing.

Less-sophisticated campaign measurers can measure the results of only a portion of their marketing activities—and usually none of their branding activities. Because they have a long sales cycle, they have difficulty connecting the lead source to the marketing campaign, and there is an unsophisticated lead-valuation process. Generated leads, regardless of quality, are handed to the sales team or the channel, and it becomes their responsibility to follow up on them. Because the leads are not qualified, it can be difficult to track the progress of leads from a particular marketing activity as the leads progress through the sales cycle. Only at the end of the campaign can the results be determined. These companies will gain significantly by implementing a more sophisticated lead-management and lead-processing system.

For less-sophisticated campaign measurers, marketers may have difficulty making marketing budget allocations based on the effectiveness of individual marketing activities. By investing in a more rigorous measurement infrastructure, even marketers with rudimentary campaign measurement abilities will be able to make better choices for the allocation of their precious marketing dollars. Although they may not be able to directly measure the impact of incremental brand awareness—or other top-of-the-funnel metrics for that matter—even knowing what drives change in brand metrics can help them to justify it to the C-Suite.

How can marketers improve their campaign measuring?

Can campaign measurers do better? Can their measurements lead not only to improved marketing results, but also to improved operational results? Can campaign measurers predict over time, and with a reasonable certainty, how their activities can impact revenue? If so, they can help the company to plan their revenue better and thereby reduce costs in operations, manufacturing, and inventory.

Purchase funnel
The purchase funnel is a key component in helping any marketer to understand how consumers process the messages that are being inserted into the market. Understanding the purchase funnel for their particular market can deliver significant value to marketers in their efforts to improve their marketing

effectiveness. Campaign measurers, especially, can improve their marketing results: they can use the purchase funnel to track the success of their marketing as customers move from low engagement with the brand—the top of the funnel—to high engagement with the brand at the bottom of the funnel. Where prospective customers lie in the purchase funnel can often be determined by surveying the prospect base.

Through a thorough analysis of the purchase funnel, marketers can uncover potential bottlenecks—where leads and prospects are not moving from one level to the next. They are either "getting stuck" or they are "leaking out." With an understanding of the causes of these bottlenecks and leakages at all levels in the purchase funnel, marketers can start to target specific marketing campaigns to "unstick" their prospects and decrease leakage. Armed with this type of analysis, marketers can significantly improve the results of their activities.

One important component of the purchase funnel has to do with determining the value of a specific marketing touch. Campaign measurers often determine the value of their marketing based solely on the attribution of the last touch, and all the prior touches are ignored. In reality, all marketing touches combine to convert a lead or prospect into a consumer.

With that in mind, the purchase funnel provides a framework through which marketers can start to determine the upper funnel value of various marketing campaigns. Marketing activities deliver value simply by touching the prospect. They generate incremental brand awareness, or brand consideration, regardless of whether the campaign is thought of as being primarily direct or indirect. Therefore, a portion of those consumers who don't convert to a sale do become aware, and put the brand into the consideration set or build brand equity. For example, a coupon campaign delivers 0.75 percent in redemptions. The coupon, however, was received by 99.25 percent of the distribution list that didn't redeem. Some level of incremental brand awareness, consideration, and purchase intent was also delivered to each of these prospects.

Case study 5 (Rebate redemption: Gas utility in North America) illustrates how a gas utility was able to directly track rebate redemptions in order to prove the success of its campaign with a major home-appliance manufacturer.

MARKETING SUCCESS METRICS

Data is critical at all levels in the continuum. All marketers require good data that measures outcomes in order to begin to connect marketing activities to results. Data must be accurate and timely, and must be representative of key responses in the customers' purchase decision-making process.

For business-to-business and consumer companies that have a large personal-selling component, marketers must find creative ways to obtain accurate data. Often, when key interim metrics must be tracked—such as the number of cold calls or the number of face-to-face visits—errors can creep into the system. This is especially true when there is a large sales team in place that must provide the data. Marketers must often find creative ways to accurately obtain this data from a sometimes obstreperous sales team. However, with accurate data, marketers can make more intelligent decisions about what works and what doesn't.

Case study 5 (Rebate redemption: Gas utility in North America) shows how marketers must segment their enterprise customers in order to provide the best marketing support for their sales team. By helping them maintain and build relationships within their client organizations, enterprise marketers can increase retention, and defend against competitive pressures.

For companies selling their products through a channel, the data received from the channel can be incomplete, or have inconsistencies and inaccuracies. Putting systems in place to correct for these errors is critical to maintaining valid and reliable results. Syndicated data from Nielsen or IRI often provides an accurate representation of the POS purchases and in-store marketing and promotions. Nevertheless, errors and inconsistencies do creep in.

Those companies that sell directly to the end-user, such as banks, retailers, or restaurateurs, have the most accurate POS data because it is gathered through their own internal systems. These systems can typically track sales by product on a daily basis. Marketers, however, must add to this data set to include in-store promotions, stock availability, and pricing. This tracking information—information that is gathered at regular intervals from a consistent data source—is ideal for many types of analysis.

MARKETING SUPPORT TOOLS

Marketing support tools fall into several categories, from the simple to the complex. Some are more appropriate for sales-driven companies, such as SFA systems, whereas other tools focus on the planning, management, and develop of marketing materials. Some examples of marketing support tools include:

- **Spreadsheets**—Spreadsheets are often the primary tools of marketers at this level to plan and measure results. They typically require the manual gathering of data.

- **SFA and CRM**—In companies with strong personal selling components, data can be retrieved from SFA or CRM tools. In some cases, analytics can be done directly in the SFA or CRM tools. In these cases, the limitations are that the analytics are typically only available for activities relating to discrete prospects and consumers known and identified in the system. Marketers must augment this data with their forecast of activities such as mass media that are targeted at noncustomers.

- **Enterprise marketing management (EMM), marketing resource management (MRM), and marketing investment management (MIM)**—These tools emphasize different aspects of managing marketing operations, but each typically assists the marketer in planning, managing, and executing marketing activities. Usually these tools support the planning of the campaign mix—as opposed to the analytics—but this seems to be changing. EMM[5] is a software system designed to help marketers manage the end-to-end process from planning and developing marketing plans to executing them and then, finally, to analyzing their results. A related term often used interchangeably with EMM is marketing operations management—although currently it may not be as all-encompassing as EMM. MRM systems are typically a subset of EMM—they manage the planning and development of marketing activities. MIM systems manage and track the financial side of marketing activities, including the financial results in terms of volume and revenue. These systems usually track results based on last-touch attribution. Their data set, however, can often be used for further analytics through other tools.

- **Marketing dashboards**—Marketing dashboards are often components of the EMM, MRM, or MIM tools. The main difference is that they deliver a real-time presentation of the status of marketing development and activities. If a marketing dashboard is designed properly, marketing executives can monitor how programs unfold in the marketplace to help uncover potential problems, or to take advantage of early positive results. Dashboards can allow the marketing executive to receive up-to-the-minute ROMI and marketing ROI calculations.

CORPORATE VALUES

Many companies are successful at measuring effectiveness throughout both the operations and production side of the company. For them to become campaign measurers, they need to instill this same value of accountability into the marketing department. These companies already have a culture of measurement and continuous improvement, but now it becomes marketing's turn to start measuring and improving, and to start demonstrating accountability. The CEO and CFO must support this change in values and culture in order for the marketing department to successfully implement this conversion from a focus on creativity to one of accountability and creativity.

EIGHT STEPS TO BECOMING A CAMPAIGN MEASURER

As mentioned previously, campaign measurers can measure the results from some, or all, of their direct-response marketing campaigns. They can measure the redemption rates from a coupon drop, the lead-generation rates by lead quality from a direct mail campaign, and the conversion rates of a Web banner advertising campaign.

There are two key components to becoming an effective campaign measurer: being able to capture and measure all of the costs of a direct-response marketing campaign, and being able to measure the success of that campaign with a hard and fast metric.

There are eight steps to becoming a campaign measurer:

1. **Identify direct-response marketing campaigns and separate them from indirect or branding campaigns**—Direct-response campaigns can be identified as having a direct and immediate call-to-action. The call-to-action can include calling an 800-number, responding to a Web site, clicking on a link in an e-mail, or redeeming a coupon. In contrast to brand, advertising, which has no call-to-action because the ad is intended to associate some type of brand image, the impact of direct-response marketing can be measured and quantified relatively easily. Certainly, the impact of brand advertising can be measured through various survey techniques to determine changes in purchase intent, brand awareness, or other brand imagery components. However, for the purposes of this discussion, I am defining campaign measurers as those that can measure the response to their direct marketing.

2. **Choose a success metric that is meaningful and yet measurable**—These can be interim measures of click-through rates, leads of a certain quality, or calls to an 800-number, but, preferably, they should be measures of direct sales conversions.

3. **Rank interim success metrics according to their value and proximity to the actual sales conversion**—For example, a click to a Web site may be of less value in predicting purchase intent than the downloading of an order form, or the search for a store location. Table 8.1 shows a sample ranking of different types of success metrics for a B2B company. Of course, your metrics may be defined differently and have a different ranking.

4. **For each interim success metric, determine the potential future value each unit might have**—For example, in a webinar campaign, each webinar participant may have a 33 percent probability of purchasing a product or service with a value of US$1,000. Thus, for a campaign that generates 100 webinar participants, the potential future value would be calculated as 100*0.33*US$1,000 = US$33,000. Each trade-show-booth visitor (non-customer) may have a probability of 25 percent of purchasing a product with a value of US$250. Thus for a campaign that generates 1,000 trade-show visitors who aren't existing customers, the potential future value would be 1,000*0.25*US$250 = US$62,500.

Table 8.1: Value rankings of interim success metrics

Interim Success Metric	Value Ranking
Click to home page	Low
Trade-show-booth visitors (non-customer)	Low
800-number calls	Medium
Webinar participants	Medium
Download of order form	High
Registrations for demonstration	High

5. **Determine the costs required to execute the campaign and calculate the prospective ROMI factor**—For the webinar campaign, it might be the cost of e-mailing prospects from a rented list of 20,000 combined with the creative development costs. If this amounts to US$20,000, and the costs of hosting the webinar are US$1,000, then the prospective ROMI for this webinar campaign, using the revenue potential from step 4, would be US$33,000 ÷ US$21,000 or 1.6. That is, for every dollar invested, the campaign is expected to generate US$1.60 in revenue at some point in the future.

   For the trade-show program, if the cost of the trade show was US$50,000, including all personnel, travel, and booth-related costs, and 50 percent of the costs was ascribed to noncustomers—with the other 50 percent ascribed to current customers—then the prospective ROMI for this campaign would be US$62,500 (see step 4) ÷ US$25,000 or 2.5. That is, for every dollar invested, the campaign is expected to generate US$2.50 in revenue at some point in the future.

6. **Track actual results and calculate actual ROMI factors**—In order to track results, it is crucial to have some type of marketing source tracking capability. For leads, this might be a SFA system. For coupons, this might be a coupon redemption code. For calls to an 800-number, this might mean having separate 800-numbers or extensions for each campaign and simply counting all calls to a specific 800-number or extension. For other campaigns, A/B testing or split cell testing may be used to determine the incremental revenue generated for the specific marketing activity. If

instead of 100 webinar participants, the campaign delivered 121 participants with an actual close rate of 30 percent then the actual ROMI would be 121 *0.30* US\$1,000 ÷ US\$21,000 = 1.7.

7. **Save, secure, and make available your results in a knowledgebase to help guide future decisions**—It is critical to make your results information available for future campaign planning. The information can also be used to generate a full bottom-up budget that is more closely related to supporting the achievement of the corporate sales plan.

8. **Widen the scope of measurement to include all direct-response marketing activities**—With these functions in place, connecting the dots to specific direct-response marketing campaigns is now possible. When this information becomes available, you will be able to see whether some campaigns were successful and worth repeating—and improving—and if others were marginally unsuccessful and worth fixing, or were completely unsuccessful and not worth repeating.

My experience in business-to-business environments is that over 50 percent of the marketing activities can be discarded because they provide little or no value. Of the remainder, only 25 percent are successful, and the remaining 25 percent are worth fixing. If this were the case for you, what would be the value of effective ROI measurement?[6]

CASE STUDIES

CASE STUDY 1—A/B TESTING: PLUMBING REPAIR SERVICES IN NORTH AMERICA

A/B testing is an invaluable methodology to determine marketing effectiveness. This case study illustrates how a U.S.-based chain of plumbers utilizes A/B testing to measure the success mass media can have at driving short-term results.

BACKGROUND

Plumbing services for existing homes are called on for emergency repair and planned renovation. Selecting a plumber in an emergency can be done based on your neighbor's recommendation, a quick look in the phone book, or a quick search on the Web. The extent of the emergency determines the amount of time available to search for a plumber. Brand awareness and imagery are key elements in influencing the selection process.

How could the marketing team determine whether mass media would have any impact on revenue when mass media has never before been systematically employed? What would be a reasonable method to set up as a testing regimen to determine if mass media has any effect and to what degree?

ACRS Plumbing has locations in several major cities in the southeast, with coverage of ten counties in and around Dallas–Fort Worth (DFW), Texas. The category is very fragmented and there are no real national market leaders, although ACRS Plumbing is one of the top ten brands. The company has been successful—growing organically, primarily through the use of billboards, telephone book advertising and, more recently, a strong Web presence in many city-oriented search sites.

SOLUTION AND REQUIRED DATA

The company had some success with radio in other, smaller cities, but now the marketing team wants to place a major bet to determine whether radio advertising could have a measurable, repeatable, and scalable effect on sales in one of their larger regions. If it is successful in their largest region, they could then repeat it across their second-tier cities.

The marketing team decided to run a controlled test around morning and evening drive-time radio in one of the neighboring towns to DFW. They used DFW itself as the control. The radio stations were chosen such that there was little if any overlap with DFW. The company ran a series of advertisements for a 12-week period. The marketers did their best to make certain no other changes were made in terms of marketing or sales, as well as pricing and service offering, in order to keep the experimental design as rigorous as possible. Also, because of the close vicinity between the test and control cities, differences in weather and other seasonal factors, as well as competitive set, were limited.

In order to determine the ROMI factor for this experimental marketing activity, the following data is required:
- The weekly sales for the test city for the prior and current years
- The weekly sales for the control city for the prior and current years
- The cost of the advertising—separating creative development from production and insertion costs
- The tracking of other activities (competitive, partner, consumer, exogenous) such as competitive entries/exits, advertising, and other promotions

RESULTS
Within two weeks after the experiment began, sales started to noticeably ramp up in the test location. This continued mass media test drove incremental revenue for a few more weeks and then started to level out. Throughout the 12-week test period, and for weeks thereafter, the increased level of sales was maintained. The test was discontinued 3 weeks after the conclusion of the advertising campaign. Fortunately, because the success of the test was so obvious, the company immediately began to change their advertising campaign—planning to add the control city 3 weeks after the conclusion of the test campaign. Because the control group advertising was changed only 3 weeks after the conclusion of the test, it was not possible to clearly measure medium and longer term effects. Nevertheless, the test validated that mass media can drive incremental revenue for plumbing services.

Results are calculated as illustrated in Table 8.2. Assuming all else being equal, the incremental sales over the 12- week period for the test location versus the control city represents the incremental sales due to radio advertising.

Table 8.2: Sample ROMI calculation for test/control group measurement

Calculating the impact of marketing on the test city versus the control city		
	Prior year revenue for the 12-week period plus 3 weeks after the end of the test period	Current year revenue for the 12-week period plus 3 weeks after the end of the test period	Calculated percent growth
Year over year sales for the test city	US$2,840,000	US$3,120,000	9.9%
Year over year sales for the control city	US$35.660,000	US$36,111,000	1.3%
Attributed growth to radio advertishing in the test city			8.6% (=9.9%–1.3%)
Calculating ROMI		
Assumed increased revenue due to radio advertising	US$244,240 (=US$2,840,000 * 8.6%)	
Marketing spend (not including creative development)	US$18,000	
ROMI factor	13.6 (=US$244,240 ÷ US$18,000)	

CHALLENGES, ISSUES, AND OPPORTUNITIES
One of the key assumptions is that "all else is equal." This is a critical factor in validating that the ROMI result was valid and objective.

Key considerations include:
- Were there differences in the weather (e.g., a freeze outside of the city that didn't take place inside the city) causing increased repair requirements?
- Did the competition open or close any of their locations during the test period?
- Is it possible that there would have been any crossover from the test locations to the control locations?
- Were there potentially any other considerations that could have influenced the outcome?

Other potential business questions not evaluated in this particular study were the medium- and long-term effects of the advertising campaign. This campaign lasted only 12 weeks, but revenue continued to remain high even after the advertising ceased. This medium-term effect could be evaluated had the test been able to conclude without any changes in the media to the control group. Because the medium- and long-term effects are ignored in this calculation, the above ROMI factor understates the full long-term value of the advertising.

Media flighting is one opportunity that can also be explored with this testing method. Once the results of the media reach a plateau, different flighting can be tested to determine the decay and growth rates in revenue when the media is turned off and on. With this information, the flighting of the media can be further optimized by flighting it in such a way that awareness is maintained and revenue remains relatively flat even though less advertising is inserted into the market.

PROCEDURE
1. Choose test units to form a test group. These can be cities, locations, products, or other clearly defined units within the market that will only receive the test marketing.
2. Manage and purchase media to make certain that the test units receive the media and the control groups

do not. (This method could be reversed, where the control groups receive the media and the test group does not).

3. Track all marketing expenditures, including creative, production, and insertion costs associated with the test group. Expenditures relating to one-time production and creative need to be excluded in order to estimate the potential ROMI of the insertion in the control market. Expenditures that are volume-related (i.e. the difference in size between the test and control markets) may also need to be adjusted as well.

4. Track all appropriate success metrics (such as revenue, clicks, or leads) over the time period and compare them with a prior equivalent time period. These time periods can be hourly and daily—in the case of the Internet—or weekly, or monthly, depending on the business question.

5. Track and monitor all outside influences for both the test and control groups; for example, competitive actions, changes in the channel, changes in consumer behavior, and changes in exogenous factors.

6. Calculate results, keeping in mind potential sources of error or inaccuracy—"experimental noise." Errors can creep into the test from many sources, such as those mentioned in Point 5 above.

CASE STUDY 2—DIRECT MARKETING AND CRM: MOBILE TELECOMMUNICATIONS COMPANY IN ASIA

Using analytic techniques to improve one-to-one relationships can significantly enhance customer retention and provide up-sell and cross-sell opportunities. This case study illustrates how an Asian telephone company was able to use valuable information extracted from its database, combined with publicly available data, to improve marketing ROI.

BACKGROUND
Using analytics to improve retention of customers is critical to improving marketing results for one-to-one marketers. ModernTelCom—one of the five largest telephone companies—has operations in over ten countries throughout Asia-Pacific with over five million customers. They provide a complete suite of telephony services, including mobile, fixed line, broadband Internet, and television. To increase retention, up-selling, and cross-selling throughout the Asia-Pacific market, ModernTelCom has a team of five analysts supporting 30 campaigns per month with simple to complex analytics and customer segmentation. Because of the level of call volume in today's modern communications environment, ModernTelCom generates over 70 million rows of detailed call data per day in the mobile communications segment alone. As with most mobile communications providers, the handsets are heavily subsidized and consumers have become accustomed to being able to afford the latest handsets as their contracts come up for renewal.

As in most maturing Asia-Pacific countries, fixed line usage is being substituted with mobile telephony. On the other hand, the penetration, in this country, of mobile telephony has reached nearly 90 percent of the available market. Because of these two trends, smaller telephone companies, ISPs, and other recent entrants are consolidating with the larger players and their pricing is becoming increasingly competitive. Retaining customers is more cost effective than acquiring new customers (of whom there are few).

The company uses sophisticated data mining to evaluate customer usage and behavior, service levels, and product usage in order to predict potential churn (attrition), and to respond to, and counteract, inactivity, as well as up-sell and cross-sell potential new services. For example, data analysis can determine with some specificity when users attend specific concerts, such as Britney Spears and, following the concert, provide concert-goers free Britney-related wallpapers and ringtones. Although the data-warehousing solution provides very detailed behavioral information, matching users with publicly available demographic information offers some challenges. Because the mobile customer can be anyone in the household, mobile customers can only be matched at the household level—not individually—with publicly available information, such as household income, age of the home, and competitive telecommunications services.

SOLUTION AND REQUIRED DATA

Customer behavior and usage data are captured in a real-time integrated data warehouse. The various internal customer databases are joined to form a single "view" of the customer, where the analysts use structured query language (SQL) combined with statistical data-mining tools. Typical analyses include over 500 columns of data, which are used as inputs into predictive and clustering models.

MOBILE CHURN MITIGATION THROUGH SEGMENTATION AND ANALYSIS

The over one million post-paid (as opposed to pre-paid) mobile phone customers in the country were segmented by monthly billing to those spending over US$20 per month. About 35 percent of the customer base had billings under US$20 per month and were deemed not to be profitable analysis opportunities—leaving 65 percent of the customer base for analysis and targeting. In this target segment, the average mobile phone bill was just over US$35 per month. Identification of the top 5 percent high-churn-risk customers represented 2.5 percent of the customer base, where about half of these customers would churn to another provider and the remainder would churn for health reasons, holidays, and/or late payment—indicating potential credit risk. Based on demographic and behavioral data, subsegments of this customer set were targeted with retention-marketing programs. As part of the ongoing promotional design execution, control groups were used with every offer to validate the level of reduced churn for each marketing promotion.

FIXED LINE SEGMENTATION

As opposed to mobile usage behavior, fixed line usage is household based. Actual behavior is determined by the usage behavior of each of the household members, so segmentation can only be accomplished at the household level. With the right segmentation, it can be used to target up-selling and cross-selling offers.

Seven behavioral segments were developed using cluster analysis, with each segment representing from 6 percent to 25 percent of the customer base. This was then overlaid with demographic information. One of the key segments—customers with heavy international dialing— represented a key profit opportunity in which customers who were typically expatriates were using their fixed line phones to dial home outside of the country. Fifty percent of the average monthly spend in this segment was on international calling. Churn rates for this segment were typically the highest of all the segments—many times over the average of 2 percent per month.

RESULTS

MOBILE CHURN MITIGATION THROUGH SEGMENTATION AND ANALYSIS

Based on analytics and retention-based offers, the churn rate was demonstrably reduced by 0.2 percent per month. This reduction represented just over US$50,000 in revenue per month and a reduction in the churn rate from 1.6 percent to just less than 1.25 percent. The cumulative effect of the ongoing retention marketing and analytics after the first 18 months of continuing analysis represented an annualized revenue saving of over US$1.1 million.

FIXED LINE SEGMENTATION

As an initial test, a group of 6,000 customers was selected and offered participation in an international dial-saver program, at a recurring monthly cost of US$5.00 per month, combined with a lower international dialing rate plan. Although this offering reduced short-term international dialing revenues, it led to a reduced churn rate to well under 0.5 percent per month and significantly higher long-term revenues; the lack of lost revenue due to reduced churn outweighed loss in revenue due to the lower international dialing rates.

CHALLENGES, ISSUES, AND OPPORTUNITIES

Many of the challenges in delivering improved churn rates have to do with being able to continually prove that the churn rate has been actually reduced. This can only be done by rigorously maintaining a control group to validate that the churn rates were actually reduced.

Organizational challenges exist, and some marketers still believe that "carpet-bombing" all of their customers with a specific offer is a more effective approach than just marketing to specific, prospective high-yield customer segments. Through rigorous testing and experimental design, these ingrained attitudes can be slowly overcome. The reduced costs of the smaller mailing campaigns can be redirected and used to enhance the quality of marketing materials.

PROCEDURE

1. Clean the data by making certain that billing addresses accurately match other data and can be accurately linked with externally purchased demographic data.
2. Set up a data warehouse or data mart for analysis. Verify internal procedures concerning the use of the data mart to make certain that they comply with spam and other direct marketing regulations in the country.
3. Determine the type of analytics, beginning with, for example, recency, frequency, and monetary (RFM) value. Define the success metrics (e.g., reduced churn or increased monthly revenue).
4. Advance to more complex analytics, such as neural networks, once the organization has accepted the value of analytics.
5. Iterate as necessary to deliver continuous improvement.

CASE STUDY 3 — LAST-TOUCH ATTRIBUTION: DENTAL EQUIPMENT SUPPLIER IN NORTH AMERICA

This case study illustrates how last-touch attribution can be used in a business-to-business environment to help a dental equipment supplier improve its marketing effectiveness throughout the marketing and sales process in the United States.

BACKGROUND

Teeth, Inc. is a distributor of digital X-ray devices that provide digital snapshots of a patient's teeth directly on the screen of the dentist's PC. No longer do the dentist and patient have to wait for the film to develop. Now dentists can remain in the room while they consult with the patient and reviews the results in real time.

Teeth, Inc. used direct mail, newsletters, search engine optimization, and pay-per-click advertising to drive leads to their internal sales force. The leads fell into four broad categories:
- Unqualified
- Those that converted immediately in inside sales
- Those that needed to be nurtured further
- Those that required immediate further contact in the field sales team

Once the leads were qualified, most were handed off to the outside field sales team to be converted; there were only a few leads converted over the phone in inside sales. The company initially assumed that the Web-lead generation was highly effective, because both of these sources generated a high quantity of leads. Unfortunately, the quality of those Web leads was not tracked, so the company couldn't determine which lead source provided the highest returns, as measured by revenue.

SOLUTION AND REQUIRED DATA

The company decided to track the marketing lead source for each lead. Although there was some overlap and some inaccuracies, each of the leads that responded in some fashion was assigned one of the four lead sources. With the lead sources assigned the associated monthly costs were determined and the marketing costs per lead were calculated as shown in Table 8.3.

Table 8.3: Marketing sources

Marketing source	No. of leads	Monthly costs	Marketing cost per lead (calculated)
Search engine optimization (SEO)	190	US$2,500	US$13.16
Pay-per-click advertising (PPC)	160	US$5,000	US$31.25
Newsletter	33	US$5,000	US$151.52
Direct mail	75	US$6,500	US$86.67
Total leads	458	US$19,000	US$41.48 (av.)

Based on the table—prior to a rigorous end-to-end analysis—the company wanted to increase their investment in SEO and PPC, and significantly reduce investment in their monthly newsletter and direct mail programs, because the cost per lead was so much lower for the first two options

A detailed cost analysis, however, tells a different story. Leads generate follow-on costs in order to process and convert them. The first cost associated with a lead is the qualification process. Qualified leads must be sorted out from the unqualified leads. For Teeth, Inc., this is a manual process performed by the inside sales team.

The sales team was comprised of three individuals—not including the manager—each working actively on leads about 75 percent of the time. The rest of their time was spent on administrative tasks, training, and personal days (vacation and sick days). Including benefits and an estimated level of commissions, their costs per year were determined to be about US$60,000. One-third of their active lead-processing time was spent on lead nurturing, while two-thirds was spent on lead qualification. Based on this allotment of their time, the lead-processing cost was determined to be, on average, US$16.38 (= US$60,000 * 3 ÷ 12 ÷ 458 *75%* 2/3). This represents the actual cost per lead to qualify leads in inside sales, regardless of quality.

RESULTS[7]

The last piece of information required in order to provide a more accurate picture of the marketing effectiveness for this dental equipment provider is the conversion rates per lead source. The revenue per sale was, on average, US$26,000. These are shown in Table 8.4.

Table 8.4: ROMI factor calculations by marketing source

Marketing source	Monthly marketing costs	Monthly inside sales processing costs	Total costs (marketing + inside sales)	Conversion rate	Revenue	ROMI FACTOR (marketing 7 inside sales)
Search engine optimization	US$2,500	US$3,112 (=US$16.38 * 190)	US$5,612	3%	US$148,200 (US$26,000 * 190 * 3%)	26.4
Pay-per-click advertising	US$5,000	US$2,621 (=US$16.38 * 160)	US$7,621	5%	US$208,000 (US$26,000 * 160 * 5%)	27.3
Newsletter	US$5,000	US$541 (=US$16.38 * 33)	US$5,541	40%	US$343,200 (US$26,000 * 33 * 40%)	61.9
Direct mail	US$6,500	US$1,229 (=US$16.38 * 75)	US$7,799	40%	US$780,000 (US$26,000 * 75 * 40%)	100.9
Total leads	US$19,000	US$7,502 (=US$16.38 * 458)	US$26,502		US$1,479,400	(av.)55.8

ROMI factors were calculated by dividing the revenue generated per marketing source by the investment made in both marketing and inside sales per marketing source. This shows that the best response was direct mail, followed by the newsletter program.

CHALLENGES, ISSUES, AND OPPORTUNITIES
Calculating the costs to process a lead needs to take into account the value of personnel costs of the sales team. Certainly, if the number of leads increased drastically then additional sales capacity would need to be hired. If, however, the number of leads increased only slightly, then the processing costs per lead in sales would actually go down because the slight increase in leads wouldn't warrant the addition of sales staff. In other words, there would be more leads to process without the addition of any new costs.

If, on the other hand, the company significantly changed its investments, leading to the hiring of additional sales personnel, the calculation would have to take into account this new cost structure.

Last-touch attribution ignores all prior touches and any mass media. These assumptions must be tested in order to validate whether they might impact the result of the decision. In many cases, the differences in results between the various media will be large enough that these effects can be ignored.

PROCEDURE
1. Track all leads by lead source. Capture the actual costs per month applied to each media type.
2. Track all costs in the sales department. Determine the full costs of the sales team in order to assign costs to the average amount of time required to process a lead, depending on the quality of the lead. Include commissions and other variable costs, if applicable.

3. Calculate the full cost to generate a lead in marketing, to process the lead in inside sales, and to convert the lead in field sales.
4. Calculate the ROMI factors for each media type, dividing the actual revenue generated by the costs from step 3.

CASE STUDY 4—LOYALTY MARKETING: INTERNATIONAL HOTEL CHAIN BASED IN ASIA

Travelers have many choices for their hotel stays. Hotels must cater to both business and leisure travelers. Loyalty marketing—a component of CRM—can help hotel chains stay top-of-mind with their important customer base—the frequent traveler—and to help keep them coming back. This case study reveals how an Asian four-and five-star hotel chain was able to build its brand and increase revenue through loyalty marketing.

BACKGROUND
Hotel chains in Asia are experiencing high growth and occupancy rates due to the economic growth in the region, especially in the emerging markets. Profits are tempered due to increased competition and increased capacity. Hotel quality is roughly described through the one- through five-star system. Regardless of the number of stars, a particular hotel or chain might have high customer expectations for service and quality.

APHotels has a long history of a very effective loyalty program. Over the last few years the company revamped their program and data infrastructure to take advantage of modern analytical capabilities to drive retention and revenue. APHotels defined retention at two levels: High retention was defined as those customers returning within three months, moderate retention was defined as those customers returning with 12 months.

Loyalty programs can deliver incremental revenue by maintaining and nurturing the relationship with their most frequent travelers. Tiers in the loyalty program are based on a combination of the number of stays and the length of the stays. For each tier in the program, different levels of services and rewards are offered. As is common in the industry, APHotels' loyalty program is aligned with other frequent traveler programs for air and car rentals. Depending on the alliance, points can be exchanged and travel options enhanced. Promotions are offered through the loyalty program for vacation packages and related services, such as car rentals and dining.

The company invested in both loyalty and brand-related marketing—spending just over US$500,000. One third of their budget was targeted to their existing customer database using a combination of direct mail and e-mail. The remainder was spent on mass media—on branding, on TV, and in print.

SOLUTION AND REQUIRED DATA
In many companies, customer information is scattered across many databases. APHotels is no different and has over 10 databases containing customer and behavioral information. Through the loyalty program, online and offline customer behaviors can be tracked and offers made based on the customers' loyalty program level and recent activity.

The customer base was segmented, based on demographic and behavioral information, into seven segments spanning eight countries. RFM (recency, frequency, and monetary value) analysis was used to manage and plan campaigns by segment. In addition, online searches were matched against offline behavior.

RESULTS
Because of the long-term value of a loyal customer, both the short- and long-term behaviors needed to be measured. In some cases, effects due to marketing were not noticeable for over six months. Based on initial

testing and through the use of RFM analysis and other analytics, three-month retention rates were improved by over 9 percent and 12-month retention rates were improved by over 6 percent, delivering a marketing ROI for their loyalty marketing of over 175 percent.

CHALLENGES, ISSUES, AND OPPORTUNITIES

As in any database-centric marketing approach, aligning databases and cleansing the data can often be an overwhelming task. For APHotels, offline and online behavior needed to be integrated in order to be able to target specific personas with specific offerings. To drive the most benefit a cross-functional team was set up between sales, marketing, and customer service. It supported the smooth flow of data gathering and manipulation, and provided a broad range of strategic options that could be explored.

The length of time required to detect a measurable difference caused the analytics to be scaled back in the first year. However, as verifiable results began to be noticed after the first six months, investments were put back on track and investment in the program was intensified.

PROCEDURE

The building of marketing programs to maintain loyalty and retention, and to build cross-selling and up-selling opportunities, must start with a concise data strategy. The many databases housing customer demographic and behavioral data must first be identified, and a strategy must be put in place to build a usable data warehouse with accurate and fully aligned data. Once this is done, various analyses can take place, beginning with the simplest and then moving to the more complex.

CASE STUDY 5—REBATE REDEMPTION: GAS UTILITY IN NORTH AMERICA

This case study illustrates how a U.S.-based gas utility can use the redemption of rebate offers to measure the impact of direct-marketing campaigns and determine their success over time.

BACKGROUND
Improving the marketing and selling of natural gas—whether to commercial or residential customers—must take into account a number of factors:

- Demand is very seasonal, with heating being the primary driver, whereas cooking and hot water are basically nonseasonal. This is especially pronounced in states in the north.
- For the residential segment, total consumption is based on two primary factors: the number of homes connected, and the number of burner tips (such as stove tops, furnaces, fireplaces, or water heaters) and the usage of gas at each of those tips.
- In most states, the rates paid by consumers are heavily regulated, although a few states have now deregulated and opened up the actual marketing of the gas (as opposed to the delivery of gas through the pipes) to competition.
- Marketing must drive conflicting messages into the marketplace; not only must the message drive more consumption, but it must also provide a message to increase energy conservation.
- Residential construction methods, efficiency improvements, and conservation typically reduce overall demand by about 1 percent per year.
- Availability of gas to the home or commercial structure is determined by whether there is a pipe under the street and a connection to the home. Thus the number of new home or commercial structure connections is determined primarily by the developer and the homebuilder. Homes and commercial structures that aren't connected when they are built are generally not retrofitted.
- Gas is perceived as a premium option that will increase a home's resale value and is therefore not typically made available for homes under a certain floor area and dollar value.

- For new home construction, the gas sales team must "sell" the developer to bury gas pipes under the street and connect up the new homes. In order to increase the number of opportunities for increased consumption, they must further "sell" the homebuilder to not only provide gas for heating, but also gas hot water, stove tops, and fireplaces. Because gas is a utility, and essentially a monopoly—leaving aside the states where gas is marketed by independent gas marketers for the moment—very little "branding" is required to influence the decision of the developer or the homebuilder. It is primarily decided by the size and dollar value of the home, and by the amenities assumed to be desired by prospective home buyers.
- Homeowners, as well as commercial gas users, often disconnect in spring and reconnect in the fall in order to save the recurring monthly connect charges during the summer months.
- Residential customers may be set up with a gas connection to the home, but it can be active or inactive. If it is inactive for a long period of time—18 months—the meter is removed so that the utility can reuse this asset with other, active customers.
- The health of the housing market can significantly influence the net number of connections. In a down market with a high foreclosure rate, homeowners downgrade to smaller homes or apartments where gas usage is less prevalent. On the other hand, a high number of new housing starts directly influences the potential number of future connections.
- When a gas-related appliance breaks down—for example, a furnace or air-conditioning unit fails—the homeowner may decide to replace just the failing unit with gas or electric or replace both the furnace and air-conditioning unit with all-electric. This is heavily influenced by the HVAC repair person when it comes to the furnace and air conditioning, the plumber when it comes to the water heater, and house remodeler when it comes to the stove and oven. It may also be influenced by any of the home improvement retailers, such as Lowe's® and The Home Depot®.

Against this backdrop, gas marketing must deliver incremental revenue and improve its effectiveness in order to help the company grow the business and meet corporate objectives.

MNO Gas is based in the western part of the United States, with franchises in a number of northern and southern states. It spends about US$10 million per year on marketing, and has inside and field sales that primarily target commercial customers, developers, and homebuilders. Most of the marketing investment is spent on the largest—yet least profitable—residential segment. And, because new connections are primarily driven by the sales team through selling efforts with the developers and homebuilders, marketing's objectives and success is primarily driven by retention (that is, lack of attrition), reconnection and, to a lesser extent, increased consumption—i.e., an increased numbers of burner tips.

As with many companies operating in regulated, less-competitive markets, data systems and infrastructures are less than cutting edge. They are often designed to handle only the billing function, but can't support the data manipulation required of complex analytics on consumption behavior and other factors.

SOLUTION AND REQUIRED DATA
MNO Gas implemented a monthly tracking method that separates its residential and commercial customers—capturing the number of newly activated customers and the total number of active connections, where the net difference equals the calculated number of lost customers (attrition). This is the number marketing is responsible for. After deseasonalizing these numbers, the monthly and year-over-year growth and decline can now be more definitively determined and trends can be deduced.

RESULTS

ROMI CALCULATION

MNO Gas significantly reduced all advertising and marketing to the residential market for the five-year period prior to 2006. For the first year, the number of net new customers continued to grow, yet in the following four years the numbers steadily declined at a rate of about 1.5 percent per year. In 2006, advertising and marketing efforts were reinstituted and sales immediately started to increase—leading to a 2.1 percent year-over-year increase based on a budget of about US$10 million. The increased sales due to these marketing efforts were 3.6 percent or US$149 million delivering a ROMI factor of just less than 15. This ROMI factor was calculated based on a simple 12-month estimate of future revenue, as opposed to a more detailed calculation of the long-term impact (i.e. customer lifetime value). The actual ROMI factor would be significantly higher if the lifetime value of the retained customers was considered.

Through improved trend analysis, MNO Gas was also able to discover the lag time of specific marketing activities and properly attribute the impact to the specific event. In particular, a June promotional rebate using radio, billboards, and print advertising was offered to homeowners to support the financing of a new furnace (US$200) or a new water heater (US$100). Rebate redemptions were received primarily in July (73 percent), with some in August (22 percent), and the rest in September (5 percent). The direct value of the promotion was determined with this tracking information and determined to deliver US$12.5 million in incremental revenue for the year. The marketing spend was about US$1 million, whereas the revenue was worth an annualized US$26 million when the full 12 months of annualized revenue was calculated. This yielded a ROMI rate of 26.

SUBSIDY

However, in order to make this calculation more accurate, subsidy effects must be considered. Subsidy, in a marketing context, refers to those customers who would have nevertheless bought the new gas furnace, water heater, or stovetop had they not received the rebate. The subsidy effects were estimated by comparing the attrition rate from the prior year with the attrition rate immediately following the promotion. In this instance, the attrition rate was reduced by an estimated 0.2 percent versus the prior years' attrition rates. This yielded an estimated ROMI for the promotion of 17, after subsidy.

CHALLENGES, ISSUES, AND OPPORTUNITIES

The biggest challenge for MNO Gas is to determine the value of an improved data infrastructure. At this time, the customer database can't run large queries for the marketing team. Every time the idea comes up to invest in a new database, it is put off for other investments. Without knowing the value of an improved customer database, the marketing team is completely missing out on many direct-marketing opportunities. This limits the ability of the company to improve retention, up-selling, and cross-selling. Without accurate knowledge of active and recently inactive customers, the company can't devise creative programs to influence their customers' behavior.

COLLINEARITY

In highly seasonal businesses, determining the seasonal impact on sales and deseasonalizing the numbers can be impacted by collinear marketing activities. If, for example, the company always runs a June promotion of furnaces and water heaters, it will not be possible to separate out the impact of the seasonal influences from the marketing influences. In the case of MNO Gas, where no marketing was undertaken for the four years prior to 2006, the seasonal effects on retention can be reasonably well estimated.

CUSTOMER LIFETIME VALUE

Many companies use customer lifetime value calculations to support their marketing decisions. With an estimate of a customer's lifetime value to the company, the company can now make more accurate investment decisions. The customer lifetime value represents the discounted estimate of the sum of all the expected revenue and margin a customer will pay the company over the expected time period that he or she is a customer.

Some companies use other approximations to calculate the expected future revenue value of a customer. Because many companies are worried about the revenue to be generated during the fiscal year, they simply calculate the expected revenue for each customer through the end of the fiscal year. From a marketing perspective, this can skew the analysis of the results of marketing activities. This method can tend to front-load marketing activities in the first few months to gain many new customers early in the year in order to garner as many months of revenue as possible.

Other companies, such as MNO Gas, simply measure the value of the customer based on the expected revenue for the first 12 months with the company. This can also be a reasonable approximation of the success of marketing to deliver annualized revenue. Adding in an expected attrition rate can provide reasonably accurate estimates of future revenue generated through the acquisition of new customers. Other companies use an estimate of the first month of revenue, the average revenue per user (ARPU), to calculate the value of a particular marketing effort.

Only when calculating customer lifetime value can investments in retention marketing versus acquisition marketing be accurately compared.

PROCEDURE
Calculating monthly retention and attrition:
1. Capture, on a monthly basis, the number of new customers and the total number of active customers.
2. Add the number of new customers in this month to the total number of active customers from the prior month. Subtract the total number of active customers from this month, yielding the attrition for the month.

3. Choose a weather variable—such as the minimum temperature, the average temperature, or the maximum daily temperature in the region—to approximate the impact of the seasons.
4. Adjust for the number of days in the month.
5. Capture the level of advertising on a monthly basis. Investigate potential lag and adstock factors.
6. Regress these variables against the monthly attrition to deseasonalize and determine the impact of advertising and seasonality on retention.

CASE STUDY 6—DIRECT MEASUREMENT: ENTERPRISE SOFTWARE IN THE ASIA-PACIFIC

This case study illustrates how an Asia-Pacific enterprise software company—STC Company—can use segmentation and direct campaign measurement to determine marketing effectiveness when selling at the enterprise level.

BACKGROUND
The selling and marketing of enterprise software to large enterprises and organizations is one of the most difficult types of revenue generation. The sales cycles are long, and the sale can be easily derailed by many forces, including the prospective company missing the numbers for the month, a single naysayer, or just another project that may be perceived to be better aligned with corporate objectives.

Enterprise software services are often a combination of one-time installation and consulting services, and recurring license and maintenance fees. This combination complicates the calculation of financial success.

How do the two revenue components add up when one is a one-time service that may or may not be repeated and the other is a recurring revenue stream derived over many years of continuous service?

Enterprise marketing is also more complex than most other marketing activities because all of the accounts are known, and may already be, or have been, customers. In this case, marketing can only support the revenue generation process through retention, win-back, up-selling, and cross-selling. In some cases across the Asia-Pacific region, marketing must help win an account back in one country while supporting retention in others. In some countries, the competition is a mix of local providers and other multinationals.

With an enterprise salesperson in the mix, all the credit will be grabbed by him or her, even though it is clear that marketing has added some value. The question for the enterprise marketer is how to prove their value. If you ask a salesperson how their month went, you would hear that they made their numbers without any help from anyone else. On the other hand, if you said to the same salesperson that all marketing had to be slashed in the next two quarters, complaints would begin to flow. Even though there is recognition that marketing supports the selling process, there is no credit given. Somewhere in between lies the truth as to whether marketing contributes to revenue achievement or not.

In an ideal world, every touch with the customer would be measured, qualified, and tracked. Leaving mass media and PR aside for the moment, this would include all direct-marketing touches as well as all sales touches. Sales touches can include every phone call, e-mail, proposal submission, meeting, and so on. Direct touches can include all e-mail, Web visits, webinars, events, or other communications, mechanisms developed by the marketing team.

Because the customer base is well known and the company already has some relationship with some or all of the contacts within the account, enterprise marketing is often primarily focused around the hosting of events. In enterprise sales, events fall into two categories: informational and relationship building. Informational events are defined as having a strong marketing message associated with them, and often accompany the launch of a new technology, solution, or capability. They include conferences, summits, seminars, lunch-and-learns, and webinars.

Relationship-building events are defined as having no sales message associated with them whatsoever. For members of the C-suite they include golf outings, or tickets to a wine-tasting party or other high-value, entertainment-focused event. For STC Company in the Asia-Pacific, the C-suite is actually a misnomer, because the actual enterprise customer's C-suite may not be based in Asia-Pacific but in the U.S. or Europe. Because most of the C-level executives of STC's customers reside at their customers' headquarters in Europe and North America, this term is defined to mean the top-ranking manager in the region and in each country.

STC Company—a multinational corporation based out of Europe—is one of the top three enterprise software providers worldwide. Its Asia-Pacific headquarters are located in Singapore, and it has sales offices in just about every Asia-Pacific country—from Australia and New Zealand in the south to South Korea in the north and India to the west. Marketing has direct staff in the larger countries and uses local agencies in the smaller countries. For both China and India the company is in acquisition mode, whereas in just about every other country the company is looking only to retain its existing customers and potentially grow its customer share of wallet. With the exception of Japan, all of the countries are managed out of the Asia-Pacific headquarters, although it is expected that in a few years both China and India will be managed as separate regions.

Although the company was interested in determining its marketing effectiveness in India and China, the immediate need was to determine budget allocation for all the other countries where most marketing functions were retention and up-selling/cross-selling focused as opposed to acquisition focused. In countries where English isn't the native language, much of the marketing effort is consumed in translation of printed materials and the Internet presence.

Many of the customers of STC Company have a major presence throughout most of the countries in Asia, and therefore have—or should have—multiple touchpoints in each country. Although purchase decisions for enterprise software are sometimes made, or influenced, at corporate headquarters in Europe or the U.S., local services are also put out for bid between local and multinational providers. Depending on the competitive situation at the time, one competitor may simply buy the business by offering an extremely low price. In these cases, selling and marketing efforts may not be successful in overcoming this very competitive pricing action. Once the customer is lost, they may remain lost for up to three years—depending on the length of the contract with the competitive service provider.

SOLUTION AND REQUIRED DATA

ACCOUNT SEGMENTATION

In the past, marketing efforts were split evenly between all customers, regardless of size or potential value to the company. By not segmenting their customer base, marketing opportunities may be missed and resources may be misaligned. STC Company therefore implemented a marketing classification scheme segmenting enterprise customers into "A," "B," and "C" segments. The A customers were defined as the top 10 percent of customers by revenue. The B customers were the next 50 percent, and the C customers were the remaining customers. This classification scheme followed the classification scheme within the sales department, although some adjustments were made to account for high-potential-value customers that currently didn't represent high revenue.

Marketing implemented a plan to dedicate resources accordingly. The A customers would receive 50 percent of the marketing investment and measurement. B customers would receive 40 percent, and the C customers would receive the remaining 10 percent, and would potentially piggyback off events focused on the A or B class customers.

Once this classification scheme was defined, the goal of the marketing team was to improve the breadth and depth of event participation within each A and B account. In the past, the contact strategy was determined by the sales team. Instead of extending invitations broadly across the customers' management teams, they tended to invite their "friends" within the account to all events. Because it was often the case that a single naysayer or friend of the competition could stonewall the relationship, a contact strategy targeted broadly across all key touchpoints within the customer organization would tend to mitigate the impact of this one potentially unfriendly individual.

MARKETING BUDGET ALLOCATION
Because marketing funds are not unlimited, A accounts were set to receive broad and deep marketing support. This included invitations to events across the C-suite at the regional and national levels. The C-suite includes the top regional managing director or CEO, the CIO, the CFO, the networking manager, the networking security manager, and other top-level line positions directly touching the enterprise software infrastructure decision.

TOUCHPOINT PROFILE DEFINITION
Marketing needed a scoring system to determine how successful their activities were in touching all key influencers at the C-level within their accounts by country and region. Three touchpoint profiles were defined, as shown in Table 8.5, such that a broad touchpoint profile (top-tier) would indicate that all top-level managers were touched by a marketing event in the year, whereas a narrow touchpoint profile would indicate that only one of the top-level managers—typically the CIO—was touched. A mid-tier touchpoint profile was also defined.

The prior two years' marketing touchpoint profile was benchmarked with the results as shown in Table 8.5.

Table 8.5: Benchmark of actual touchpoint profiles for A customers

Touchpoint profile	Touchpoint profile definition	Percentage of all A customers	
		2 years ago	Prior year
Top tier	All top-level managers within an account were touched at least once with attendance at an event during the course of the year	0%	3%
Mid-tier	One or two top-level managers within an account were not touched with attendance at an event during the course of the year	45%	48%
Bottom tier	Only one of the top-level managers (usually the CIO) was touched with attendance at an event during the course of the year	55%	49%

Similar benchmark results were determined for the B and C customers, (not shown). Based on this benchmark, it was determined that for A accounts over the past two years the breadth of contact was very low. As a matter of fact, only a few of the A accounts in the last two years had a completed top-tier touchpoint profile.

SALES TEAM INFLUENCE

In the analysis, changes in the sales team profile must be controlled for. Key influences include salesperson tenure, training, and selling abilities. To account for these potential influences, tests were made to determine whether a salesperson's tenure, or other influences, were detectable. By analyzing the results at the country level, these influences were controlled for.

EXIT SURVEY ENHANCEMENT

In the past, success for events was defined as receiving high ratings from the exit surveys and maximizing the number of event attendees, regardless of position and function, within the customer organization. The ratings were based solely on whether the attendee "enjoyed" the event. To align the exit survey more closely with any improvement in the relationship, and with the consideration of STC's solutions, questions were added relating to the pertinence of the discussed technology to the customer's business requirements and whether the technology would be recommended either internally or externally to their peers. These two specific questions allowed the marketers to determine whether consideration for the solution was stimulated by the event and whether the customer could relate to the solution enough to want to recommend it to others—either internally or externally.

As part of this solution, the event-tracking mechanism was enhanced to track these questions. In addition, each event was scored based on the breadth of attendance and level of attendee. This scoring mechanism was also added to the event-tracking mechanism.

SALES AND MARKETING OBJECTIVES COORDINATION
Although there were clearly opportunities to improve the coordination between the sales and marketing strategies, during the initial phase of this restructuring little change was made to the sales strategy other than to support, where possible, the marketing strategy. Compensation plans and staffing levels remained unaffected. Once this program took hold, modifications to the sales targeting could be made.

The marketing budget as a percentage of plan revenue remained unchanged.

RESULTS

EVENTS MUST MATCH THE TARGET AUDIENCE
The redefinition of successful events forced the marketing team to define new types of events that would appeal to the contact audience. Financial managers wouldn't attend a technology event, but would, for example, attend an event discussing the calculation of total cost of ownership

and ROI for different types of solutions. Success of these new event types illustrated how the customers' nontechnical staff perceived the enterprise software provider.

THE EVENT EXIT SURVEY

The event exit survey was enhanced to inquire whether the presented material related to the attendees' business and whether it was something they would recommend internally or externally to their peers. As the year progressed, both these survey results and the event scores improved in the first two quarters by over 20 percent.

RESULTS BY TOUCHPOINT PROFILE

Objectives for each touchpoint profile were set for A, B, and C class customers. Although objectives were set for the C customer segment, the marketing priorities were based on those objectives set for the A and B customers. Table 8.6 shows the objectives and achievement for the year:

Table 8.6: Objectives and actual achievement of touchpoint profile by segment

Touchpoint profile	Top tier		Mid-tier		Bottom tier	
	Objective	Actual	Objective	Actual	Objective	Actual
A Customers	80%	55%	20%	9%	0%	0%
B Customers	40%	61%	40%	24%	20%	15%
C Customers	50%	38%	50%	38%	50%	62%

RETENTION RATES

As a result of the attainment of these objectives, retention rates increased as shown in Table 8.7.

Retention rates for A accounts remained relatively unchanged. Because of the relationship in general at the headquarters level, local marketing events had little effect on retention. However, retention grew significantly for the B and C accounts.

Table 8.7: Retentation rates by segment year over year

	2 years ago	Prior year	Average of prior 2 years	Current year (increase %)
A Customers	92%	90%	91%	93% (2.2%)
B Customers	73%	68%	70.5%	88% (24.8%)
C Customers	79%	73%	76%	84% (10.5%)

REVENUE IMPROVEMENTS

In addition to the improved retention rates, total revenue and the revenue profile for all three segments improved as shown in Table 8.8.

Table 8.8: Revenue profile by customer segment

	Revenue change		
	2 years ago	Prior year	Current year
'A' Customers	73% increased	78% increased	83% increased
	27% decreased	22% decreased	17% decreased
'B' Customers	66% increased	58% increased	71% increased
	34% decreased	42% decreased	29% decreased
'C' Customers	63% increased	61% increased	58% increased
	37% decreased	39% decreased	42% decreased

Overall, total revenue for the Asia-Pacific region increased by 8 percent, compared with a 3 percent increase in the two years prior, versus only 4 percent and 2 percent for the rest of the world. Only for the C customers did the number of customers with increased revenue decrease.

SHARE OF WALLET

Revenues were tracked for each of the attendee, invitee, and noninvitee accounts. The cost of gathering the share of wallet data and the associated analysis across all accounts in detail was cost prohibitive. However, analysis of a sample of attendee versus nonattendee accounts showed that those accounts with the highest attendance scores for both A and B accounts improved STC's share of wallet versus the competition. In many cases in enterprise sales, a particular account may not implement a specific solution simply because it doesn't apply to its business. In these cases, enterprise accounts may not attend an informational event simply because the solution won't apply to their business environment. On the other hand, attendance at any event may improve the relationship for any of STC's offered solutions, regardless of the type of solution presented at the event. Because of this halo effect, a true measure of the success of an event needs to include the gathering of specific competitive information surrounding the offered solution. Because gathering competitive information at the account level is extremely time-consuming, expensive, and possibly inaccurate or not provided, it was deemed that this analysis would be made across only a small sample of accounts, with the objective of delivering only a directional answer. Although the specific results showed a positive correlation, the answer isn't robust enough to be presented here. This positive correlation was, however, validated in general through the publication of share data at the country and regional levels from third-party analyst reports.

CHALLENGES, ISSUES, AND OPPORTUNITIES

In any large direct-selling organization, coordination between the sales team and the marketing team is always difficult. The sales team is on the front line and must juggle customer relationship issues, uncover new needs, and close the business. The marketing team must support the sales team and their relationship-building efforts, and provide the right tools to position the sales team for success. With the marketing objectives more closely aligned with the customer segments, tighter coordination between the sales activities and marketing activities has uncovered many opportunities for further improvement. In particular, the following year's compensation plan will be realigned to coincide with the breadth and depth of objectives of the marketing team.

Sales compensation plans don't often change mid-year and the sales executives aren't going to change their compensation schemes with an unproven marketing initiative. This limitation can slow companywide adoption of improved coordination between the marketing and sales objectives. To some extent, this can be mitigated by piloting the modified compensation plans in one or two countries.

One of the challenges facing the sales and marketing team is the understanding of the required incentives to improve the breadth of contacts even further in the A and B accounts. Because of the improved success in the B and C segments, marketing investment will be increased to improve the breadth of the touchpoint profile within these two segments at the expense of the investment in the breadth of the touchpoint profile within the A accounts.

Many top-level executives, especially in multinational companies, are often unable to participate in specific events. If appropriate, they will delegate one of their subordinates to attend. Although this isn't ideal, it is certainly better to have some representation from the specific functional area than none at all. The scoring of the success of the event, if necessary, can be weighted slightly lower than if the designated senior executive actually attended.

Coordination of the data infrastructure is also important. CRM and SFA tools exist in large organizations, and are implemented with some level of capability. Unfortunately, these tools are very sales-centric and often don't have the capabilities to support the marketing function at the account and contact level. Enterprise marketers require the ability to track marketing actions and results against customer segments and touchpoints. In many cases this can be achieved by using off-the-shelf software applications dedicated to the marketing function.

PROCEDURE

Defining segments, target contacts, and goals for enterprise accounts at the regional and country levels:

1. If they don't already exist in the sales department, define customer segments based on actual and potential revenue.
2. Define the key internal functions that will make up the target C-suite. For example, IT, business manager, CFO, and CEO. Define the touchpoint profiles.
3. Gather contact names and information for A accounts. This can come from the sales team or a purchased list. It can also be gathered through public information or through research within the company.
4. Determine rules to handle regional-level customers versus country-level customers.
5. At the account level, benchmark for each segment the marketing actions touching these accounts, including invitations and attendance. Include prior years' revenue totals by product line.
6. At the segment level, benchmark prior years' revenue growth and retention rates.
7. Enhance the exit survey to include questions concerning business relevance and likelihood to recommend. Set up an event-tracking and scoring method to gather and track survey results and attendee profiles for each event.
8. Set up a regular tracking mechanism to capture invitation and attendee activity by account and contact.
9. As the project unfolds and initial data begins to show results, explore ways to enhance the coordination of the achievement of marketing objectives with the sales team.

This case study uses actual measured differences in time to process (on average) a lead, depending on whether it is qualified, unqualified, or converts in inside sales. (This example assumes that the lead-conversion rate after nurturing is the same across all marketing lead sources. It also assumes that the outside sales conversion rate was the same across all marketing lead sources. Initial studies determined that was true with an error of plus/minus 8 percent.)

ENDNOTES

1. Under the definition of A/B testing, I am also including pre- and post-testing, test/control group testing, split cell testing, multivariate testing, and Taguchi testing.

2. This calculation ignores subsidy, synergy from other marketing activities, and cross-selling. It uses last-touch attribution.

3. Guy R. Powell, *Return on Marketing Investment: Demand More From Your Marketing and Sales Investments,* (Atlanta: RPI Press, 2003).

4. For a more indepth discussion of ROMI hurdle rates, please see Guy R. Powell, *Return on Marketing Investment: Demand More From Your Marketing and Sales Investments,* (Atlanta: RPI Press, 2003).

5. Dave Sutton and Tom Klein, *Enterprise Marketing Management: The New Science of Marketing,* (Hoboken, NJ: John Wiley & Sons, 2003).

6. Hint: If you were able to identify the 50 percent of activities that weren't successful and were able to make them either successful or worth fixing, the revenue due to marketing would double.

7. For simplicity this case study, as presented here, will ignore the following effects. For a more accurate calculation of ROMI factors, these would need to be included. The appendix shows the results with this calculation:
   • The successful conversion of nurtured leads
   • The difference in processing time for different types of leads. For example, those that are qualified usually require additional

sales-processing time in inside sales. Leads that are unqualified typically require less processing time.
- The costs of field sales and conversion rate in field sales are also dependent on lead quality. In addition, commission rates for "won" sales must be calculated into the final cost per marketing source.

9

MIX MODELERS

MIX-MODELER CAMEO

Mary—the database marketing manager for a midsized bank called First National—received an e-mail from John, the CEO. She was initially very concerned, and delayed opening it. It was sent with a timestamp of 7:30 in the morning. That meant that the CEO was either up late the night before or, worse yet, got to work very early that morning. The CEO had sent various data requests with impossible deadlines in the past, and the answers that he was looking for were always very difficult to obtain. Hopefully, this e-mail wasn't the same.

"Whew, it wasn't," Mary thought. This e-mail was very different: it asked a question that Mary had always wanted to answer but for which she had never had the necessary tools. And, she had almost a week to get to the bottom of it. That she could handle. She knew that at her previous job there

was a group in another division that used statistical analysis of the database marketing activities to develop a true model of their division's marketing mix. It sure looked like the CEO wanted to get a similar model from her.

She began to key in a response, but decided it might make more sense to stop by John's office and make sure she properly understood what he was looking for. That way the e-mail wouldn't come across wrong, and she definitely didn't want to get a "John-o-gram" back from him. On her way over, she stopped in to see her boss, Joellyn—the VP of Marketing—to let her know that the CEO had sent another request, and to find out if there was anything else behind the request that might help them both look good in front of the CEO.

Apparently, John had just returned from a conference where he had been introduced to the concept of marketing mix modeling and he wanted to see if it could be applied to First National Bank. He must have written the e-mail on the plane and it got transferred to Mary's inbox when he finally connected in the morning.

Mary began to explain to Joellyn some of the things that were done at her prior company. Joellyn interrupted her. "We don't have the data to do that. I wish we could do it, but I just don't think we have the right data."

"We would have to capture every activity we ever ran. We don't know how many impressions were executed and we definitely don't know how to quantify the quality of any of our marketing activities, other than by looking at the number of calls that come in."

"Yes," said Mary, "but we do agree that brand-awareness activities, such as our PR, do help to improve the response of our other direct-marketing activities. If we could get a handle on the connection between our brand activities and our direct activities, then we could really see what's working and what's not working. Besides, I think it would be fun to try and figure out, so I would love to take this project on."

"Alright, but be careful, and don't overpromise and underdeliver," Joellyn warned, giving in to Mary's persistence. "Go see what this is all about and let me know what happens."

"You know, one thing that we could maybe start with is analyzing all of our past campaigns against our sales with our prospects and consumers in our database," Mary started thinking. "We could see how many touches each one of them

received and, with some weighting scheme, we may be able to determine the impact each campaign had on the improved response rates."

"Well, there are actually some good statistical analyses that can be done to provide real correlation between the two," Joellyn interjected. "We did this at the marshmallow division where I used to work, but we had to pay quite a bit for data. In this case, though, maybe we could figure out how to use the data we have so as to avoid spending any of our precious budget dollars on the analysis. I'm tired of our budget being pulled in every direction except generating revenue," Joellyn groaned and thought to herself, "and my bonus!"

After a quick walk down executive row, she stepped into John's office. "Mary, good morning. I'm glad you stopped by. Did you get my e-mail?" John asked. "George and I were just talking about some of the things I learned at the marketing management conference and he had some suggestions as well." George was the VP of the contact center, who happened to be in John's office going over the expansion plans, which included a new automated phone dialer.

"Yes, I got your e-mail and I had a few questions for you. Joellyn and I were talking about it, but I just wanted to make sure we understood your question before we went too far," Mary responded. She was glad to get the pleasantries out of the way.

"Yes, what I wanted to do was to figure out how we can improve our marketing response rates. We generally have an idea of what works and what doesn't work, but we don't seem to be able to value the branding activities, nor any of the synergies between activities," John replied, with a little bit of frustration in his voice. "Joellyn always talks about integrated marketing campaigns, but, at the end of the day, all we talk about is how well the direct mail and e-mail campaigns did. We can never pull it all together. That's all I want."

"Well, I would love to dig my teeth into this. I know I shouldn't say this, but I'm certain we can measure the results of all of our campaigns, including the branding campaigns, in order to know exactly how well each of them is producing. Once we've done that, we can maybe even figure out how to improve our marketing mix." Mary said, going way out on a limb. "We could even..."

George interrupted before Mary fell out of the tree. "I know I've seen other companies do this. We just need to know what kind of data we need and I'll be glad to help," George offered, knowing that would win some points for next month's annual review. "If it works, we could even re-evaluate the program effectiveness every month so that we could make some quick corrections, if needed."

Mary left knowing that she may have overcommitted herself. "But, why not?" she thought. "I've almost completed my MBA, and maybe I can position myself for that Director of Marketing Operations spot that's going to open up when Fred retires. I've been thinking that there has to be a better way and, if this works, I could set up a position that would need to become permanent once the value of this program became apparent."

Point #1: It takes commitment throughout the organization to move up the marketing-effectiveness continuum.

Mary knew that, in order for this to work, she needed to determine exactly where the data sources were and what the requirements were for the data. She was in for a surprise when she found out she needed, ideally, three years of weekly data across the 4Ps, 3Cs, and 1E. "Yikes," she thought, "That's going to be tough." She realized, though, that George may have also bit off more than he could chew. He would have to provide some of the sales and contact center data, and it would be interesting to see if he could dig it up.

"The good news," she thought, "is that, as a bank, we have direct contact with prospects and customers." They didn't have to worry about getting data from the channel. She started making a list. "We have our brand-advertising data, our direct-response data, and the number of branches. We also have perfect information on the number of accounts, the value of the assets and the types of accounts. We could start by determining the success of our marketing at bringing in new credit cards. John was always interested in this high profit area, so let's start with that."

"So, who in the organization knows the number of branches and when they opened?" she thought. "I'll bet the facilities guy could get me that. I had better talk to the CFO first, just to grease the skids."

Point #2: The cost of data is not zero, whether it is purchased or gathered internally.

Mary walked into Joellyn's office and told her the good news. Joellyn wasn't surprised. "Did you know we have three new branches to launch next month? How do you think we're going to do this and make sure we don't screw up the launch of those three branches?" she asked. Joellyn breathed deeply, regretting what she had just said and added, "All right. Let's think about this a second. What have you got so far?"

Mary recounted that she thought she had the sales data—focusing initially on new credit card accounts. Joellyn wholeheartedly agreed. They had the marketing data, and George inadvertently committed to putting together data from the contact center. "That'll teach him," Joellyn thought, remembering all of the heated battles they'd had over the years. "I wonder if we can get John to pay for some of the competitive marketing data from his budget."

Joellyn smiled. "Our budget is committed for the next two quarters to the launch of the three branches in Chicago this quarter and the six in Des Moines next quarter." Joellyn smiled further. "If we play our cards right, maybe we can get John to spring for a real analyst and some real market research data, as well."

Mary started walking back to her office. She wondered, "What else do we need in order to do this right? How are we going to get pricing data for a credit card? Should we use the interest rates or the fees, or both?"

Point #3: The key data streams need to be carefully considered to make certain that the right business question is being asked and answered.

"I think I understand the data requirements for our credit card offering—the product. But we need to think through what the price is, and how we handle customer satisfaction," Mary thought. "What is the price that a credit card holder pays for a credit card? Essentially it's free, other than some nominal fees. But that only applies to those who pay off their balances every month. And two-thirds of all of our customers don't do that. So, we may need to segment our credit card holders into two groups based on this behavior: those who

pay off their balances and *those who don't. But, on the other hand, the price for our credit card—our interest rate—hasn't changed very often. Actually, we only changed it when the competition raised their rates. Our relative rates are on par with everyone else, other than a few small banks trying to buy into the market. And our fees have been constant forever. Maybe we could put it into our marketing materials that we don't change our fees—ever."*

Later that afternoon, as Mary had her data plan just about complete, she started walking over to Joellyn's office to give her a quick update. Mary walked right in after noticing that Joellyn wasn't on the phone and was alone in her office. "E-mail is a never ending battle," Joellyn said, clearly happy to take a break from catching up with her e-mail queue after having been out of town the prior week. "I only have twenty-eight left," she said as she pushed her chair back.

Mary sat down. "Yep. George has already sent me a couple of e-mails. I think he's realizing that he may not have wanted to volunteer so quickly. It looks like the bellyaching is going to start. Anyway, I was thinking about how to handle customer satisfaction in our model, and wondering if and how we can include it. It's definitely part of the service that they buy from us, but the number of people that actually complain is pretty low," Mary said, coffee cup in hand.

"Hmm," Joellyn murmured. "We really don't lose many customers because of bad service. We only had that one incident when our Internet line went out last year, and we were able to smooth that over pretty well. We hardly ever get any complaints. Plus, I don't think that when new customers sign up they're taking into account our reputation for good or bad service. Since it doesn't change that much, I'd ignore it."

"Well, I thought it was a clear attribute of our product," Mary said, "which it is. But you're right. It doesn't change much, and we haven't really lost many, if any, customers to it. I don't even think we lost any last year when the backhoe decided to dig up the street and rip out our water and Internet. It was nice not having to do e-mail for half a day."

"So we're just about ready. I think we have all of the data we need to start doing some statistical modeling…"

MIX MODELERS

Mix modelers drive their marketing based on a model of the mix of the 4Ps: product, price, place or distribution, and promotion or advertising. Traditionally, the concept of the 4Ps is used to describe the strategy of a particular brand or company. But, at the execution level in the Marketing-Effectiveness Framework, it can be used to describe the influence of incremental changes in any or all of the 4Ps in driving further marketing effectiveness and higher marketing ROI.

Although these models typically ignore the long-term value of advertising, they do help significantly in understanding the shorter term components of what drives customer response in the market. There are, however, some advanced techniques that can take the longer term value of advertising into account as well.

From a promotional level, all types of marketing media can be modeled. This can include TV, radio, coupons, and print—as well as outdoor, PR, channel promotions, and sales personnel and their activities, such as call volume. In addition, the comparable value of one creative to another can also be determined.

Case study 7 (Marketing-mix modeling: Regional restaurant chain in North America) illustrates how a regional restaurant chain was able to improve its marketing mix by reviewing all of its key marketing media elements. In addition, the chain was able to increase its pricing in order to invest further its advertising budget.

As much as marketers want to take full credit for the superior impact of their marketing activities during good times, they don't want to be blamed for less-than-stellar performance during bad times. The influence of exogenous factors, including the economy, the weather, and seasonality, can be included in the model. This allows marketers to understand how each factor influences consumer response, so that in both good and bad times they can receive credit where credit is due. They can also use this information to make certain they are taking advantage of seasonal opportunities—or mitigating the risk of unforeseeable weather influences.

Once the budget mix has been determined, it is up to each of the marketing media managers to optimize their activities based on their budgets. This involves taking advantage of both the synergies between marketing media, and the halo or cannibalization between products or brands in order to deliver the highest profit for the given investment. The TV manager optimizes the TV media plan in terms of placement and flighting. The direct-mail manager optimizes the media plan in terms of the creative for the various pieces, the call-to-action, the synergy with other media channels, and other factors.

On a regular basis—let's say once a year—the model is reviewed and recast to take advantage of any major changes in the marketplace and to reallocate funding between the media.

Marketing-mix models (MMMs) can be built using a number of methodologies, but they are typically built using least squared statistical regression analysis. "Statistical models," "regression models," and "econometric models" are terms used synonymously with "marketing-mix models." However, marketing-mix models can also be built using other techniques, such as system dynamics, structured equation models, and agent-based modeling. Each technique has strengths and weaknesses in terms of its data requirements and the predictability of its results. But, under the right circumstances, they can provide marketers with insight into their markets that would not be achievable through last-touch attribution or other methods.

Case study 8 (Marketing-mix modeling: Kids' snacks in the United Kingdom) is a great example of using a statistical modeling process in order to determine the effectiveness of a launch in a complex, new category. It also illustrates how the right analysis can uncover insight into the actions of the channel that might negatively impact the brand.

Accurate and periodic data on both the marketing activities and the dependent variable is critical for good model predictability. The dependent variable can be a success metric such as point-of-sale (POS) data, clicks to a Web site, calls to a call center, or visitors to a store. This variable "depends" on the inputs to the model or independent variables. Independent variables are the inputs to the market. These are the variables defined for your business question in the 4P3C1E framework.

In statistical models, this data must be based on a time series. Time-series data is collected at regular intervals in the same way. It could be collected on a daily, weekly, or monthly basis. For marketers, this means collecting at regular intervals both the 4P3C1E data and the desired success metrics of the marketing-accountability framework. If the data sources are limited, then the scope of the business question that can be addressed by the model must be narrowed to accommodate for potential limitations in the model's predictability and accuracy.

CHALLENGES FACING MIX MODELERS

Many companies are already utilizing the results of marketing-mix models to improve their marketing effectiveness. Many of these are consumer marketers, such as consumer packaged goods (CPG) companies, but some large business-to-business, industrial, and original equipment manufacturing (OEM) companies are also finding value in this capability—although they are faced with some limitations. Marketing-mix modeling applies well to companies and categories in which many marketing activities take place simultaneously and continuously throughout the year.

INDUSTRIAL AND OEM COMPANIES

Few companies in this area have influence on their consumer purchases. Those that do, however, are candidates for the use of marketing-mix modeling. Ingredient brands, such as Intel and the Intel Inside campaign, can take advantage of MMM by optimizing their advertising—assuming they have access to accurate POS data in a time series across all of their consumer channels. Limitations for Intel include the availability of accurate POS data into their business channels. However, Intel can also use other success metrics, such as traffic to their Web site, as their dependent variable. Industrial and OEM companies that have many customers, such as home electrical wiring suppliers, may also be able to use MMMs in a limited way.

BUSINESS-TO-BUSINESS COMPANIES

Larger business-to-business (B2B) companies can take advantage of marketing-mix modeling if they have good time-series purchase data about their products and services at the end-user level. Some allowances may need to be made if sales volume can be heavily skewed by a few significant new consumers, but these may need to be seen as outliers,[1] and separately modeled. In some cases, unit volume might be a more appropriate dependent variable, but in others it may be that "new consumers" are more appropriate. Business-to-business marketers might also be able to use other interim metrics, such as visits to a Web site, as their dependent variable. In this case, they could identify which marketing activities drive the most prospects to a Web site, and then use other conversion metrics to determine the probability of conversion through each level in the purchase funnel to final product purchase.

CONSUMER COMPANIES

Consumer companies have utilized marketing-mix models in just about every category. Whether in automotive, CPG, pharmaceutical, or durables, marketing-mix modeling can help consumer marketers to measure ROI in the past and deliver improved ROI in the future. In addition, the results from marketing-mix modeling can be used to develop media plans in order to improve the timing and flighting of all media. A number of obstacles can be overcome as more marketers begin to understand the value of this approach. Then, as data is properly collected and the channel begins to collaborate with their manufacturers to provide them with better time-series-oriented sales data at the POS level, even more advancements can be made.

CHANNEL COMPANIES

The channel has an advantage over manufacturers in developing models because they have the most accurate POS data. Marketing-mix modeling is appropriate for channel companies with high, continuous spend in the marketplace. Medium and large retailers fall into this category.

Large department store chains and other big-box retailers can use marketing-mix models to help them understand the many different facets of their marketing. MMMs can answer questions at the product level and the department level, and look at the cross-impacts between departments and between products.

Channel companies in general, however, can reap rewards from marketing-mix modeling by providing—even potentially selling or licensing—their POS data back to syndicated data providers, or directly back to the manufacturer. Because channels are working with their suppliers, this data can be used to the mutual benefit of both in developing a more predictive and accurate model of particular categories.

On the other hand, wholesalers have similar problems to some manufacturers, in that they must also gather POS data from their channel partners. Depending on their position in the marketplace, wholesalers can then make decisions similar to those made by manufacturers.

OTHER COMPANIES—POLITICAL, CHARITIES, NGOS, GOVERNMENT, BUSINESS-TO-GOVERNMENT

Marketing-mix modelers require time-series data on results, preferably on a weekly basis. For government organizations that are advertising to support a cause—as in cause marketing—success metrics may only be available through ongoing tracking studies. Unfortunately, many of these tracking studies may only be available on a monthly or quarterly basis, which makes statistical analysis difficult. Because of the high expense of ongoing tracking studies, it may not be perceived as economically viable to track results in this fashion—making other analytic methods potentially more viable.

Political advertising has an additional challenge in that the results are only available once—on Election Day. Unless accurate tracking data exists from opinion polls, marketing-mix modeling may not be a viable solution.

CATEGORY-SPECIFIC CHALLENGES

Companies that have good solid weekly data going back more than three years can develop very insightful marketing-mix models. Even with one or two years of weekly data, marketers can begin to develop models to answer key marketing-effectiveness questions. These models can also account for competitive advertising and marketing, channel marketing, and exogenous factors. In addition, synergies, adstocks,[2] and diminishing returns—as well as halo and cannibalization—can be included in the model.

Regardless of what type of marketer you are, this statistical modeling technique can be used to determine:
- How offline marketing drives clicks to the Web site, or calls to the call center.
- The impact of mass media, such as TV and radio, on incremental store visits and revenue.
- Which marketing media delivers the most leads of a certain quality.

- The relative lift from different creative concepts.
- The influence and control for exogenous events, such as the weather, economic factors, and many others.

Both mass marketers—such as Proctor & Gamble, Kraft, and Unilever, which use television, radio, and other mass marketing media channels—and one-to-one marketers[3] can use this technique to improve their marketing mix. One-to-one marketers can correlate the mix, number, and type of impressions with revenue. They can determine the attribution for each media element employed and advance past last-touch attribution. Once they know the correlation between revenue and impressions, they can calculate their return on marketing investment (ROMI) factors based on revenue and contribution margin (mROMI), as well as marketing return on investment (ROI).

CALCULATING mROMI AND MARKETING ROI

Marketing-mix models typically result in correlation coefficients, such as incremental revenue per gross rating point (GRP), or incremental revenue per impression. These must then be converted into ROMI factors, based on either revenue or contribution margin, and into marketing ROI for the CFO and CEO.

Table 9.1: Calculating ROMI, mROMI, and marketing ROI

Calculation assumptions	
Incremental revenue	US$40,000
Cost per GRP	US$12,000
Contribution margin (as a percentage of revenue)	45%

ROMI factor	Definition	Example
ROMI =	(Revenue per GRP) ÷ Cost per GRP	(US$40,000 revenue per GRP) ÷
mROMI =	ROMI * (Contribution margin percentage as a percentage of revenue)	(US$12,000 cost per GRP) = 3.33 3.33 * 45% = 1.50
Marketing ROI	(mROMI – 1.00) * 100%	(1.50 – 1.00) * 100% = 50%

There are complexities surrounding the use of marketing-mix modeling. Here are a few that must be considered when developing actionable results from a model:

- **Long or highly differentiated sales cycle**—Sales cycles lasting more than six months pose challenges in correlating marketing activities to customer response. For example, if some customers respond to media within 30 days, and others take six to nine months, then it may be better to use a combination of approaches. Marketing-mix modeling can be used to determine the impact of marketing on generated leads of a certain quality. Sales-tracking systems, such as a sales force automation (SFA) system, can be used to track the lead as it moves through the sales cycle. Conversion rates by lead quality can be determined to complete the ROMI calculation. This is the norm for business-to-business marketers, for whom a two-step approach is often required.

For consumer markets with long sales cycles, such as in the automotive category, the consumer is considered "in-market" when they are intending to purchase. During the in-market phase, the consumer—now often called an intender—is actively making choices concerning needs, features and models. A purchase is made at the end of the in-market phase, with a replacement purchase not taking place for another five or six years on average. In this case, marketing has both a short- and long-term effect. For intenders, marketing must be targeted to prompt consumers to keep their brand in the consideration set as they get closer and closer to a purchase. During the time between purchases, the consumer is out of the market. Any received media for consumers not in-market doesn't build purchase intent, but does build brand awareness, consideration, and equity. Other categories with long sales cycles include banking, financial services, and home ownership. In the case of life insurance, a consumer may only be in-market once in a lifetime. Marketing-mix modeling is very effective at correlating the short-term impact of marketing media on sales, but may miss the longer term brand value built up between purchases.

Nevertheless, marketing-mix modeling can provide valuable information about the short-term allocation of spend as it relates to the short-term purchase actions of the consumer. As for the more complex consumer decision-making process, consumer analyzers, which are described in the next chapter, will help to provide a more accurate model of the purchase process and consumer decision dynamics.

- **Lack of data from the channel about both revenue and instore promotional activity**—This is probably the most common challenge facing marketers using modeling techniques. Many channel partners are reluctant to share their POS revenue and promotional data with their suppliers. This is evolving in many industries, as the channel partners realize that they can increase their overall volume as well by sharing data. If data is not made available, marketers can build less accurate models based on shipment data. Shipment data is based on shipment volumes to the channel, as opposed to POS data, which represents purchases by the consumer. These models are often more directional in nature. Directional indicators help marketers determine the general direction of incremental or decremental spending, but don't indicate in an accurate fashion how much the spending should be increased or decreased between media channels.

- **Lack of data across all channels**—Sometimes only certain trade partners provide their data. In this case, marketing-mix models can be built by using the dependent variable from the trade partners that did provide the data and using assumptions extrapolated from the shipment data for the other channels.

- **Highly seasonal sales and one-time events**—Seasonal manufacturers, such as those in the toy category, must develop a model based on limited and often nonlinear circumstances. The marketing of blockbuster movies falls into this category as well—a marketer is trying to optimize the marketing and distribution of a movie that will only be in high demand for the first few weeks after its debut. On the business-to-business side, farm products, such as feed, have highly seasonal or one-time demand equations. There can be many different factors influencing consumer behavior for these types of products, including:
  - The mix and preference of the products that are available, and which ones are "hot" that season.
  - The economy and the weather for farm products, which vary from year to year.
  - The mix of competitors in the market, which can also vary each year.
  - The amount supplied, which can either exceed or fall below demand, causing stockouts or end-of-season price cuts.

In the case of toys, marketers must carefully balance the amount of production—which is typically made in a onetime buy in preparation for the Christmas holiday buying season many months in advance—with the level of marketing spend. This must be done to avoid stockouts or inventory returns. Combined modeling approaches can be developed to support manufacturers in these cases.

- **Capacity constrained businesses**—Marketing-mix modeling assumes that there is always stock on the shelves when a model is built. If there are stockouts, then the true consumer response will be understated. In industries where high utilization is critical to business success, stock-outs— or 100 percent utilization—take place on a regular basis, causing a nonlinearity in the supply function. This is the case in the travel industry for airlines, hotels, and rental cars, as well as for gasoline. When demand reaches near 100 percent capacity, pricing is adjusted and marketing is abruptly halted. Yield management is a methodology designed to help marketers manage price and demand and, to some extent, their marketing in order to improve utilization rates and profits. Combining an accurate model of consumer response to marketing with sophisticated yield management systems can help take marketing effectiveness to the next level. The success metric is to maintain almost 100 percent utilization as much as possible.
- **Low distribution**—In the reverse case, demand may be difficult to measure because there is very little on the shelf at any given time. Is the lack of a sale, which is what gets reported, due to lack of demand or lack of supply? The modeling process must take stockouts into account as they do when a manufacturer is at 100 percent utilization in the capacity-constrained case above.

MEASUREMENT AND MODELING CHALLENGES

Modeling techniques have limitations on how they can determine the effects of marketing on the success metric. With the knowledge they provide, however, marketers can make changes in the way they execute their marketing plans in order to measure and model the effect of their marketing to deliver improved results. These changes include:

- **Variance**—Media must have built-in variance in order for most modeling tools to be able to discern an impact. For example, if a company consistently has an advertisement on one page in the Saturday newspaper throughout the modeling time period, then, because there is no change in the input, there won't be any change or correlation detected in the output. This doesn't mean that the Saturday newspaper has no effect. It means, however, that its effect can't be detected using many approaches, including statistics. In this case, the marketer has two options. One technique is to build in variance to the media component so that on some Saturdays there might be two pages, on others there might be no pages, and on still others there might be three pages. Another technique is to use "share of voice" in the Saturday newspaper with advertisers in the same category. If the competition varies their advertising then the modeling input variable may then be the share of voice between all competitors in the newspaper.

It can also be difficult to discern the impact that billboards have on sales. Billboards are usually in place for six months or more, six delivering little variance as a marketing input. The impact of the billboard is generally determined by the dates of presence and the traffic in the vicinity of the billboard. If there are varying amounts of billboards present in different locations around the country, then the input variable may be the number of billboards multiplied times the amount of traffic on a weekly basis in the vicinity of the billboards. Other signage—such as that found at baseball stadiums or other venues—also falls into this category.

Sponsorships are also usually long lasting and may not vary over the modeling period. For example, the impact of a NASCAR or NBA sponsorship may not be discernible using a statistical approach. In this case, a surveying method may be necessary, after which its results can be incorporated into the model in a combined fashion to make it more complete and comparable across the entire marketing mix.

Combined measurement and modeling methods can include the combination of marketing-mix modeling, A/B testing, and survey techniques—each handling the specific nuances surrounding each specific media. If they are properly normalized, the modeling results across the different media types can then be compared to make actionable decisions.

- **Collinearity**—Collinearity is similar to the variance issue discussed above. Not only does each marketing medium need to vary, but it also needs to vary in relation to other media. For example, if TV is always followed by a corresponding amount of print advertising, many modeling approaches will not be able to discern the individual correlations to revenue between the two media. It will, however, be able to determine the correlation for the combined TV and print marketing activities.

In certain marketing activities, including PR, marketers can gather more indepth measures in order to accurately determine their impact. Merely counting the number of articles covering the product or brand often doesn't provide enough information to develop a strong correlation. Instead, mix modelers are moving toward measuring PR based on their net effect impressions. Impressions for a brand found in newspaper articles and TV news programs are now weighted based on the type of article, the circulation of the publication (or the viewership for TV), and the quality of the article—e.g., above the fold, with a picture, etc.—among other factors. With this measurement of the net effect impression, the impact of PR activities can now be more accurately modeled.

Through marketing-mix modeling, marketers are now able to begin to determine the effectiveness of both their direct and brand advertising across most, if not all, marketing media types. As they become more advanced with their marketing-mix modeling, marketers will develop more sophisticated business questions, which will in turn lead to more detailed answers. Data collection strategies will improve in terms of timeliness, accuracy and frequency, as well as depth and breadth, across more channels and promotional elements.

MODELING TO PREDICT THE FUTURE

Predictive models make certain assumptions about the future. Either the future is very dynamic or it is static. If the future is like the past, then marketing-effectiveness measurements from the past can be assumed to still hold true for the future. In this case, both marketing-mix modeling, using statistical regression analysis, and campaign measuring, using just about any method described above, can be reasonably predictive. They both assume that competitors will make no major changes along any of the 4Ps, that the consumer base will remain unchanged, that the channel is constant, and that there are no major exogenous events that would change consumer response. However, they do not allow for major product launches or changes in the 4Ps to such an extent that the future is no longer like the past. With these caveats, both last-touch attribution and marketing-mix modeling using statistical regression analysis can be expected to be reasonably predictive.

But what do we do when we want to launch a new product, or when the future is unlike the past? In this case, these tools are significantly less predictive and other techniques must be employed. This will be discussed in depth in the next chapter under consumer analyzers.

HOW CAN MARKETERS IMPROVE THEIR MIX MODELING?

Mix modeling is the first level in the continuum where marketers can finally begin to measure the impact across all of their marketing elements. Finally, with mix modeling, the direct and indirect effects of all marketing elements can be accurately determined. With this newfound insight, marketers can significantly improve the allocation of their scarce marketing funds. And now, advertising campaigns that aren't designed to have a significant impact this quarter can be better defended when the budget axe comes swinging.

ADVANCED TECHNIQUES

Marketers can now ask more questions and deeper questions. Advanced topics can include:

- **Advanced success metrics**—Although this may stipulate improved data collection methods, other success metrics can be examined, such as:
  o Customer satisfaction
  o Retention
  o Loyalty
  o Recommendations, testimonials, and referrals
  o Ratings and reviews in social media Web sites.

With data at each level in the purchase funnel—from awareness through purchase intent and loyalty—marketers can now determine whether there are any bottlenecks or significant leakages that must be plugged.

- **Synergies**—Marketers can begin to uncover the synergistic components between brand advertising (TV, PR, and others) and the more direct marketing elements, such as Web advertising, direct mail, and e-mail.

Due to this new-found knowledge, marketers can now use advanced analytical techniques to look at how they plan their media and make certain they can both determine the impact they are having on revenue and adjust accordingly.

TOOLS

Mix modelers primarily use statistical regression analysis to deliver insight into the value of each of their marketing components. In fact, marketing-mix modeling has become synonymous with statistical or econometric analysis of the marketing mix. In reality, any tool that provides accurate factors relating marketing activities to success metrics and dependent variables can be used to model the marketing mix. Here a few different examples:

- **Last-touch attribution**—Although it ignores many aspects of consumer response, this technique, too, can be used to determine and improve subsets of the marketing mix. Either direct-response mechanisms can be used to measure incremental results or alternatively, A/B testing can be used to measure the value of some or all marketing activities. To some extent, Case study 3 (Last-touch attribution: Dental equipment supplier in North America) illustrated how to use last-touch attribution to evaluate the marketing mix. Under the assumption that no synergies exist between the marketing activities and prior activities, this can be a reasonable tool to evaluate the marketing effectiveness across the mix.
- **System dynamics and structured equation models**— These tools use different approaches to relate marketing inputs to specific consumer responses that can be measured in the marketplace. These often reveal how consumers move through the purchase funnel through variables based on marketing elements across the entire marketing mix.

- **Marketing-mix models**—As already mentioned, marketing-mix modeling is an approach that correlates sales, unit volume, or some other dependent variable with the 4Ps, competitive spend, and exogenous factors—the independent variables—using least-squared statistical regression analysis.
- **Agent-based modeling and simulation**—This technique uses a detailed understanding of how consumers process information, make choices, and fall into segments to determine the impact of marketing on consumer response.

FINDING A PLACE FOR BOTH CAMPAIGN MEASURING AND MIX MODELING

One of the most difficult concepts to accept—especially with the presence of a strong personal-selling component in the marketing mix—is that both campaign measuring using last-touch attribution and mix modeling can simultaneously provide valuable management insight for an organization. In the case of the personal-selling function, even though the sales team is taking all the credit for every sale and every dollar in revenue, some of the credit or attribution still belongs elsewhere in the marketing mix. Managing any direct marketing function, whether it is direct mail, coupons, or personal selling, requires them to optimize their results, ignoring the contribution of the other marketing components. It is when all components are managed together that another level of marketing effectiveness comes to light. Mix modelers can now provide another level of improvement over that based on last-touch attribution alone. Mix modelers can begin to deliver results that make sense across the entire marketing budget. Mix modeling and campaign measuring can operate in tandem to support marketing allocation decisions between media. And, together, they can optimize tactics for each specific media to improve the overall effectiveness of the marketing function.

SEVEN STEPS TO BECOMING A MIX MODELER

Mix modelers can measure the results from their marketing across the 4Ps in order to determine and improve their marketing effectiveness. They can measure the relative impact of each of their marketing activities in highly dynamic markets where various marketing inputs are active in parallel with many other marketing inputs at any given time.

Although there are other methods, statistical regression analysis is the most popular. It requires time-series data across the marketing-accountability framework. In an ideal world, each input across the entire framework is used. In practice, however, some components can be aggregated or eliminated altogether.

The two key components of a marketing-mix model are the dependent and independent variables. Dependent variables are the success metrics measured over time throughout the modeling period. The independent variables are all of the 4P3C1E marketing inputs measured throughout that same time period. Some of these variables may be transformed using lags, adstocks, diminishing returns and breakthrough, and synergies. To get started, data must be gathered to represent each of the key elements of the 4P3C1E framework. The steps are as follows:

1. **Clearly define the business question**—For example, to determine ROMI coefficients for all marketing inputs in driving incremental unit volume, dollar volume, channel volume, or many others.

2. **Assemble independent variables**—Based on the business question, determine required data inputs, such as:
   a. **Marketing inputs**—Collect all of the company's marketing inputs in a time-series fashion, that is, on a weekly basis over the last 2–3 years.
   b. **Competitive marketing inputs**—Primarily those similar to yours, although this may be aggregated across all competitors. A data stream might be the sum of all advertising, the weighted average price, channel-marketing programs, or new product introductions.
   c. **Channel marketing inputs**—A data stream might include the change in number of stores per channel type, or the channel-marketing activities supporting your product or category.
   d. **Customer inputs**—This is represented through a data stream for the size and growth or decline rate of the particular target consumer group.
   e. **Exogenous factors**—Several data streams would represent what could potentially be the most influential external factors, such as weather, economic factors, and seasonality.

3. **Assemble dependent variables and success metrics**— Collect data for sales, preferably at the POS level, over the two to three year modeling time-period. Depending on the business question, a separate time-series data stream for each of the success metrics may need to be assembled. These might include sales by channel, unit volume, store traffic volume, new accounts, leads, clicks of a certain type, and others.

4. **Run the model**—Adjust for data transformations as necessary, determine which variables are the most predictive, and follow standard statistical best practices. Calculate and verify the goodness of fit by looking for outliers, calculating R-squared[4] and comparing the results for the modeling time-period against the results for the holdout[5] time-period.

5. **Calculate ROMI factors and other results**—Use costs per GRP, or other marketing inputs in relation to their impact on results, to determine relative weightings. Calculate price and other elasticities.

6. **Use ROMI factors to diagnose marketing response and to reallocate marketing funds**—If marketing media delivered less-than-expected results, it may be that something went wrong in the execution of the media. It may be possible to determine what went wrong in order to deliver improved results from that particular media type. If this is not the case, then the various calculated ROMI factors will help the marketer determine how best to allocate the marketing budget across each of the media types. The allocation can take into account potential nonlinear responses and limited media opportunities, such as saturation and other factors, to deliver the best results possible.

7. **Calculate new revenue goals**—Use the reallocated budget to calculate new goals—assuming the future is like the past.

Marketers who implement marketing-mix modeling can see enormous value in terms of increased revenue and profit. I've seen typical revenue gains on the order of 5–10 percent and profit increases of 10–20 percent without any increase in marketing budget. What marketer can pass up these advances in marketing effectiveness?

CASE STUDIES

CASE STUDY 7—MARKETING-MIX MODELING: REGIONAL RESTAURANT CHAIN IN NORTH AMERICA

This case study illustrates how a regional restaurant chain was able to improve its marketing effectiveness and drive increased growth by answering a number of critical marketing questions using econometric modeling.

BACKGROUND

A regional restaurant chain had 140 outlets, launching about 12 new restaurants per year—about one per month. The management team was concerned about a number of key business questions, including the optimization of the launch marketing mix, the optimization of the mix for established restaurants, and the impact of marketing on the changeover in its menu. Because of the fast growth of the chain through the launch of new restaurants, a number of key components of the modeling process had to be accounted for:

- Separating out the effects of the new restaurants and their associated marketing from the marketing surrounding established restaurants (that is, those in place over a year, often called comparables)
- Any competitive activities that could have disrupted the success of these launches
- Separating out the effects of the quality of the menu from the quality of the marketing associated with the launch of the new menu

During the 4 year analysis period, 36 new stores were added, with 12 new stores added in the last year. Five stores closed. In addition, during the modeling time period there was one change in its creative concept. The restaurant chain had three primary formats: stand-alone, strip mall with no anchor, and shopping center with major anchor, such as Wal-Mart or another big box retailer.

SOLUTION AND REQUIRED DATA

A marketing-mix model was built using four years of data consisting of:

- Regional weekly advertising for TV, radio, direct mail, and outdoor
- Daily store-level revenue
- Daily store-level transaction volume
- Daily traffic to the Web site
- Date of implementation of the new advertising creative concept
- Dates of changes to the menu
- Dates of introduction of new stores and their formats
- Marketing expenditures related to the launch of a new location
- The net number of stores open per month
- Weekly competitive advertising (TV, radio, print, and outdoor) in the region for the top three competitors

The six-month holdout time-period was used to validate the goodness of fit.

RESULTS

Results from the model indicated the following:

- The advertising associated with the launch of the new menu was very successful, with radio delivering the highest ROMI (>10), and direct mail delivering the next highest ROMI—also greater than ten. TV and outdoor delivered the least.
- Adding new locations delivered incremental revenue for the region, with little cannibalized revenue from other locations (less than 10 percent). That is, for every dollar of incremental revenue generated by a new location, less than 10 percent was cannibalized from other locations.
- Revenue and ROMI rates for each marketing element were calculated and determined to differ by store format, but the rank-order of the elements didn't change. Radio was again the most successful element, with direct mail a close second and TV and outdoor being the least.

- Downloadable coupons were tested during the modeling time-period, and the effectiveness was calculated separately using last-touch attribution. They were determined to be slightly more effective than radio. Downloadable coupons were not able to be included in the statistical regression analysis because of the low volume of coupons downloaded from the Web site.
- The new creative concept implemented during the modeling time period delivered just over 1 percent incremental revenue versus the creative concept running at the beginning of the modeling period.
- Price elasticity was determined and was generally inelastic, meaning that an increase in price would yield an increase in revenue. Therefore, price increases would be sustainable, delivering increased profit overall. It was determined that for every 10 percent increase in price, revenue would decline by just over 4 percent.

Based on the results of the model, recommendations included an increase in radio and direct mail spending, and a decrease in TV and outdoor. This applied to both new and existing locations. With these marketing-mix modifications, and without increasing the marketing spend, revenue could increase by up to 7 percent. By increasing the price by 3 percent, an additional 1.2 percent profit could be achieved. Half of this estimated increased profit was to be invested in the advertising budget, which would increase the marketing budget by just over 10 percent. The investment of this additional 10 percent in marketing was calculated to be able to deliver another 3 percent in increased revenue across all locations.

CHALLENGES, ISSUES, AND OPPORTUNITIES
Marketing-mix modeling can provide some very important answers to help a company to improve marketing effectiveness. It can support decisions concerning the marketing mix and provide insight into opportunities across the 4Ps. The marketing team can now make information-based decisions concerning pricing and advertising to deliver higher revenue and profit.

Other potential business questions could be answered:
- The company could determine the advertising effectiveness of promoting specific menu items.
- With additional data stretching back further in time, the long-term effects of advertising could also be determined.
- Analysis against transaction size could also be done to determine potential marketing activities that could drive larger transaction sizes.

Because the extent of the Web-marketing activities during the modeling time-period was relatively small, the response to the Web activities was not able to be determined using a statistical marketing-mix modeling approach. Direct-response measurement using last-touch attribution provided a first estimate of the Web coupon ROMI factor.

PROCEDURE

The procedures for econometric modeling are as follows:

1. Determine the business questions to be answered by the model.
2. Determine the associated success metrics required to answer each of the business questions.
3. Collect insertion and cost data from internal sources as per the marketing-accountability framework.
4. Determine the data that must be purchased from outside sources, such as competitive media and exogenous factors, as per the marketing-accountability framework.
5. Clean data and perform transformations, such as lagging or adstocks, where necessary.
6. Build a model for each of the success metrics and business questions. Validate the model using various statistical methods.
7. Calculate the ROMI coefficients.
8. Simulate potential marketing plans and determine potential increased revenue, profit, and share.

CASE STUDY 8—MARKETING-MIX MODELING: KIDS' SNACKS IN THE UNITED KINGDOM

This case study illustrates the use of marketing-mix modeling in a large western European country, and highlights the difficulty in defining a category and the difficulties surrounding the marketing of children's products.

BACKGROUND

Marketing to children is complicated by the fact that the end-consumer of the product is not the purchaser. Most children's products start by marketing in parallel to parents—particularly mothers, and children. By stimulating demand in this way, the brand can usually be certain that when the children ask the parents to put their product into the shopping basket, the actual purchase will take place. Brand KidSnack is primarily targeted at children aged 8–10, with a broader audience of children of 6–12 years of age. Understanding the dynamics of the dual-purchase decision model was required in order to improve the success of the launch of the new brand.

Marketing a new product type and brand brings further complication because the competitive set isn't clearly defined. This particular new brand and product falls into the complex overall snacking market, but also has attributes that fall into sweet snacks, chocolate, fruit confectionary, cookies, fruit, and others.

Due to the popular—yet incorrect—notion that TV advertising is dead, the campaign to launch brand KidSnack had to engage children in a very special way on TV, the Web, and through other media. In fact, a few specific Web sites were brought online that led to significant engagement during the early part of the campaign, yielding hundreds of thousands of unique visitors with time-on-site numbers averaging greater than 12 minutes. Only after engagement with children was underway was the campaign to market to the purchaser—the parent—rolled out.

SOLUTION AND REQUIRED DATA

In order to determine the effectiveness of the campaign, an econometric model was built, with average pack price, distribution, TV GRPs and adstock, PR, and Web site visit counts as independent variables. In addition to capturing data to build the econometric model, a number of tracking studies were used to determine penetration and the level of trial-and-repeat sales for households with children. For example, the first and second trials, over the first nine months after launch, reached 51 percent and 65 percent, respectively, of households with children.

As part of the rollout, distribution reached 80 percent in grocery within the first three months and grew further to just under 90 percent over the next 12 months. Other than a short decrease around the Christmas holiday week, distribution remained at the 90 percent level thereafter.

RESULTS

Based on the econometric model, the total contribution due to communications was 22 percent of the total volume. This led to a ROMI of just over 0.94, based on the model in the distribution channels where volume tracking data was available. Because the model only covered 65 percent of sales, the actual ROMI was estimated to be higher by another 54 percent—leading to a ROMI of just over 1.45. Although TV was the largest contributor to incremental volume, visits to the newly created Web sites drove a direct contribution of 6.7 percent of volume and PR drove another 1 percent. The process was complicated by the flavor aspect of the product. One of the flavors actually ran out of stock, causing a short, one-month-long decrease in sales by about 30 percent, and slowing its phenomenal post-launch growth.

CHALLENGES, ISSUES, AND OPPORTUNITIES

Because of the few Web-measurement solutions available at the time of the launch, the contribution to volume due to Web advertising was not able to be accurately deduced. This meant that the indicated numbers underestimate the actual volume contribution due to Web advertising. Although the direct viral effect of PR was captured in the model, the indirect viral impact of PR was not able to be fully captured for lack of appropriate data.

The measurement of marketing effectiveness in a multistage marketing environment led to some interesting questions not addressed in this case study. For example, the impact of Web site visits on incremental contribution was determined, but what drove the number of Web site visits? What was the impact of the various online and offline media on visits to the Web site? In order to answer these questions, the company would need to build a two-stage model to capture the full effects of all of the media elements on incremental volume. For example, initially Web site visits were driven primarily by PR and online media, but once the TV components began, visits to the Web sites were primarily driven by the TV activities.

PROCEDURE
See the procedure outlined in Case study 7 for developing an econometric model.

CASE STUDY 9—MARKETING-MIX MODELING: MOBILE TELEPHONE SERVICE PROVIDER IN ASIA

This case study illustrates how an Asian mobile telephone service provider was able to measure the success of its major media components using marketing-mix modeling. This case study uses the indirect approach found in marketing-mix modeling as opposed to simply measuring the direct effects as discussed in the earlier Case study 2 (Direct marketing and CRM: mobile telecommunications company in Asia).

BACKGROUND
One of the global mobile phone service providers needed to launch a new service into one of the more mature, mid-sized, Asian countries.

Advertising was spread primarily across television and out-of-home. Out-of-home advertising included unique banners on static locations, such as trackside on the metro lines, travelators, and billboards, as well as mobile advertising on buses and taxis. TV displays were also purchased in airport concourses and "computer malls." PR was used to introduce the capabilities of the new service to the media. Lastly, retailers, and even restaurateurs, provided unique advertising opportunities for signage, including stairways, pole wrappers, and others.

SOLUTION AND REQUIRED DATA

An econometric model was developed to determine the value that each of the media elements was able to deliver. Although data was available on a weekly basis, the analysis only stretched back 18 months in time, allowing the regression of about seven or eight variables.

In addition to the econometric analysis, a brand-tracking study was run to help to determine the effectiveness of the individual out-of-home advertising venues. It also provided valuable information comparing the impact of the advertising campaign on women versus men.

RESULTS

The analysis delivered some interesting results see Table 9.2

Table 9.2: Marketing ROI results by media type

Media channel	Marketing spend	Marketing ROI
Out-of-home	US$354,000	450%
Online	US$172,000	423%
Direct mail	US$753,000	198%
Television	US$3,040,000	178%
Newspaper	US$439,000	147%
Total	US$4,758,000	207%

Synergy effects between television and the other media were studied and it was determined that it provided a significant lift to the results for out-of-home, but less lift for online and direct mail. These synergy effects are included in the marketing ROI calculations shown in Table 9.2.

Spontaneous advertising recall was gathered for four of the out-of-home media channels and the results by gender are shown in Table 9.3. Results indicated insignificant differences in the responses between men and women—meaning that the out-of-home messages could remain gender-neutral.

Table 9.3: Advertising recall by out-of-home media type

Media channel	Men	Women
Billboards and buildings	47%	46%
Transit video screens	33%	24%
Mobile out-of-homes—bus and taxi	31%	33%
Metro	28%	28%

With these results, the next major campaign, which would take place six months later, was optimized for each of these media to deliver a projected 14 percent improvement in ROI. The most significant shift was away from newspapers and into static out-of-home displays.

CHALLENGERS, ISSUES, AND OPPORTUNITIES
Econometric models have strict guidelines that must be followed to deliver highly robust models. If the data is limited, detailed answers across all media elements cannot be determined. In order to determine marketing effectiveness across the full spectrum of marketing activities, other survey-based tools often need to be employed. Advertising recall and brand-tracking studies

are just two ways to understand the impact of various advertising media on the short- and long-term impact of the advertising.

PROCEDURE
See the procedure outlined in Case study 7 for developing an econometric model.

CASE STUDY 10—MARKETING-MIX MODELING: PREMIUM LAGER BEER IN EUROPE

This case study illustrates how a premium lager importer (SSS) was able to measure the success of its marketing and understand its component drivers. It explores the importer's success in keeping its price at a premium versus the other providers by using a combination of marketing-mix modeling and brand-tracking studies.

BACKGROUND
Marketing beer in Europe has a number of complicating factors not found in other fast-moving consumer goods (FMCG) industries. Purchase of beer takes place both on-premise in bars and restaurants and off-premise in grocery, liquor, and convenience stores, and there is a strong interaction between both purchase paths. Because of the continuing growth and strength of off-premise consumption, some of the premium lager brands have become members of the top ten brands of all brands sold through the grocery channel. In parallel, the trading up phenomenon (see Michael Silverstein and Neil Fiske's Trading Up)[6] has been driving the growing demand for premium lagers in a category where overall beer consumption has been declining. Growth in the premium lager share of all beer sales has tripled over the last ten years.

The premium beer market is made up of nine major brands, all of which sell Europe-wide, and some represent major global brands. On-premise sales represent just under two-thirds of beer sales and off-premise about one-third.

One of the interesting impacts from advertising is the indirect effect it has on driving distribution in the pubs and bars. As a brand grows in stature, it drives both on- and off-premise demand. As on-premise demand grows, it forces the bar and pub owners to stock it and offer it on tap—accelerating demand growth even faster. Availability in the bars and pubs then feeds back to consumers the desire to consume it off-premise. In so doing, brand growth is accelerated even further.

Bar and pub outlets are made up of both large and small chains, as well as many independents. Each of these chains can have commitments with different beer brands, and, depending on the interaction between the competitive brands, there may be an exclusive long-term contractual relationship. On the other hand, most of the independent bars and pubs are free to choose the brands they wish to offer. Although it is the responsibility of the brand sales team to negotiate the best deal and terms for the brand, that team must also help the bar or pub with signage and other on-premise promotion. In the case of SSS Company, the brand had grown so strong that bars and pubs were quickly switching over from other commitments to the SSS brand as soon as their competitive contracts allowed.

SOLUTION AND REQUIRED DATA

Spain was one of the larger export markets for SSS Company's brand, and analysis of the company's premium lager marketing in Spain was done using econometric modeling. The model was built to answer a few separate questions about the impact of short-term marketing inputs, but also to determine the longer term marketing effects of a clearly successful marketing campaign. Where marketing campaigns in the past had delivered only marginal growth, the current campaign, which began about five years ago, was delivering extraordinary growth, exceeding all expectations. Because most of the data inputs were only available on a monthly basis, only a handful of input variables were employed in the model.

In addition to the standard short-term advertising, pricing and distribution effects, the marketing team also wanted to determine the long-term sales effect. This was done by first stripping away all the short-term effects and then correlating the remainder with long-term brand affinity as measured through an ongoing brand-tracking study.

Monthly brand tracking across the category for the top nine brands was done—providing valuable input surrounding all of the brand imagery. For those aware of the advertisements, brand tracking tracked a number of attributes including taste, quality, and "genuinely continental," with the SSS brand ranging from 10 percent to 30 percent better than the average of the other premium brands for these three attributes.

RESULTS

ADVERTISING

The model showed that, at the time, the new advertising concept delivered a short-term ROMI factor of 10.3—delivering €10.3 for every advertising Euro invested. The long-term advertising effect was that for every Euro invested in advertising, the long-term effect delivered another €3.5 in incremental sales.

PRICING

As a result of the advertising, the SSS brand was able to maintain its premium pricing versus other premium lagers even though the premium lager segment became more and more crowded. As with just about any other successful and well-known, fast-moving consumer goods, a temporary price reduction (TPR) can drive short-term volume in the off-premise channels for the brand. In addition, the channel can use the TPR to increase overall volume for the chain. This is a very effective tactic for a retailer, and the food channel would often drive down the price of their premium products in order to drive increased store traffic. For brand SSS it was no different, although over the analysis period SSS was able to maintain consistently higher pricing over the average of the rest of the premium lagers—from 9 percent to 10 percent in the first three years and 14 percent for the last two years of the study—even in the face of generally declining pricing across the premium lager segment.

PRODUCT
As with any premium beer, the product doesn't change for decades at a time. Its formula and brewing process remains fixed, constant, and consistent. What does sometimes change for the off-premise channel, however, is the packaging: changing from one type of bottle or can to another.

For the on-premise channel, beer is sold in an unbranded glass where the only obvious signage may be the tap symbol or font at the bar and even this doesn't change very frequently. For brand SSS the signage remained unchanged during the analysis time-period.

EXOGENOUS FACTORS
As household disposable income grew between 0 percent and +2 percent per year over the analysis period, household expenditures on brand SSS grew from 20 to 25 percent, significantly outpacing any of the top premium lagers.

DISTRIBUTION
During the analysis time-period, distribution in independent bars and pubs grew from about 18 percent to just less than 40 percent, while the share in the major chains grew from just under 30 percent to just under 50 percent.

The analysis showed that an incremental €1 million spent on advertising drove €2.5 million in incremental revenue through the bars and pubs. Consumers were either changing their choice of bars to those with brand SSS on tap, or were changing their choice of beer to brand SSS once they were in the bar.

CHALLENGES, ISSUES, AND OPPORTUNITIES
In this study, most of the data was available at the monthly level, limiting the granularity in the model. Had the data been available at the weekly level, the model would

have been able to provide even more granular answers. Nevertheless, the model provided some robust answers, clearly showing the marketing ROI for the campaign and the creative, separating out distribution, pricing, and long-term effects.

PROCEDURE
Generally the modeling process follows the procedure outlined in Case study 7. In this case study, because brand affinity values were available on a monthly basis through a monthly brand-tracking study, the long-term effects of the marketing activities were able to be regressed against the advertising.

ENDNOTES

1. Definition of "outlier"—a value far from most others in a set of data. *The American Heritage® Dictionary of the English Language,* 4th ed., (Boston: Houghton Mifflin Company, 2006).

2. The impact over time of any single marketing communications event.

3. One-to-one marketers have a direct relationship with their consumers (and often their prospects). Examples of one-to-one consumer marketers include cellphone, insurance, banks, and utilities. Many business-to-business marketers are one-to-one marketers.

4. "R-squared" is a statistical term saying how good one term is at predicting another. If R-squared is 1.0 then given the value of one term, you can perfectly predict the value of another term. If R-squared is 0.0, then knowing one term doesn't help you know the other term at all. More generally, a higher value of R-squared means that you can better predict one term from Trade Ideas, http://www.trade-ideas.com/Glossary/R-Squared.html, (accessed July, 2007).

5. Holdout data—also called the validation data set—is data not used to build the model, but to validate the quality of the model. A model is built using the modeling data and then projected

forward against the holdout data to see how predictive the model is against unknown data. For more information see http://www.statisticssolutions.com.

6. Michael J. Silverstein and Neil Fiske, *Trading Up: Why Consumers Want New Luxury Goods—and How Companies Create Them,* (New York: Portfolio, 2004).

10

CONSUMER ANALYZERS

CONSUMER-ANALYZER CAMEO

This story is about a major consumer-package-goods (CPG) company called Multi-brand, Inc. They had been operating for many years in a number of consumer categories, and developed a number of successful consumer brands. Some of the brands were acquired, but, for the most part, the company has been successful through organic growth. Unfortunately, though, in a few categories they have not been able to understand why their traditional planning tools continue to fail. Their judgment seemed to be off at every turn.

The categories were very dynamic, with at least one launch of a major new competitive brand or variant per month, on average. Shelf space was getting squeezed and they had been relying more and more heavily on trade promotions in order to maintain their relative sales volume.

Nick, the brand manager who was recently reassigned from one of the sister brands, was trying to make his mark on the category. He had just learned of a new competitor, Jenny Co., entering the category. Apparently, this competitor was in the category about six years ago, but finally left after two marginally unsuccessful years. Jenny Co. pulled out primarily because they needed to restructure after suffering some major setbacks in two of their other, more-strategic categories, and not because they failed in that particular category. They had recently been very successful in entering a related packaged-food category, and now Nick was responsible for managing his brand while staving off this new onslaught.

The good news was that he had competed against the same brand in his old category, so he had a good idea of what to expect. His prior experience told him that they typically lead with 80 percent of their spending on TV, combined with delayed spending on coupons and display. It always puzzled him that they didn't do more in parallel, but he was ready for them. What he didn't know, however, was the exact preference that the consumers would have for their new formulation, but he had a range of guesses that he and the other members of his team thought made sense. Armed with this information, he was confident he could predict a range of good responses in order to minimize his risk as he put together his marketing plan.

One thing was clear: Nick would need some new techniques to make sure that he is making the right decisions. He just finished reading some consumer testing about results on the new variant he was about to launch—chili crème chocolate, affectionately known as CCCs around the company, and they look very promising. But with all of the activity in the marketplace, and Jenny Co. about to re-enter the market in a big way, he needed to clearly understand how to launch his CCCs at the right price, with the optimum level and timing of promotional support. Then, he needed to make sure his defensive marketing would actually deliver as he had always assumed. In the past, he led with simple pantry loading right before a rumored competitive launch, but now he wanted to know whether this really works. If it did, he wanted to see how that, combined with some neat word-of-mouth activities, might keep his brand growing.

Pontiac was extremely successful with their Oprah giveaway in 2004 and Nick wondered whether the investment for a similar action might pay off. Plus, he needed to submit his operating plan for the next year and, in order for him to make his bonus, he had better make sure he can make the numbers.

Point #1: Traditional approaches that assume the future is like the past won't provide the insight necessary to win in a highly dynamic market.

Nick knew the company had a lot of information at the consumer level, and felt they were one of the top marketers in all categories. They had been doing marketing-mix modeling and other analytics, but it never seemed like these tools handled the dynamics of the categories he worked in. They also didn't help in determining how best to develop the marketing mix for a product launch. Nick needed a method to analyze the market from the consumer's point of view. He also wanted to be able to simulate the future against a range of scenarios depending on how Jenny Co. would launch in order to determine what his best response might be. Although there may have been other alternatives, ultimately, he wanted to be able to simulate a number of Jenny Co.'s potential marketing plans and see how his own would deliver against them.

Point #2: In dynamic markets, marketing effectiveness can be heavily gauged based on the actions of your competition.

Nick and his boss were commiserating the fact that if you look at the market with blinders on, you may miss the latent opportunities to take advantage of when planning against the competition. This can include not only how the competition launches new products, but also how they advertise in the steady state or during seasonal fluctuations. With a few alternative guesses about their competition, Nick could build a few scenarios of the future to test and simulate.

Point #3: Models that include both a deep understanding of the consumer and the competition will provide significantly more robust results than those that only look in the rearview mirror, or only look at optimizing your own activities.

Nick thought that it would be even better to simulate how the competition would react to the launch of CCCs. He knew that his biggest competitor, AllBrands Advantage, always tried to do some pantry loading and pull forward their advertising to defend their position. His brand was the second largest competitor in the category, but Advantage was definitely on a spree; they were growing at twice the rate of the category. Nick realized that knowing how consumers will respond to your marketing actions—in the context of all of your competitors' actions and reactions—is a quantum leap above simple marketing-mix modeling, system dynamics, or other measures of marketing effectiveness. You can now understand the effects of your marketing, and that of your competitors, with a clear and concise model.

Point #4: Competitors act in predictable and unpredictable ways.

Nick spent a lot of time learning how his competition acted in the past and was confident that he knew how they were going to act and react now. It seemed that a few of them always tended to do things the same way. Others seemed to always try to be different—often with disastrous results. He laughed to himself, "Brand managers are paid to make changes, regardless of whether they're good or not." The good news was that the launch marketing mix for Jenny Co. was reasonably predictable. However, the timing, the actual product attributes, and the consumer preferences for those attributes were unpredictable. But, within the level of unpredictability, there was a top end and a bottom end, across which a range of potential actions and responses could be simulated and optimized. He knew they weren't going to spend less than US$10 million, but they were probably not going to spend more than US$15 million. Even in an uncertain future, the level of uncertainty could still be bounded and overall business risks reduced.

CONSUMER ANALYZERS

Being the first in a category to have a superior, future-focused approach can create a profound first-mover advantage. Being able to accurately and quickly simulate the impact of a competitive threat—and then being able to plan and execute the most optimal response—can have enormous payback. Investments in superior marketing methods yield not only direct results, but also a more competitive company. Brand managers gain insights not available through any other means. They can "learn from the future."[1]

Critical to this forward-looking approach is a model of how consumers will respond to your actions, your competitors' actions, actions in the channel, and even exogenous factors. With this type of response model—based on keen insight and analysis of consumer behavior—accurate projections in highly dynamic markets can be developed. The most popular tool I've found that can support this method of modeling is called agent-based modeling and simulation.

Consumer analyzers develop a model across the entire Marketing-Effectiveness Framework. They have a deep understanding of how consumers and segments make purchase decisions, how they evaluate brands, how they choose a channel, and how they process information from themselves and their competitors. With the right tools at their fingertips, they can develop robust models to project the response to their, and their competitors', potential actions. Armed with this knowledge, they can seek out and analyze potential opportunities, and compare different levels of risk.

Consumer analyzers have lots of consumer data available to them at this level in the continuum. This data comes in different forms, with different levels of granularity and periodicity. To utilize this data to its fullest extent, consumer analyzers must have, and use, the right tools to build models that make sense.

One of the primary advantages of a model based on the consumer is that it includes the consumer-response behavior based on all of the influences in the marketplace. One key variable, not easily accounted for in most other analytical modeling methods, is the value of the brand equity built up in the minds of the consumer, based on the messaging they've received and any engagement they've had with the brand. Because the value of the brand changes slowly in comparison with most marketing elements, marketing-mix modeling and campaign measuring— which primarily model short-term variations in sales volume— can't easily account for these long-term changes. This is a key differentiator in modeling methods based on the consumer.

In addition, because this type of modeling takes into account how consumers go shopping, and whether there is availability in the channel, this modeling process can now also explicitly take into account nonlinear effects, such as stockouts and capacity-constrained manufacturers.

Because consumer response is consistent over a wide range of changes in the marketplace, models based on consumer-response behavior can be very robust in the face of these dynamics. *When the future is no longer like the past*—whether it's due to the launch of a new product, the entry of a new competitor, or the big run-up in gas prices—then these models can deliver accurate projections of the future.

CHALLENGES FACING CONSUMER ANALYZERS

Many companies have been capturing, tracking, and gathering the data needed for analysis at the level of a consumer analyzer for years. What hasn't taken place until recently is companies putting that data into a comprehensive model that covers the entire category. Overall, these models require additional types of data than other modeling techniques, but not much more than what is already available to many of the larger business-to-business (B2B) and consumer marketers. With these models in place, brand managers can simulate the impact of upcoming events to project which strategy delivers the best results in an uncertain and dynamic future.

Once these types of models are in place, brand managers must shift their thinking. Brand managers must now begin to thoughtfully plan how they need to respond to competitors' actions with their own marketing plans. They need to build reasonable scenarios—made up of these potential competitive plans—against which they can test their own marketing strategies. Then, based on their expectations of the most likely scenarios, they can place their bets on the future. In this way, brand managers can take their marketing effectiveness to the next level, because they can act more presciently, and react more quickly and accurately, with much less risk to deliver much higher marketing return on investment (ROI).

Case study 11 (Agent-based modeling and simulation: Consumer packaged goods in North America) illustrates how brand managers can think of the market in terms of how each of the competitors will act, and through this optimize their plans accordingly. Armed with an understanding of how competitors have acted in the past, brand managers can now determine the impact of those same actions on their brands if they were to be repeated under similar circumstances in the future. With this knowledge, brand managers can more accurately assess the risk of their actions in the context of prospective competitive actions.

INDUSTRIAL AND OEM COMPANIES

Ingredient brands and other industrial and original equipment manufacturing (OEM) companies that are marketing, or contemplating marketing, directly to the end-consumer can take advantage of this type of modeling and simulation. Instead of simple shipments data, this type of modeling requires data at the end-consumer level. Otherwise, this type of modeling requires a large number of potential customers, as opposed to end-consumers—as in the case of the electrical equipment provider selling to contractors, and not homeowners—in order to deliver value for the industrial or OEM company. This limitation may make it difficult for an industrial or OEM company to take full advantage of the modeling techniques available to consumer analyzers.

BUSINESS-TO-BUSINESS COMPANIES

Business-to-business marketers have similar limitations to industrial and OEM marketers—they must also market to many businesses in order to be able to take advantage of the tools available to consumer analyzers. Ideally, they would have small- and medium-sized businesses in their target customer sets. This might include shipping companies, such as FedEx and UPS, as well as providers of office supplies, such as 3M and Avery, in which there are many customers and, in the modeled segments, there aren't single customers that might skew the results of the model.

CONSUMER COMPANIES

Consumer marketers are the primary members of the consumer-analyzer group. They typically operate with many consumers and spend heavily on advertising. They can justify the investment in this level of modeling sophistication—where a single share point can mean success or failure for the brand. This category includes those companies making big bets in the marketplace and those that are concerned about the impact of new competitive actions and need to determine their best response.

Smaller consumer companies can also take advantage of this type of marketing-effectiveness analysis; they can use it to battle effectively against their larger competitors. Also, smaller companies operating against considerably larger competitors are making significantly larger relative bets. Just about every category can gain from this type of analysis, whether it is CPG, pharmaceutical, media, and entertainment, or financial services.

CHANNEL COMPANIES

Large consumer-channel marketers—rather like consumer marketers—can gain from becoming consumer analyzers. Department stores, fashion retailers, restaurateurs, and other large consumer-oriented channel marketers can all benefit from using their point-of-sale (POS) information and their knowledge of their consumers to support their strategic decision-making.

OTHER COMPANIES—POLITICAL, CHARITIES, NGOS, GOVERNMENT, BUSINESS-TO-GOVERNMENT

Large political marketers, charities, NGOs, and government marketers would gain in a similar fashion to large consumer marketers. Given the level of spend and the import of the service that these organizations offer to the community, moving to the consumer analyzer level could be critical in delivering the requisite value to their stakeholders.

Even though the desired output can't be measured in terms of revenue, it can often be accurately measured in terms of votes, donations, or recruits. Interim polling data can be used to further refine the model.

The best consumer analyzers can combine all of their consumer and competitive information into a lucid and consistent model of the marketplace. With this model in place, they can run simulations based on their understanding of how each and every aspect of their marketing can drive incremental revenue or results for their cause. They use the model to their advantage by developing scenarios with which to optimize their actions and reactions in order to maximize returns and minimize risk. They know exactly how to launch a new product, enter a new market, and take advantage of word-of-mouth marketing, and they understand what their best response might be to any competitive action.

Many consumer analyzers, however, have a lot of good information but don't know how to act on it. They receive PowerPoint presentations of great findings, but act only partially or inconsistently on them. They're swimming in data, yet still act based on their gut instinct. This is why they need a specific tool, or suite of tools, to be able to pull it all together into one decision-support framework.

Consumer analyzers understand in detail how their consumers act within the Marketing-Effectiveness Framework. They understand:

- How to segment their consumers along different dimensions— whether based on attitudes, behaviors, or lifestyles. In many cases, they build a single segmentation that allows them to gather data across the consumer set in a consistent fashion.
- The ways that each of these segments processes information, building awareness and brand equity
- How the segment's develop utility for products in the category, based on each segment's preference for product and brand attributes and their disutility of price
- How each of these segments consumes products, chooses a channel, and goes shopping

Armed with this information, consumer analyzers are the most sophisticated marketers in determining the ROI of past marketing activities and optimizing their marketing spend in an uncertain, dynamic future.

Projecting the future

Consumer analyzers now have a tool with which they can optimize their marketing, given an uncertain future. But consumer analyzers must minimize their risk of uncertainty by making informed choices about how that future is going to unfold given different potential scenarios. The unknowns fall into four areas, made up of the 3Cs and 1E:

- **Competitive actions**—No marketer can know exactly how a competitor will act or react. But, in many cases, brand managers act with some consistency. When they launch a product, their marketing mix—the 4Ps—follows a pattern. They do certain things, and not others, when they react to a product launch. In order for marketers to make projections about the competitive environment of the future, they must develop scenarios of how the competition will act and react, especially in regards to the 4Ps. The discussion below will add more detail to this key component of optimizing the future in the face of uncertainty.

- **Consumer changes**—Changes in the consumer base are easier to predict. In general, consumer-response behavior remains consistent over a wide range of stimuli. If a model of consumer-response behavior can be built—for example, by using agent-based modeling and simulation based on the Marketing-Effectiveness Framework—then consumer actions over the foreseeable future can be gauged with some predictability. Some elements of the consumer base do change—including how the different segments grow or decline in size—but these can be estimated based on past history. Alternatively, if the business question dictates it, a robust model must be able to project outcomes across a range of potential varying growth rates.

- **Channel actions**—The channel is also reasonably predictable. They may add more outlets, advertise more—or less—or they may change their policies related to manufacturer instore advertising and promotion. The information relating to these changes is usually provided directly from the channel partner through the ongoing relationship between the manufacturer and the trade partner. What might be less predictable is the impact of mergers, acquisitions, or bankruptcies of specific channel partners. If this were the business question, then a model relating to these larger changes would be able to inform the marketer what their best course of action might be.

- **Exogenous factors**—As we've seen, exogenous factors fall into a number of categories. Each of these has an impact on outcomes in the market. For most modeling exercises, we just need to make certain that we have accounted for all of the major impacts of the exogenous factors on consumer-response behavior. If there are significant changes in any one of these factors, a robust model will be able to answer questions such as, "What is the best way to respond to an event like Hurricane Katrina?" For most business questions, it is not necessary to determine beforehand what would happen if a catastrophic event took place. More important to the brand manager is what the best actions are when the unforeseen, extraordinary event has passed.

Because we must understand how competitors act and react in the marketplace in order to improve our marketing, we must put together a framework of potential types of actions that they might take in response to prospective events in the category.

MAKING PROJECTIONS OF POTENTIAL COMPETITIVE ACTIONS AND REACTIONS

Competitors can act, react, or do nothing. They can either enter or exit a market. They can either spend more, less, or about the same. In each of these cases, in order to make projections about the future, we need to look at the range of possibilities and the level of precision necessary in our projections.

- **Small competitors**—Unless small competitors have the wherewithal to spend significantly more than they have in the past, these competitors can, for the most part, be planned for with a low level of specificity. They can be planned for as a group, because together they could represent a significant portion of the share in the category, but individually their actions can be assumed to be the same as past actions at the first level of planning granularity. However, the introduction of new technologies, offering of new attributes or significantly lower prices, and the development of potential market changing channels or communications media, such as social networks, need to be monitored and potentially modeled.
- **Mid-sized and large competitors**—Often these competitors have the wherewithal to deliver significant change to their marketing mix by either spending heavily or not supporting their strategies. Because of this, each of these competitors needs to be modeled individually. Competitors, however, fall into a number of classes: some react very aggressively to changes in the market; some act very aggressively when they launch new products; and others simply act as if they have blinders on. Still others act unpredictably. A review of past history can give some indication of how competitors may act or react. Surprisingly, though, most competitive actions that relate to new product

introductions are inadvertently leaked or made known to the marketplace, often three to six months in advance. This can give ample time to develop strategies to optimize your marketing plans. Depending on where each of your competitors lies in this competitive action matrix, you can develop potential marketing plans for each of these scenarios. Secondly, you may not know exactly how they will act or react, but you know that their actions will fall within a certain range. That is, they will launch a new product with US$10–15 million in support. With a robust consumer-response model you can project what the range of impact might be across this uncertainty and you can determine what your best response should be.

- **New entrants and exits**—These fall into the same categories as those above. Analyzing how potential entrants enter or exit a category can help you predict what their marketing plans might be across a certain range of possibilities. With this information, and a robust model and simulation capability, you can determine what your best response should be across that range.

This area of study is a complex one, but it is also bounded, which makes it tractable. Based on some reasonable estimates, marketers can now begin to look at the future, develop potential scenarios, and optimize across those scenarios. A good starting point—sometimes called a baseline scenario—is often to assume that competitors are going to repeat what they did in the prior year. This is, by the way, what mix modelers assume—statistical methods, system dynamics, and last-touch attribution methods make no accommodation for changes in competitive actions. Once the baseline scenario is set, new scenarios incorporating modifications to the baseline can now be examined. Once that is complete, the marketer can estimate the risks and probabilities associated with each of these new scenarios to minimize risk and optimize results.

By putting all of this together, we can build a series of scenarios with varying levels of certainty:

- **Things we know with reasonable certainty**—Typically these are trends in consumer and channel behavior and growth, as well as exogenous factors. Discontinuities may occur, such as with the passage of a regulation specific to the category or the entry of a channel, but these are variables that can easily be simulated.

- **Things we know with some uncertainty that will have only minor impact, or won't substantially impact, the business question**—This could include competitive behavior of some smaller to larger competitors that we can narrow into a small range of possibilities, based on our knowledge and intuition. The impact of these actions will have little impact on our success.

- **Things that are uncertain, but against which we can make reasonable, educated guesses**—Larger competitors often act in predictable ways. There are four designations describing their potential actions and reactions based on an analysis of past actions:

1. **Blinders**—These competitors act in isolation and appear not to respond to any major competitive thrusts from the top brands in the category.

2. **Reactive**—These competitors generally react in some way to others in the category. They may respond with a copycat product, or otherwise try to subvert the success of your actions.

3. **Proactive**—Proactive competitors also act in the marketplace with innovation and daring. Because marketers can never know exactly what a competitor is going to do, there is always a measure of uncertainty surrounding their actions. However, even within this uncertainty there is some level of certainty. For example, when these competitors launch a new product they often use a standardized formula for their marketing mix. When they launch a new marketing campaign, they also follow a relatively predictable playbook. Lastly, although the exact marketing support may not be known ahead of time, a reasonable guess can be made as to the range of potential investment by the proactive competitor to support a product launch or react to one.

4. **Unpredictable, but bounded**—These competitors act erratically. For these competitors, brand managers have the greatest difficulty determining likely scenarios. A brand manager's best guess, or the prior year's actions, may be good starting points. Other potential actions and reactions can also be tried to determine the level of effect these potential uncertainties might have on our success.

- **Things we can guess with varying levels of certainty over a range of uncertainty**—In the case of proactive competitors the relationship of the various mix elements may be fairly predictable, yet it may be that the level of investment is uncertain. For example, a competitor may respond or react with a certain mix, but the volume of marketing spend may be uncertain. Will the launch investment be at US$10 million or at US$20 million? That it will not be greater than US$20 million or less than US$10 million is reasonably certain. In this case, we need to be able to simulate across the range of potential spend to project the impact of the competitive spend on our market position. Through this study we can then understand what the risk of our response might be across this range of uncertainty. We can bound the results, and test various marketing plans within these bounds of competitive action, in order to optimize our response.

- **Things we don't know—aka, "the failure of imagination"**—When the *Challenger* space shuttle was destroyed during launch, investigators determined that a specific sequence of events took place that ultimately led to the catastrophic failure of the external solid-fuel booster rockets. The particular failure sequence had never been imagined. If the business question is to determine the potential risk of totally unplanned occurrences, then a consumer model based on consumer response to all competitive, channel, and exogenous factors would be the best way to answer the question. However, the brand manager must take solace in the fact that not all catastrophic events can be imagined. Only if the business question warrants it should a brand manager spend time worrying over things that are in the wild reaches of his imagination. In general, because those events are highly unlikely, understanding the things that are more likely will provide significantly higher returns, and reduced risk.

  For most business questions, these category-changing events will not impact how the brand manager and the company are going to make their money. Of course, there is always the possibility of hurricanes, terrorist attacks, fires, earthquakes, and acts of God. If these occur, we need to be able to have a tool in place to help us dig out of the mess after the fact more quickly and more efficiently than the competition. Consumer analyzers have the tools to analyze the possible outcomes of these occurrences, and to recover from them if they ever do occur.

How can marketers improve their consumer analyzing?

Often consumer analyzers have the data, but what they haven't done is to pull the data into one cohesive model spanning the entire Marketing-Effectiveness Framework.

- **Purchase funnel**—Understanding the purchase funnel is critical to success at this level of the continuum. Many consumer analyzers use brand trackers to measure and track brand imagery elements for their brands.
- **Data**—Requirements for data include tracking data for POS promotions and purchase volume, for purchase and shopping behavior by segment, and for awareness and other measures.
- **Tools**—There are many tools and survey methods that provide information to support components of the consumer model described in the Marketing-Effectiveness Framework. These are listed below, but these tools only represent a piece of the analytical puzzle. They don't pull it all together into one cohesive, consumer-centric model. The only tool I've found to do this is called agent-based modeling and simulation. It is also described below.

  o **Latent-class segmentation**—There are many types of segmentation, and defining an appropriate segmentation scheme is critical to making the right decisions at this level of the continuum. One of the segmentation analysis tools is latent-class segmentation, which identifies an optimal clustering of consumers based on the available consumer data.
  o **Conjoint and discrete-choice analysis**— Understanding how consumers make choices can be done through survey methods such as conjoint analysis and discrete-choice modeling. These methods ask consumers to evaluate a series of real and hypothetical products that are defined in terms of their attributes, prices, and brands. Analytical methods determine consumer preferences for these individual attributes—isolating the relative value of each attribute to determine relative utilities derived for the tested products.

○ **System dynamics**—System dynamics tools use a top-down approach to define relationships between actions in the marketplace. They are typically used to develop a model of how marketing communications activities affect consumer purchases.

○ **Test marketing**—Test marketing can be used to test many of the components of the Marketing-Effectiveness Framework. These can be very expensive, but provide good information for the marketer when launching a new product. However, they can be misleading if the competition tries to disrupt the test with marketing tactics of their own.

○ **Agent-based modeling and simulation**—Agent-based modeling and simulation defines simple algorithms or rules for the way individual agents—or virtual consumers—act in the marketplace. Each agent processes information and builds awareness and equity, consumes products, goes shopping, chooses a channel, and makes purchase choices. When taken as a whole, agent-based modeling and simulation delivers a behavior that closely mimics how consumers behave in the real world.

EMERGENT BEHAVIORS AND THE TIPPING POINT[2]

Emergent behaviors come about if individuals act in unplanned ways when they come together in a group. The behavior that emerges out of the combined actions of many individuals can have an enormous impact on revenue. In the marketplace, emergent behaviors often reveal themselves as fads, trends, or price wars. Depending on how consumers respond in a market, their actions can reach a tipping point, and have a dynamic all of their own.

In nature, emergent behavior can be seen in many animals. Cattle on a rampage or ants marching in a straight line between the food source and the nest are great examples of emergent behaviors. There is no single command telling the ants to go directly in a straight line from the nest to the food source, pick up a morsel of food, and bring it back. In fact, they are responding to a series of preprogrammed actions built into their DNA that are leading them to act in this way.

For marketers, the most obvious emergent behavior is market share. There is nothing telling consumers to purchase x% of one brand, y% of another, and z% from a third. Yet the sum of all the consumer responses in the marketplace leads to consumers spreading their purchase choices out amongst all competitive products, which creates market share percentages. There is no store where marketers can buy share. Marketers can only build market share by offering products at certain prices in certain channels with certain messaging that consumers respond to—based on their preferences and shopping behaviors. Market share emerges based on the sum of all actions of all consumers in the marketplace.

The concept of "tipping points" has been popularized by Malcolm Gladwell in his book, *The Tipping Point*, which describes how the combined actions of many individuals can "tip" once they reach a certain critical mass. These inflection points provide marketers with the greatest positive volume impact—if a tipping point takes place in their favor.

Such unexpected outcomes are difficult to predict with traditional modeling tools. The method of "system dynamics" only models relationships that are known in advance; it can provide some insight into the direction of social networking factors, but has difficulty predicting tipping points. Marketing-mix models based on statistical regression models assume the future is like the past, and therefore totally miss the inflection of a tipping point. Agent-based modeling is the only technique that creates a comprehensive model that can effectively reproduce emergent behaviors.

The Marketing-Effectiveness Framework help us to understand these results, and to give marketers the tools they need to have confidence in the results, because it includes all influences in the marketplace—competitors, the channel, products and their attributes, consumers, and external factors.

BECOMING A CONSUMER ANALYZER

Consumer analyzers use an intimate knowledge of their targeted consumers to drive increasing marketing effectiveness. They can look into the past and determine the ROI of prior marketing activities. More importantly, they can look forward into the future and simulate the response from any number of marketing plans across a set of scenarios to optimize their results and reduce their risks. Brand managers can decide what they believe to be the most probable scenario and act accordingly, knowing they have chosen their best path for this scenario. Responses to traditional and nontraditional media can be determined. The market is modeled not by the best statistical fit, but by the simulation of consumer response across all segments, brands, channels, and exogenous factors in the category.

Although there are many ways to model a consumer base, the one most widely used is what I have described in the Marketing-Effectiveness Framework. The five key components are:
- Segmentation
- Information processing and the purchase funnel
- Product choice
- Channel choice
- Consumption and purchase behavior

Many consumer analyzers have developed effective, yet partial, models that include some or all of these components. Only a handful of these analyzers have combined all of these elements into a complete and logical model.

Once the model is complete, the fun can begin. The future can be simulated. "What if" scenarios can be run and market responses can be calculated.

Initial partial steps can include the following studies. Not all of them are required in order to develop a robust and accurate model:
- Behavioral-segmentation studies
- Conjoint or discrete-choice analyses
- Brand-imagery-tracking studies
- Brand-switching studies
- Penetration analysis

With these studies and analyses in place, brand managers can now make significant progress in modeling their markets.

Although there may be other technologies that can combine these studies into one comprehensive, category-wide model, I've found that only agent-based modeling and simulation can deliver a complete model and simulation tool. With this model in place, now marketers can estimate the potential future actions of key competitors and see how their marketing plans stack up. Their marketing plans can be optimized against the most likely scenarios, and they can see increased revenues, profit, and share.

Case study 14 (Agent-based modeling and simulation: Unsweetened tea in Japan) illustrates in detail how a category can be modeled and critical insights gathered about consumer behavior.

To date, I've found only a handful of companies that understand this level of marketing effectiveness. That number will clearly grow as marketers continue their quest for ever-improving tools, analytical methods, and concepts to help them improve their marketing effectiveness. Many marketers already have most of the components necessary to becoming a consumer analyzer. The missing element is a tool to bring it all together. Agent-based modeling and simulation does this, and it will begin to be adopted as marketers continue to move closer and closer to their consumer base, and as they learn what their best options are to act and react in the marketplace.

CASE STUDIES

CASE STUDY 11 — AGENT-BASED MODELING AND SIMULATION: CONSUMER PACKAGED GOODS IN NORTH AMERICA

This case study illustrates the use of agent-based modeling and simulation to support the launch of a new brand into an existing category in the U.S.

BACKGROUND

Consumer packaged-goods companies compete in very dynamic categories. New brands, products, and variants are launched, and lackluster brands and variants are discontinued. With category sizes in the billions of dollars—and marketing budgets in the tens and hundreds of millions of dollars—every share point is hotly contested. Brand managers have enormous data available to them, yet they often resort to gut feel and intuition to make their decisions. Many analytical tools and techniques can provide them with a view of the past and some insight into the next few months, but brand managers must make decisions looking 12, 18, or more months into the future.

Measuring the ROI of past marketing operations is valuable, but predicting ROI into the future for different potential scenarios is critical to improving marketing decision-making and reducing risk.

XYZ Company—a major personal care provider—operates in four categories. It launched a new premium (high priced and high quality) brand into a new category—one in which they had not participated before. The brand manager needed to know what the optimal marketing mix would be for the launch, given a handful of scenarios based primarily on expected competitive response. The category was fragmented, with hundreds of variants and about 20 major brands. Only four of those brands had the financial and marketing power to make radical responses to the launch of a new brand. The remaining brands didn't have the wherewithal to respond with major competitive action that would significantly impair the success of XYZ's launch.

Based on these expectations, the brand manager needed to determine the optimal price in each of the retail channels, and the optimal marketing mix, to launch the product in order to maximize margin through the end of the following year—roughly 20 months. The feature set of the brand variants was already decided and would not change. Neither would the distribution channels—food, drug, mass, and value—change.

SOLUTION AND REQUIRED DATA

The marketing mix and price were optimized with the media budget set at US$35 million to support the launch and sustain the media throughout the rest of the year. A baseline scenario was developed assuming that the competition would exactly repeat their marketing from the prior year. Against this backdrop, scenarios were run to optimize the marketing mix, display, and pricing. With the entry of this brand into the category and the increased overall advertising investments, it was expected that the category would expand slightly, although for simplicity of the model, these effects were ignored.

Data required for an agent-based model includes time-series data for:
- Syndicated POS data across all channels, including price, volume, display, and distribution
- Coupon drop dates, distribution sizes, and redemption value
- PR net effect impressions
- Media spend across all competitors in the category
- Brand imagery

Also included in an agent-based model is static data, such as the intrinsic and extrinsic attributes of the product and brand, as well as consumer preferences for each of these attributes.

As part of the building of scenarios, each of the top four competitors' past marketing actions was analyzed to build a series of likely future actions. One of the competitors—Competitor B—was known to be launching a new brand into the category immediately prior to the XYZ brand launch. A second competitor—Competitor D

—was known to be launching a major new product variant with unknown attributes. Reviewing each of these four competitors' marketing actions over the last four years revealed the following:

- Competitor A was known to defend their brand by pulling forward their marketing media. Based on this assumption, it was estimated that they would do the same for this launch and pull US$10 million in spend out of Q3 and Q4 of the upcoming year, then place it in Q1 and Q2 to precede the launch of these two new brands. Minor pricing actions were also expected, but were determined to be less important and not long lasting. Other marketing elements were analyzed and not expected to change in significant ways. The actual flighting and the spending level were unknown, but it was expected that the spending would range between US$8 million and US$16 million with a "best guess" at US$10 million.

- Competitor B was known to be launching their new brand in February—two months before XYZ's launch in April. Based on launches by Competitor B in other categories, XYZ assume the launch mix would be heavily weighted with TV media, coupons, and display. Although the exact launch spend was not certain, the "best guess" was that this competitor would spend about US$40 million, spread between the launch and support throughout the rest of the year. Overall, it was assumed that they would spend somewhere between US$25 million and US$50 million. It was also assumed that this brand would be a premium brand—as Competitor B had done in other categories— somewhat higher in quality and higher in price.

- Based on analysis of the past four years Competitor C was found to be erratic and chaotic in their marketing; it was not possible to determine any particular flighting or spending expectations. A number of potential assumptions were made, and several scenarios were developed. Marketing spend was estimated to range from US$5 million to US$20 million.

- Analysis of Competitor D's marketing activities showed that, in general, they ignored all the other competitors. Only when they were planning their own launch did their marketing activities change in any meaningful way. It was estimated that they would support their new variant with about US$15 million, but it could be as low as US$5 million and as high as US$25 million.

RESULTS

With these assumptions made several interesting results emerged:

- Competitor A was able to gain market share by pulling their spending forward, but the achieved gains were lost by the decreased spending in the following quarters. This did, however, cost XYZ's brand a projected 0.1 percent share.
- The launch of Competitor B's new brand had the most impact on the category and on XYZ. Projections showed that this launch—depending on the amount of spend—could impact XYZ by anywhere from 0.3 percent to 0.6 percent share. To circumvent this impact, the most beneficial solution was to raise XYZ's price, which could help the brand afford to increase its marketing budget by US$5 million.
- Projections of the impact of Competitor C had some interesting implications for XYZ. At the high end of the range of marketing spend, it could impact XYZ by 0.25 percent. At the low end the impact was under 0.1 percent. Again, raising prices to fund increased marketing spend helped to mitigate this impact on XYZ.
- The launch of Competitor D's new variant had little impact on XYZ. Because this new variant had little overlap with XYZ's assortment, the impact was projected to be less than 0.1 percent.

CHALLENGES, ISSUES, AND OPPORTUNITIES

Determining the impact of past marketing activities can help to improve marketing results in the future. But with a consumer-centric model, brand managers have the best opportunity to look into the future to determine what will work best. Part of this analysis, though, must include the brand team's best guesses and expectations of competitive actions and reactions. Once this is added to the equation, the brand team can now develop potential scenarios with which they can optimize their actions to minimize risk and maximum results.

Only with a clear understanding of potential competitive actions and reactions can brand teams mitigate risks in the future. With modeling and simulation tools at their fingertips, brand managers must now develop formal infrastructures to gather critical competitive information in order to improve their best guesses of potential competitive actions. As their guesses improve, the managers will be able to significantly improve their ability to reduce risk and maximize results.

PROCEDURE

Agent-based models have four basic phases:
1. Gathering, cleansing and transforming the data
2. Calibrating the model such that past results can be replicated by the actions of the virtual consumers—agents. This also includes validation of the calibrated model against a holdout period, and other statistical error validity checks.
3. Development of scenarios for each of the competitors, including potential changes in the consumer base, channel structure, and exogenous factors
4. Analysis of scenario results and optimization of marketing plans. Evaluation of associated levels of risk against expectations for each scenario.

CASE STUDY 12—AGENT-BASED MODELING AND SIMULATION: CARBONATED SOFT DRINKS IN NORTH AFRICA

BACKGROUND

The carbonated soft drink category is one of the most competitive. Many exogenous influences drive volume in the category. For countries in North Africa these include:

- The weather and climate, including both rainfall and temperature
- The political environment and exceptional events, such as boycotts and war
- Religious holidays, such as Ramadan and others
- The economy, such as growth in gross domestic product, population, and tourism

For this modeled North African country, the top five brands represent just less than 80 percent of the unit volume of the 12 major brands in the category. In addition, four major competitive brand launches took place in the last year of the study. Beverage Company A needed to optimize its spend in the category across the brand portfolio, and successfully defend against the new entrants. Success depended on both quantifying interactions among the brands in the portfolio, and accurately projecting the performance of the four new competing brands just launched in the category. The potential success of these new brands and of Beverage Company A's brands, was expected to be significantly affected by a boycott of American brands following American political actions abroad.

SOLUTION AND REQUIRED DATA

Because of the large impact of exogenous variables, monthly data for each of the key influences listed above was required. In addition, tracking data for instore pricing, promotions, and mass media, and other marketing activities, was necessary. This data was used to build an agent-based model allowing simulation of a number of key business questions. These questions concern the impact of a price change on two secondary brands, the marketing mix of the top brand, and the best way to respond to an ongoing boycott of American brands in the country.

Five segments were modeled representing the key channels in this category and geography:
• Hyper- and supermarkets
• Large and mid-sized urban grocery stores
• On-premise, fountain
• Small rural convenience stores
• Small urban grocery stores

Marketing activities in the category included the following, with data available on a monthly basis:
• Distribution percentages by brand and channel
• Monthly media spend by brand, campaign, and media type
• Nonpromoted price by month and channel
• Sales volume by brand and channel
• Special consumer promotions, such as mountain bike sweepstakes and other activities

RESULTS

One of the key outcomes of an agent-based model in a consumer category is the deduced preferences by segment of the various product and brand attributes. This information is critical in supporting decisions that concern the launch of a new brand or product.

With the simulation in place, Beverage Company A learned that consumers would pay more for the two secondary brands—up to 10 percent more—with little impact on volume. This price rise delivered increased profit of over 7 percent.

In addition, it became possible to optimize advertising spend across Beverage Company A's portfolio, which allowed a significant reallocation of investment—shifting away from the flagship brand to the secondary brands. This was determined to have little effect on the flagship brand, but significant net share increases of over 2.5 percent for the secondary brands.

To counteract the impact of the boycott, data showed that advertising should be substantially increased—by over 30 percent. Although this wasn't possible from a budget perspective, the advertising was able to be increased by 8 percent, leading to a substantial increase in volume. The results of the model accurately projected the response to the 8 percent increase in advertising investment. This allowed the brand to increase even further the total advertising investment in the following year. In addition, the model accurately projected the response to TV, radio, and billboards, allowing the brands to shift spending away from TV to radio and billboards.

Finally, the model was able to accurately forecast the expected market share for the four new entrants, informing Beverage Company A on the optimal competitive strategy to defend against this competitive threat.

CHALLENGES, ISSUES, AND OPPORTUNITIES

Challenges in building accurate and predictive models in North Africa have to do with the availability of data. Accurate statistical models typically require weekly data over two or, preferably, three years. If this data were available across the category, the cost would be prohibitive for the size of the market. Models for smaller countries must nevertheless provide actionable results based on available data—whether it is weekly, monthly, quarterly, or annual. Because of its consumer-centric approach, agent-based modeling provides this possibility.

Furthermore, emerging markets face many new brand entrants from existing global brands and new local competitors. Statistical models—because of their exclusive reliance on historical data—cannot say anything about new entrants. Agent-based models, however, are uniquely suited to forecast consumer response to new entrants, because they use historical data to reveal how consumers respond to a wide array of marketing inputs, including sets of inputs that were not seen historically (such as new brands).

PROCEDURE
See the procedure outlined in Case study 11 for developing an agent-based model and simulation.

CASE STUDY 13—SYSTEM DYNAMICS: FAST-MOVING CONSUMER GOODS IN INDIA

This case study illustrates some of the challenges brand managers face in India in markets that are hampered by changing demographics and ecological forces.

India offers unique challenges in both marketing and analytics. Although there are many large cities, over 70 percent of the population live in rural areas and are dependent upon agriculture for their income. There are over 200 million households with 4.5–5 members per household. The channel is made up of up to 90 percent "mom-and-pop" stores where goods are held behind a counter. Only 10 percent of the stores are self-serve grocery stores, whereas in the mom-and-pop stores, goods are requested from the clerk over the counter and a store clerk retrieves them for the shopper.

TV penetration is approximately 119 million homes,[3] covering about 50 percent of the households, with cable connectivity extending to 62 million homes—or about 55 percent of the homes with televisions. For marketers, this means that they must find creative ways to reach the remaining households and shoppers with their marketing messages in order to gain full market coverage.

BACKGROUND
Fast-moving consumer goods (FMCG) offer specific challenges not found with other types of products. Advertising and marketing activities are done throughout the year, based on the season, the launch of a new set of stock keeping units (SKUs), response to competitive actions, and the launch of a new campaign. In India, the detergent category includes brands from the major American and European manufacturers and a number of smaller brands from other multinational and local manufacturers. A typical brand has over 150 SKUs servicing 25,000–30,000 retailers across seven channels. Major variants include regular powder and concentrated (for improved stain removal when handwashing), and a variety of detergents intended for use in washing machines.

In India, where some regions have current and impending water deficiencies, detergent brands must accommodate by offering solutions that can reduce the amount of water required. Women on lower incomes are looking for detergents that require less water to use and to carry, yet still deliver clean clothes. On the other hand, women are not ready to sacrifice the cleanliness of their wash for the ability to reduce water consumption. The laundry detergents must still deliver clean clothes, even if it requires more water. For a premium brand to appeal to this segment in the market, it must offer very clear benefits and yet still be reasonably priced in comparison with the competition. Even though Brand QQQ was competitively priced at two rupees, the consumer perception was that the premium brand afforded a premium price, and it was therefore not attractive to lower-income segments that could still afford the product.

SOLUTION AND REQUIRED DATA
Qualitative and quantitative research was used to understand the issues and the underlying messaging that concerns the need for a water-saving product. Response data was mapped against the extreme water-deficient pockets in the south and west. Further regions were

mapped against regional meteorological data to determine those areas where the benefit and the message would be most widely accepted.

In addition to the local opportunity for low-water-use detergents, the brand needed to leverage existing marketing assets in order to reduce costs in targeting this subsegment of the market. By leveraging the widely recognized advertising creative, the brand was able to deliver a significantly stronger brand message at much lower cost. It delivered an advertising recall of nearly 94 percent of the price message of two rupees per wash. Although the low-income segment was typically hard to reach because of low TV-viewing frequency, TV was nevertheless chosen as the primary media vehicle to insert the message into the marketplace. Other unique media included branded taxis, and both stationary and mobile out-of-home advertising.

Brand-tracking data was correlated against the media investment to determine the effectiveness of the overall marketing.

RESULTS
Penetration in the low-income segment nearly doubled within six months. The brand became the highest growth brand, and it re-emerged as the top brand in the country. It also led the other brands by almost a year in the low-water-use, quick-rinse attribute. In addition, the brand was able to maintain its two rupee pricing. Brand-tracking data showed the level of increased brand association with its key messages.

The increase in brand awareness of the two key messages (price and water savings) in the regions and segments correlated with the increased sales in the region showed that a rupee in advertising delivered 1.8 in increased revenue. Because the pricing and distribution remained relatively constant, these effects were not instrumental in contributing to increased volume. Unfortunately, it was not possible to separate out the overall effect of each of the primary marketing media.

CHALLENGES, ISSUES, AND OPPORTUNITIES

Econometric modeling has not yet taken hold with most brands in India. For a number of reasons—primarily concerning the availability of syndicated weekly data with the right granularity and periodicity—econometric models will be slow to find their way into the marketing analyst's toolbox. Given the constraints on available data, other methods, such as system dynamics, will need to be applied in order to deliver actionable answers.

PROCEDURE

The company was able to track, on a monthly basis, brand imagery, distribution, and media investments both by value and by impressions. Using this monthly data and ignoring changes in distribution and pricing, which were minimal, the impact of media overall was determined.

CASE STUDY 14—AGENT-BASED MODELING AND SIMULATION: UNSWEETENED TEA IN JAPAN

This case study illustrates the use of agent-based modeling to support the launch of a new brand in the unsweetened tea category in Japan.

BACKGROUND

Unsweetened tea is becoming a significant category throughout the world, but in Asia—especially Japan—the category is quite mature. It is available in a number of different packages and sizes, ranging from large one- and two-liter PET plastic containers to cans and small 250 ml paper bottles. In Japan, there are seven major manufacturers delivering 15 brands with over 100 variants, where the top five brands represent over 75 percent of the category volume. The channels for unsweetened tea are similar for most fast-moving consumer goods, including small, medium, and large grocery stores, convenience stores and general markets. In addition, unsweetened tea is also sold through vending machines and on-premise. The primary product attributes include package size, flavor (oolong, green, blended, mineral, and health) and hot versus cold.

Seasonality and the weather are key drivers in demand for unsweetened tea in Japan. Seasonal consumption for hot tea grows by a factor of 10 in winter as temperatures fall. Annual consumption of cold tea, however, far outweighs the sales of hot tea by a factor of 8:1 with relatively little variation in winter versus summer.

The market was becoming increasingly crowded, and that crowding was accentuated by the entry of six new brands into the category during the last three years. Launching a new brand into this category required the right mix of media, price, and distribution. The ABC Tea Company wanted to launch brand NTea and needed to determine the best mix, in terms of price and media, to optimize revenue and share (in yen) over the first 18 months.

SOLUTION AND REQUIRED DATA

A national model was built and developed using agent-based modeling and simulation that covered all of Japan utilizing weekly time-series data by channel for the average POS price paid, percentage distribution, volume in both units and dollars, and media by campaign and channel (radio, magazine, newspaper, and TV). Static data, including product and brand attributes and segment brand preferences, were also employed. Consumer segments were based on age in decades and gender.

Although some conjoint data was available to understand the interaction of brand attribute preference for brand NTea, one result of the modeling process is the deduced preferences for both product and brand attributes by segment across the category. In addition, the modeling process determined how preferences for some product attributes vary based on the weather (hot tea in cold weather and barley flavor in warm weather), whereas others remained constant. Brand-attribute perceptions also varied over time based on media inputs, instore display, packaging, PR, and word-of-mouth. This analysis also showed which product variants would be most in demand in which channels. In addition price elasticities by channel were also determined.

RESULTS

PRICE

Not unusual for most FMCG categories, product choice is first determined by the consumer utility derived by the product attributes—65 percent. In this category, brand is a key driver, with both the short- and long-term value of the brand attributes driving 30 percent of the utility value, whereas relative price represents only 5 percent of the choice. This indicates that the price elasticity for the brands across the category was relatively low. Low price elasticity was due to the fact that most products were priced about the same, with little activity in price promotion. Promotions in this market are oriented more towards contests, limited releases, and special packaging.

With this analysis, the brand was able to improve its launch revenue by increasing its average price in some channels by more than 25 percent over their original plans. Half of the increased expected margin was used to invest back into the media plan.

ATTRIBUTE PREFERENCES

The deduced key brand (extrinsic) attributes and preferences were supported by some recently completed qualitative market research. They included:
- Flavorfulness
- Trustworthiness
- Tea-leaf quality
- Healthfulness

Based on these preferences, the primary focus of the messaging was determined. Regional differences were explored in a second iteration of the model, helping the brand team to determine whether separate messaging needed to be used in southern Japan versus central and northern Japan. Key differences were apparent, but didn't warrant the development of significantly different, regionally based mass media for the launch. It was decided that this should be reconsidered once the main emphasis of the launch was complete.

An analysis of the preferences for the product attributes helped to support the determination of which SKUs should be initially made available. It also helped to determine which SKUs and package sizes would be next in line once the brand had established itself.

COMPETITIVE RESPONSE

Based on analysis of the expected competitive launch responses, it was determined that the top brand, with over 25 percent share, would typically defend their brand with increased media. Assuming that they would respond with an increase of 10 percent in media weight immediately following brand NTea's launch, it was determined that this could potentially impact the success of the launch by about 0.3 percent share. The second largest brand typically reacted to a new brand launch with a temporary reduction in the average price of 10 percent. Because brand NTea was entering the market at a premium, it was determined that this would have little impact on the success of the launch, with a projected impact on brand NTea's volume of less than 0.1 percent.

The largest potential competitive threat came from one of the multinational manufacturers, PC Company, which was rumored to be planning a launch of a Health Tea at roughly the same time as brand NTea's launch. If this launch took place, it was expected to have the largest impact on the success of NTea's launch primarily due to the expected media weight that PC Company would put behind the launch. This new brand launch, if it took place with the expected media weight and projected premium price of 10 percent over the norm, could potentially impact brand NTea's share by anywhere from 0.5 percent to 0.6 percent. With this information, PC Company would be closely watched and, as rumors became fact, the model would be able to assist brand NTea in determining potential responses.

CHALLENGES, ISSUES, AND OPPORTUNITIES
Tracking the competitive response to a brand launch and projecting its impact can provide invaluable insights to the brand team. It can help in improving marketing tactics, reducing risks, and managing internal expectations. This allows the marketer to not only measure the ROI in the past, but also to project marketing ROI into the future.

Availability of data is always a key issue in any modeling effort. This model was built without including sales through vending machines or on-premise. With the addition of these channels into the model, the model can be further enhanced to provide increased insight. As with any model, without specific information available, certain business questions will not be able to be answered.

PROCEDURE
See the procedure outlined in Case study 11 for developing an agent-based model.

ENDNOTES

1. Liam Fahey and Robert M. Randall, *Learning From the Future: Competitive Foresight Scenarios,* (New York: John Wiley & Sons, 1998).

2. Malcolm Gladwell, *The Tipping Point: How Little Things Can Make a Big Difference,* (New York: Back Bay Books, 2002).

3. CII-KPMG Report, "Media penetration in India," *New York Times,* February 2007 in "India's Foremost Television Network— Doordarshan," http://www.diehardindian.com/ntertain/media. htm (accessed January 27, 2008).

BRAND OPTIMIZERS

BRAND-OPTIMIZER CAMEO

This story concerns a major technology company that had been trading on the NASDAQ since it went public in the early 1990s, called CoolCo Technologies, Inc. George—the CEO of CoolCo—had always followed his stock, and it had made continually progressive gains throughout the 1990s until, of course, late 2001 when the technology bust hit. The technology bust showed him, however, that even when the rest of the market crashes, your stock doesn't have to crash—at least not as badly. Granted, he had lost many hundreds of millions of dollars in stock value in the course of a few months, but many other CEOs lost most of their net worth and their jobs.

He had long realized that great marketing not only generates revenue in the short term, it generates brand equity in the long term, and increasing stock value as well. He had always exhorted his marketers to overspend in the key investment communities of New York, Boston, and San Francisco, and it had finally paid off. Not only was the company able to sell product and make a profit, its stock had outperformed just about every other technology stock. He had been employing some sophisticated brand-value modeling services, and they were able to pinpoint the value of his brand and the impact that the company's marketing had on that brand value. Now, when he went in for the acquisition of a new technology company, he was able to understand the brand-value dynamics of the target company and make astute purchases based on the relative value of his brand and that of the acquisition target.

Point #1: Marketing can also deliver tangible, long-term, incremental value that can be realized on the stock market.

There are many factors that go into the value of an acquisition target. One driver of value is the cumulative effect of all prior marketing. Marketing builds value in the mind of the consumer, which leads to long-term purchases and increased value of the brand when the brand is to be sold or merged, or is about to acquire another brand.

BRAND OPTIMIZERS

Often overlooked by marketers is the fact that marketing activities drive more than just incremental revenue, profit, or market share. They also drive incremental share value.[1] Certainly, the share price is driven by many factors, but if we control for those factors, we can also determine that one of the underlying drivers of share value is the success in marketing. Given that this is the case—in order to determine the complete value of marketing activities—not only must the tangible results of increased revenue, profit, cash flow, or share be measured, but the indirect effects of increasing share price on the stock market must also be taken into consideration.

If marketing is able to market more effectively—squeezing more revenue and profit out of every dollar of marketing investment—the company is going to grow faster. With this incremental growth impetus, it is highly likely that the company can grow faster than the competition, and marketing effectiveness becomes a competitive weapon in itself. Marketing is now able to turn a key corporate process into a competitive advantage, leading to higher growth and—all other things being equal—higher stock value. Marketing is no longer an expense: it is an investment just like any other machine or technology that requires monitoring, maintenance, and careful scrutiny.

As the company grows faster than the competition, consumers begin to notice. Employees and prospective employees notice. Suppliers notice. And thus, the brand value increases more than the growth alone would indicate. With a higher brand value come opportunities—prospective employees may be more willing to work for a known company. The company is able to hire better employees at the same, or lower, wages. Suppliers may be more willing to extend credit. Consumers complain less. An increasing brand value—regardless of whether or not it is derived from improved marketing—has many spin-off values. These results are measurable and demonstrable, although a detailed discussion of this topic is outside the scope of this book. However, it is worth noting that there is currently research underway to develop a mechanism that can capture this value and determine how improved brand value correlates with a higher stock price.[2]

BRAND OPTIMIZERS

Brand optimizers are companies that manage the improvement of their marketing effectiveness to optimize not only their revenue, profit, and market share, but also their brand and stock value. They make strategic decisions across their entire brand portfolio to steer investments toward those brands that are able to provide higher returns, and away from those that can't. They are looking to buy, sell, or merge with another company or brand, and need to understand the relative value of their own brand or brands, as well as the target company's brands. Brand values at this level represent a combination of many factors, one of which is the accumulated impact of all prior marketing done to support the brand. A finely tuned marketing-effectiveness engine drives strategic advantage by allowing the brand to grow faster than the competition. Strategic advantage drives brand growth, which in turn drives stock value growth.

Armed with this information, the brand manager or the company CEO is able to make strategic decisions about the proper make-up and investments between brands in the corporate portfolio. These brand assets are typically the most valuable assets in the company's portfolio. Although there are many underlying complexities, at its simplest the brand value can be construed as the difference between book value and market value. It is further complicated when a corporation has many brands, each driving incremental share value among investors. In addition, complexities arise when marketing investments are made that influence the investment analysts. Additional, local advertising in New York or Los Angeles is a good example of investor-focused advertising. This advertising is intended to catch the eye of the investment community in order to have the brand appear bigger than it is.

Brand investment decisions across the portfolio are critical to the success of the company. If one brand is not performing—and there are few prospects for improved performance—while other brands are clamoring for more investment, then savvy corporate executives must shift investments toward those brands that can deliver better corporate return.

Only with an understanding of the intrinsic brand value can these decisions be made, and they are at a different level than those decisions surrounding the valuation of one marketing activity's impact on incremental revenue, profit, or share.

BECOMING A BRAND OPTIMIZER

There are a number of providers of this type of analysis[3] that can help the C-suite determine the value of the impact of marketing investments on shareholder value. For more information on this fascinating topic, please visit their respective Web sites.

A recent study, "Brands Matter: An Empirical Investigation of Brand-Building Activities and the Creation of Shareholder Value"[4] illustrates how top brands outperform by over 6% per year over seven years. The study compared the stock market performance of 111 strong-brand companies versus a similar investment in the stock market overall over the period 1994–2000. This analysis used the Fama French model, which takes into account an investment's riskiness when evaluating financial performance of the firm. This is a critical result when CMOs need to justify their investments in the long-term brand value, as opposed to short-term incremental revenue. Another key finding of this study showed that companies developing strong brands also reduced their exposure to risk. Not only do strong brands reduce the financial risks consumers face in making the wrong purchase decision, but this study links strong brands with the reduction in corporate financial risk.

In a similar fashion, the value of a brand becomes apparent when a brand is acquired. If the tangible and intangible assets are calculated and measured, the value of the brand and its associated marketing can be determined. For example, the purchase by Proctor & Gamble of the Gillette Company for US$53.4 billion illustrates how the value of the brand weighs in on the final purchase price of the acquisition. According to Brand Finance "Global Intangible Tracker 2006"[5] the value of the brands was measured at US$25.6 billion, whereas the value of tangible assets was US$4.5 billion, patents and technology US$2.7 billion, and customer relationships US$1.4 billion. The value of the brands represented just under 50 percent of the purchase price of the company.

For the merger of AOL and Time-Warner in 2000, the deal was structured as an acquisition of Time-Warner. In this case Brand Finance determined that of the US$147 billion purchase price, US$10 billion was attributable to "Brands and Trademarks."

Each of these studies indicates how marketing was able to drive incremental revenue *and* incremental long-term brand value. The methodologies behind these calculations are complex and are outside the scope of this book, but they clearly represent the next frontier of measuring and predicting improved marketing effectiveness.

ENDNOTES

1. Share value is different from share price, because the price can be artificially influenced through stock splits, dividends, and many other factors. It is the difference in share value that is affected by improved marketing effectiveness.

2. See the Emory Marketing Institute, formerly the Emory Brand Institute, http://www.emorymi.com.

3. See Corebrand, Interbrand, Brand Finance, among others

4. Thomas J. Madden, Frank Fehle, and Susan Fournier, "Brands Matter: An Empirical Investigation of Brand-Building Activities and

the Creation of Shareholder Value," 2002, http://www.hbs.edu/research/facpubs/workingpapers/papers2/0102/02-098. pdf.

5. Brand Finance, "Global Intangible Tracker 2006," p.12, http://www.brandfinance.com/Uploads/pdfs/Global%20Intangible%20Tracker%202006.pdf (accessed December, 2007).

SECTION 4
THE MARKETING-EFFECTIVENESS CULTURE

IT'S TIME TO JUST GET STARTED!

THE MARKETING-EFFECTIVENESS CULTURE

The marketing-effectiveness culture brings the Marketing-Effectiveness Framework and continuum together to drive increased revenue for every marketing dollar invested. It has three primary dimensions:
- Measurement and metrics
- Modeling and simulation
- Management and monitoring

The marketing-effectiveness culture is made up of the consistent and appropriate application of these three dimensions in many areas, including:
- Across all of the customer-facing elements of the organization

- For each brand, product, or service offering
- For each region or geography
- At the appropriate level along the marketing-effectiveness continuum
- Striving for continuous improvement
- Optimizing the acquisition of appropriate, valid, and objective data
- Utilizing valid and appropriate analytic methodologies

The marketing-effectiveness culture must support and enhance the execution of improvements within the constraints of the brand strategy.

MEASUREMENT AND METRICS

There are many things that can't be measured that, if they were measured, could deliver significant improvements in our marketing activities. In an ideal world, at every moment we would know exactly what our consumers were thinking and what would most likely influence them to purchase our products. In reality, however, we can only survey our consumers for their expressed opinions, measure their purchases, and perform other indirect measurements. Improved marketing effectiveness has to start by determining what to measure, how to measure

> **❝Not everything that can be counted counts, and not everything that counts can be counted.❞**
>
> —Albert Einstein

it, how often to measure it, and at what level of specificity. The definition of metrics specific to your marketing is critical in making certain that you can achieve improved marketing effectiveness.

- **Measurement of data at the consumer touchpoint—** Developing a culture of measurement at the appropriate points in the purchase funnel is critical to improving marketing effectiveness. There are often many hurdles that make it difficult to acquire the data necessary to improve marketing effectiveness. In many categories, the channel is reluctant to provide transactional data at the point of purchase. To overcome these obstacles, it may be necessary to find other means of approximating the required data at the point-of-sale (POS). Data collection shouldn't only include POS data, but also consumer satisfaction data, awareness and brand-value data, and many other types of data at different levels:

o **At the appropriate brand, product, or service and geographic level**—For smaller brands, products, and geographic regions, it may not be cost-effective to acquire data specific to that brand. However, it may be possible to piggyback on data collection efforts done for the larger brands to gain synergistic effects for the cost of the data collection.

o **At the appropriate level in the marketing-effectiveness continuum**—As the organization defines its appropriate level in the continuum—or plans its move up the continuum—investment in metrics can be prioritized based on this objective. It may not make sense for a military contractor to gather sales data at a daily level, but it may make sense for an Internet gambling site to monitor its Web advertising by time of day and day of week.

Activity trackers might focus their data collection efforts only on their marketing actions, whereas campaign measurers will endeavor to capture results across each of the 4Ps. Mix modelers, on the other hand, typically require marketing activities and sales in a time series, and may require key competitive marketing actions as well. Consumer analyzers require not only time-series data, but also consumer awareness, preference, and other competitive information across the category in order to effectively model their markets. Brand optimizers need similar information to consumer analyzers, but must also acquire the appropriate stock and operational data for competitors in the category or categories.

Unfortunately, the data collection expense must be tempered by the value of the decision that will result from the investment. If the cost of the data is greater than the value of the underlying business decision, then alternative means must be employed to either gather the data or to support the decision-making process.

MODELING AND SIMULATION

The types of modeling and simulation done to determine marketing effectiveness can be critical to determining the best tactics that a marketer can take to improve marketing effectiveness. At the time of writing, there are many different classes of modeling that solve different marketing questions. Many have been discussed in earlier chapters. Below are a few and their purposes:

- **Marketing-mix modeling**—to gauge the effectiveness of marketing across the mix in relatively static environments
- **Yield management**—to improve marketing and operations in order to garner the highest prices and maintain and achieve near 100 percent utilization
- **Discrete-choice modeling**—to support decisions concerning new product offerings, pricing, and messaging to specific segments
- **Latent-class segmentation**—to uncover latent segments so that it is possible to answer more sophisticated segmentation questions
- **Agent-based modeling and simulation**—to drive increased marketing effectiveness and reduce business risk in dynamic markets
- **Neural nets, decision-tree analysis**—to improve direct marketing results

MANAGEMENT AND MONITORING

Marketing scorecards and dashboards can be invaluable in gauging the success of the marketing department by providing up-to-the-minute status reports of ongoing marketing activities. They can present financial volume data, brand–tracking data, competitive data, and other consumer-tracking data to provide marketing managers with the information they need—when they need it—to make important, ongoing, mid-course corrections. In this way, in almost real time, they can take advantage of actions that are working, and discontinue those that aren't. And, finally, scorecards and dashboards give the marketer a set of information to help them make certain that their marketing spend will help the company to meet their sales and profit targets. Key aspects of managing and monitoring marketing effectiveness include:

- **Consumer touchpoints**—The Marketing-Effectiveness Culture must span customer touchpoints, including sales, marketing, and service. It must take into account actions at each level in the channel, ranging from original equipment manufacturers (OEMs) and distributors to retail and others. It must also take into account the marketing plans by media type, the timing of those investments, and the dollars and internal personnel associated with them in order to make certain that each of these investments are coordinated and delivering on their expectations.

- **Objectives based budgeting**—Budgeting is a big component of a successful marketing-effectiveness culture in terms of marketing management. Just as we segment our consumer base, as marketers we must segment our marketing investments.

> 66 You've got to be very careful if you don't know where you are going because you might not get there. 99
>
> —Yogi Berra—

The marketing budget is planned based on objectives along a number of key dimensions:

CUSTOMER

In companies with a one-to-one relationship with their customer base, marketers can target their spending in six different subdimensions. By building a budget along these subdimensions, marketers can build a bottom-up budget based on clear, achievable, and measurable outcomes:

- **New consumer acquisition**—Marketing targeted at winning new consumers
- **Up-selling and cross-selling to existing consumers**—Marketing targeted at selling additional or premium products and services to existing customers
- **Churn mitigation**—Marketing to reduce the level of churn after customers have indicated their desire to discontinue their service. For example, after a negative customer satisfaction incident, many service providers may offer a few months of free service in order to maintain and win back these customers' loyalty.
- **Win-back marketing**—Marketing to customers previously lost to the competition

- **Brand advertising**—Marketing not specifically tied to any of the other mentioned customer-oriented marketing activities. Brand advertising is done specifically to build the value of the brand, as opposed to having some kind of call-to-action. It typically covers equally all subdimensions of customer-oriented marketing, although this may vary by industry and competitor.
- **Experimental marketing**—Marketing activities executed with the purpose of trying new marketing media and ideas. Experimental marketing has no specific goal in mind, other than to see if a medium can deliver better response than existing media. Some companies dedicate a very small percentage of their budget to experimental marketing. Others use a 70/20/10 approach,[1] where 70 percent of the budget is spent on proven successful marketing activities, 20 percent is spent on marketing activities that are known to be successful, but have a new angle to them, and 10 percent of the marketing activities are very different to any other previous activities.

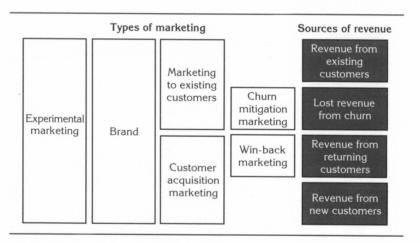

Figure 12.1:   Objective-based marketing budgeting

PRODUCT

In a similar vein, marketers must look at how to target their marketing to support the launch of new products without cannibalizing revenues of existing products. In addition, they sometimes need to invest marketing dollars to clean out inventory and clear the shelves of discontinued products in order to make way for new products.

CHANNEL

Channels are often being grown, supported, or discontinued. Although channel marketing often already has a line item in the budget, the funds to support the addition of new channel partners, or the discontinuation of old partners, are sometimes missing.

COMPETITOR

Sometimes, marketers must invest in less-than-desired results in order to block a competitor from having access to a particular medium or position in the marketplace. This could be the prime location at a trade show or the sponsorship of a one-of-a-kind baseball stadium.

The marketing, sales, and service teams must divide their activities and budgets across each of these dimensions and subdimensions in a coordinated fashion to help the company meet its revenue and profit objectives. In many instances, little effort is required to maintain existing accounts, due to contract terms or high short-term switching costs. Often the existence of up-selling or cross-selling offers can be enough to maintain a healthy existing consumer relationship.

SHARE OF WALLET

One nuance of customer-oriented budgeting is marketing to increase share of wallet. Once the account is won, you may only have won a partial share of their wallet. That is, the consumer is spending more in your category, but they are spending that share with your competitors. Additional marketing can be undertaken to increase your share in that spend.

INFRASTRUCTURE SPENDING

Expenditures falling into the "got-to-be-there" or "can't be in business without it" category are more controversial. These include the annual industry trade show. Often the sales team complains, "If we aren't there, consumers and suppliers will think we aren't in the market anymore." These expenses are typically funded out of the marketing budget and can include not only the "can't be in the business without it" expenses, but also industry association fees, or annual trademark and copyright licensing fees.

Included in these controversial marketing budget items are brochures and sales collateral. The sales team could probably sell the product without them, but with them they are significantly more effective. The brochures and collateral lead to shorter sales cycles and higher post-sale consumer satisfaction. To tie these to any specific customer-oriented budget line item, however, may be difficult. Often these fall into the marketing infrastructure line item.

RISK[2]

Every line item in the marketing budget has an associated risk. Similar to investments in the stock market, those marketing activities with higher risk and uncertainty should be expected to deliver a higher return. Those with more certain returns and lower risk should be allowed, and expected, to deliver lower returns.

One reason why the CEO of business-to-business (B2B) companies with no marketing-effectiveness scores would rather invest in sales—where he or she can quickly review quota attainment—than marketing is that the risk and uncertainty of investing in sales in usually lower. Thus the risk associated with specific media and marketing objectives needs to be considered when building the budget. After all, if your bonus is based on meeting objectives, where would you rather invest your bonus, in lower risk activities or in higher risk activities?

An example of a high-risk marketing activity might include an appearance at a major industry trade show that takes place only once a year. This is typically higher risk than an e-mail campaign that can be run with relatively short planning and response time.

Low-risk activities might also include investments in the sales team or telemarketing activities—depending on the industry. High-risk activities might include brand advertising on television in a business-to-business market. On the other hand, direct-response television advertising in a consumer market may be considered as low risk.

MEASUREMENT

For many of the very successful consumer companies that operate in highly dynamic markets, investments in measuring the effectiveness of marketing and in research in general range from 3 to 7 percent of the budget—and sometimes even higher.

Sadly, a majority of marketers invest zero, or next to zero, to measure their marketing effectiveness. Unless they are willing to bite the bullet and invest in measurement and analytics, it will be extremely difficult, if not impossible, for them to improve their marketing effectiveness and meet objectives.

Other key aspects of management and monitoring include managing agencies, marketing asset management, marketing innovation, marketing process workflow, campaign management, personnel, and reporting. Although these aren't part of the topic of this book, they also represent key opportunities to improve the marketing-effectiveness culture.

CHALLENGES IN MOVING UP THE MARKETING-EFFECTIVENESS CONTINUUM

After having trained, spoken with, or consulted with thousands of marketers on the topic of marketing effectiveness, I've found certain characteristics of companies that challenge or enhance their ability to move up the marketing-effectiveness continuum. It is up to each company to work through these challenges and take advantage of these opportunities in order to drive more revenue, profit, and share from their marketing efforts. These companies either realize that they need to improve their marketing effectiveness, and actively do so, or they have organizational or other obstacles that hinder them in their quest. Marketers must recognize these challenges and overcome them. Here a few that I've encountered repeatedly in the marketplace:

- **Organizational values or lack thereof**—Some companies are quite content not knowing how successful their marketing is. They can be very large companies or very small companies, business-to-business companies, or consumer companies with well-known brands. In some cases, they may try to differentiate themselves solely through their creative quality, and fear that measurement might hinder that creativity. When confronted with the lack of measurement, they usually respond, "The company is profitable. It's growing at a steady rate and continues to beat growth expectations. Why change a good thing?" Or, "Metrics are too risky. We believe in the quality and ability of our creative to drive growth, and we don't want metrics to hem in our creativity."

Companies like this will not change until there is a strong impetus to do so. Either there must be a few bad consecutive quarters, or the CEO or CFO must begin to demand it.

- **International subsidiaries of major companies**—Both consumer and business-to-business companies often fall into this category. The current revenue—or the future revenue opportunity—might be small enough in certain smaller countries that it may never be able to afford the cost of complete and accurate measurement. This is especially true for smaller country operations of major consumer companies, and may be true for operations in larger countries if the penetration is still low. Marketers must look for ways to minimize the cost of investing in a marketing-effectiveness culture in these countries, or try to leverage the infrastructure in larger countries in order to make components of the marketing-effectiveness culture available to smaller countries at a reasonable, marginal cost.

- **Small product lines of major companies**—This applies to both consumer and business-to-business companies in which the size of a specific product line may not justify the expense of implementing sophisticated marketing-effectiveness techniques. Rather like small international subsidiaries, often this problem can be mitigated if a company has a large product line that can afford sophisticated measurement. In this case, hopefully there is enough overlap with a smaller product line that the marginal cost of metrics for the smaller product line is in line with the smaller product line's revenue opportunity.

- **Sales-driven companies**—These are companies in which the sales team is the primary driver of revenue, and in which the marketing function is seen just as support to sales. This also includes businesses in which the sales function is more business-development oriented in nature. Many small and mid-sized companies fall into this category. The marketing function includes simple brochure development and proposal writing, but little lead generation, and it is often led by the owner's executive assistant. Examples of companies in this area include consulting firms, ad agencies, and other services firms, especially those with long sales cycles and those that are very relationship-oriented. In contrast, the sales function is usually heavily measured with monthly quota-setting and attainment tracking. Because the personal-selling function is usually well defined and tracked, these companies should be classified as campaign measurers.

Clearly tracking the activities of the personal-selling function can be very beneficial for these companies. Using interim metrics, such as the number of cold calls, sales visits, second visits, proposals, or sales presentations per week, can help these companies to improve the management of their sales function.

In some cases, the marketing function—not including personal selling—may not be measured at all. In this case, there is a lot of opportunity for the marketing function to improve its marketing effectiveness through the tracking of activities and the measurement of those activities. As discussed above, instead of using revenue as the success metric in the marketing department, it may be more advantageous to use leads generated of a certain quality as the success metric. Depending on their company's size, marketers armed with this information may be able to use analytic tools in order to measure the results from their marketing efforts, improve their mix, and understand their customers.

- **Marketing sophistication**—Many times, especially in small businesses, marketing is directed from an executive who did not have formal marketing training as part of their education. A formal understanding of the marketing function is not, therefore, available within the management team. They may simply not know that there are measurement techniques that can help them to improve the success in their marketing. Hopefully, this book will begin to provide them with the stimulus to seek out ways to improve their marketing. Examples include owner-operated companies, such as an engineering firm managed by the owner—an engineer that has learned marketing through the school of hard knocks. Law firms and accounting firms also fall into this category.

Engineers track the progress of specific development projects, and lawyers and accountants track their time spent with specific clients in order to improve the operations of their businesses. Similarly, tracking their marketing activities with critical success metrics in a structured fashion can go a long way in helping these business managers to improve their marketing effectiveness.

- **Resource constrained**—These companies believe they don't have the time, or they don't want to sacrifice the budget, to measure and analyze marketing effectiveness. This comes up in all sizes of companies, more often than not. Managers feel that their precious marketing budgets are too small to sacrifice a portion to determine what works and what doesn't. They would rather not sacrifice any of their marketing activities in order to fund the metrics for all the rest of their activities. These managers believe that the opportunity cost of lead or revenue generation is too high. They believe that the incremental value and knowledge gained through measurement and analysis will not improve the results of the remaining activities enough to justify the sacrificed portion of the marketing budget. They would be willing to invest money, time, and effort, but only if it comes out of someone else's budget.

  Typical returns on implementing effective marketing metrics are between 10 and 20 percent increased revenue. If the cost of metrics is significantly less than the associated incremental contribution margin that could be generated, then there is no reason not to invest in systems to track marketing activities. How much is 10 to 20 percent more revenue worth to you?

- **Startups and new categories**—Startups have little or no market history to determine what might or might not work. The company or category has no history of marketing effectiveness, or the company may be early enough in its initial sales cycles that tracking activities across the entire marketing mix is perceived to be of little value. One or two big deals, either at the channel level or at the consumer level, will go a long way in meeting or exceeding investors' expectations. The company has yet to reach the critical mass in its revenue generation where solid conclusions can be made across all marketing activities.

  In categories where marketing has a green field of opportunity, the value of each new consumer can be determined and tracked back to a specific marketing activity. This is especially true when the value of a customer can be determined based on specific demographics or 14 "firmographics." Putting the right metrics in place early on can help significantly as the category and product take off.

In addition, while the company is in startup mode the incremental cost of tracking marketing activities is relatively small. It is always better to put systems in place early on, rather than trying to change processes later.

- **"Marketing never worked before, but we need to try something"**—Often the spending in these companies is so low that the company can never break through the noise of all the other marketing in the environment. And, to make matters worse, the company often cuts the program before it has even a slight chance of delivering results. This is especially true for small consumer businesses that sell high-ticket items, such as home repair and renovation. It is precisely this herky-jerky type of marketing that doesn't allow the company to ever get traction in the marketplace. When marketing is done infrequently, irregularly, and inconsistently throughout the year, it can seem impossible to assume that measurement can help. However, it is in just this case that marketing metrics can help determine the impact of any program so that it can be repeated, and repeated with continued and growing success. Marketers must first, however, carefully scrutinize their success metrics and work diligently toward implementing programs that will drive that success.

- **Companies in regulated or formerly regulated industries**—Companies that had their marketing function regulated, such as doctors, law firms, and public accounting firms, had little need to do any marketing per se. They were artificially limited in marketing activities, so there was little need to measure those activities. Now that some of the regulations on marketing have loosened, they have made initial steps toward developing and executing various marketing activities. They now need to take their marketing to the next level by building a marketing-effectiveness culture within their organizations.

Publicly regulated utilities—in which revenues and expenses are tightly controlled and monitored by a public regulating authority—often have only a moderate desire to measure their marketing in order to improve it. Growing the business at low cost and risk through marketing activities is secondary to the goals set forth by the regulating authority. In addition, because many of them have a monopoly in their geographies, often their marketing is designed to drive their brand value in order to improve their ability to obtain construction approval for power plants, towers, or rights of way—if and when the time comes. This type of marketing—similar to cause marketing—is often required to smooth the way to battle against the "not in my backyard" negative outcry as they begin the approval process for plant construction.

Success metrics need to be oriented toward the top of the funnel so that these companies can maintain a positive image with their target audience.

- **Categories with strong seasonal sales**—Companies with strong seasonal sales include farm and seed suppliers, toy manufacturers, or swimsuit providers. The goal of marketing in these industries is more about predicting demand for the season, building to that prediction, and selling everything that gets produced. Sophisticated modeling and analytic tools and techniques are now available to help these companies to improve their seasonal purchases, and to match their marketing investments to make certain they don't generate more demand than the produced quantity of products.

Each of these classifications provides challenges and opportunities for marketers to measure and improve their marketing effectiveness. In every case, however, gathering tracking data of their activities will go a long way toward helping them to grasp what works and what doesn't. In many cases, if the ability to tie revenue to specific marketing activities may not be possible, then it is often possible to tie marketing activities to an interim success metric, such as lead and lead quality, clicks-through, incremental purchase intent, or incremental brand awareness. Once these activities are tracked in a systematic way, marketers can begin to analyze these data sources and start linking marketing activities to corporate success.

IMPLEMENTING THE MARKETING-EFFECTIVENESS CULTURE

Moving along the marketing-effectiveness continuum in order to implement a marketing-effectiveness culture takes time, organizational energy, systems, and money. Just as you can't eat an elephant all in one bite, so, too, can't you leap to the top of the marketing-effectiveness continuum all in one step. In order to deliver continuously improving marketing effectiveness, the marketing department and the other customer-facing departments in the organization must strive for continuous improvement. It must become part of their DNA otherwise, improvement will stagnate.

The initial steps to improving marketing effectiveness must be in line with the strategy for the brand and the strategic objectives of the company. Once the marketing-effectiveness plan has been developed, priorities can be defined by product, region, growth expectations, the next big bet, profit margin, or channel and then the process can begin.

Improved marketing effectiveness, however, will only truly succeed when there is a line item in the budget specifically designated to support the three elements of the marketing-effectiveness culture. Until this happens, investments in improved marketing effectiveness are still an afterthought and will not be executed with the consistency and dedication they deserve.

ENDNOTES

1. Rex Briggs and Greg Stuart, *What Sticks: Why Most Advertising Fails and How to Guarantee Yours Succeeds*, (Chicago: Kaplan, 2006).

2. Guy R. Powell, *Return on Marketing Investment: Demand More From Your Marketing and Sales Investments*, (Atlanta: RPI Press 2003).

CONCLUSION: PUT MARKETING ON THE CRITICAL PATH TO SUCCESS

MARKETING EFFECTIVENESS AND YOU

As we have seen, improving marketing effectiveness and implementing a marketing-effectiveness culture in your organization has an enormous value for the company. It can deliver more revenue, more strategic advantage, and increased stock value. But it also has an enormous benefit for you. Whether it is someone in the C-suite looking to earn larger bonuses, mid-level managers looking to increase their salaries and responsibilities, or lower level marketers looking to prove themselves to the organization, everyone can gain enormous personal value from improving marketing effectiveness. One of the key questions for most marketers is, "How can marketing effectiveness improve my resume, help me secure a raise, or make certain that I win a new job?"

THE VALUE OF MARKETING EFFECTIVENESS

"If your business were sold today, would you be prepared to defend your marketing expenditures with strong evidence of marketing effectiveness?"[1]

When Bill Donnel, former CMO of GE Insurance Solutions, was told that his company was being acquired, he was successfully able to defend his position and his marketing organization. Upon completion of the acquisition, it was the acquiring company's marketing team that was downsized and integrated into Bill Donnel's organization, and Bill Donnel became the CMO of the acquiring organization.

Simply put, marketers who can illustrate how their actions lead to clearly measurable improved results earn more than those that can't. They stay in their positions longer, and keep their jobs when the company is bought or merged.

IMPROVED MARKETING EFFECTIVENESS REQUIRES SUPPORT THROUGHOUT THE COMPANY

Successful companies have systems and processes in place to make certain every department in the company can deliver the most from their efforts. Operations are optimized and accounting is systematized. The sales function and call centers work well. The marketing department can no longer operate in a silo devoid of accountability. For the marketing department to deliver improved effectiveness, it needs the participation of the entire company, working together in order to drive the company to its optimum performance:

- **The financial team** must provide the right numbers: costs, margins, net present values, and cash discount rates. At times they will be called upon to help with analytics.
- **The IT department** must provide the technical infrastructure: timely, consistent, robust, and searchable repositories of both hard data, such as sale figures and shipment volumes, and soft data, such as primary or secondary market research.
- **The sales team** must help gather data from obstreperous channel partners, and they must allow marketers access to primary consumers in order to get first-hand knowledge of the consumers' mindset and operating environment.
- **Operations** must trust in the data. Skepticism is always healthy, but operations must be able to deliver without delay.

In order for a complete transition to a culture of improving marketing effectiveness to occur, the CEO must be the number one champion of this new marketing-effectiveness culture. Marketing needs complete commitment in order to keep the other departments on board. Without it, CMOs' tenures will continue to shorten, companies will fail to meet their numbers, and bonuses will be curtailed. The stock value will not grow.

CEOs—and the rest of the executive team—must no longer think of marketing as only delivering pretty graphics and catchy slogans. It must not be thought of as an expense in the budget. Instead, marketing must be considered the central investment in delivering incremental revenue and profit, and increased bonuses. The CEO must demand that marketing invest in the right tools, data, personnel, and training.

PUT MARKETING ON THE CRITICAL PATH TO SUCCESS

In company after company, my experience shows this:

Marketers shoot from the hip.

They make decisions in the dark.

They have no data on which to base their decisions, and there are few analytics being done!

Why? Because unlike the rest of the company, most marketing departments don't have an infrastructure and culture of measurement and continuous improvement built into their DNA. When total quality management and continuous improvement were implemented in the rest of the company, they took a U-turn at the door to the marketing department. Marketing must now, too, embrace these critical aspects of operational efficiency and effectiveness.

In order for this to happen, a culture of measurement, metrics, continuous improvement, and accountability is a must.

Take a look at your priorities. What do you want to achieve from your marketing department? Do you have clear goals to improve its effectiveness? Does your marketing team know the steps to achieve them?

If not, get ready to begin your journey, but most important of all, just get started![2]

Act now to put marketing on the critical path to corporate success.

ENDNOTES

1. Paraphrased from Bill Donnel, CMO, GE Insurance Solutions, The Conference on Marketing, March, 2006.

2. For a free lesson, just contact the author at: www.Marketing-Calculator.com.

BIBLIOGRAPHY

BOOKS

Ambler, Tim. *Marketing and the Bottom Line: The New Metrics of Corporate Wealth.* London: Prentice Hall, 2000.

Barwise, Patrick, and Sean Meehan. *Simply Better: Winning and Keeping Customers by Delivering What Matters Most.* Boston: Harvard Business School Press, 2004.

Briggs, Rex, and Greg Stuart. *What Sticks: Why Most Advertising Fails and How to Guarantee Yours Succeeds.* Chicago: Kaplan, 2006.

Carroll, Brian. *Lead Generation for the Complex Sale: Boost the Quality and Quantity of Leads to Increase Your ROI.* New York: McGraw-Hill, 2006.

Davis, John. *Measuring Marketing: 103 Key Metrics Every Marketer Needs.* Singapore: John Wiley & Sons (Asia) Pte. Ltd., 2007.

Eechambadi, Naras. *High Performance Marketing: Bringing Method to the Madness of Marketing.* New York: Kaplan 2005.

Fahey, Liam, and Robert M Randall. *Learning From the Future: Competitive Foresight Scenarios.* New York: John Wiley & Sons, 1998.

Farris, Paul W., Neil T. Bendle, Philip E. Pfeifer, and David J. Reibstein *Marketing Metrics: 50+ Metrics Every Executive Should Master.* New Jersey: Wharton School Publishing, 2006.

Gladwell, Malcolm. *The Tipping Point: How Little Things Can Make a Big Difference.* New York: Back Bay Books, 2002.

Heinlein, Robert A. *The Moon is a Harsh Mistress.* New York: Orb Books, 1997.

Hellman, Karl, and Ardis Burst. *The Customer Learning Curve: Creating Profits From Marketing Chaos.* Ohio: Thomson South-Western, 2003.

Kaplan Thaler, Linda, Robin Koval, and Delia Marshall. *Bang! Getting Your Message Heard in a Noisy World.* New York: Doubleday, 2003.

Kotler, Philip. *Marketing Insights from A to Z: 80 Concepts Every Manager Needs to Know.* Hoboken, NJ: John Wiley & Sons, 2003.

Lenskold, James D. *Marketing ROI: The Path to Campaign, Customer, and Corporate Profitability.* New York: McGraw-Hill, 2003.

MacFarlane, Hugh. *The Leaky Funnel: Earn More Customers by Aligning Sales and Marketing to the Way Businesses Buy.* Richmond, VA: Bookman Media Pty Limited, 2004.

Miller, Scott. *How to Experiment Your Way to Increased Web Sales Using Split Testing and Taguchi Optimization.* The ConversionLab.com, July, 2006, http://www.conversionlab.com.

Moore, Geoffrey A. *Crossing the Chasm.* rev.ed., New York: Harper Collins, 2002.

Moore, Geoffrey A. *Inside the Tornado: Marketing Strategies from Silicon Valley's Cutting Edge.* New York: HarperCollins, 1995.

Peppers, Don and Martha Rogers. *The One to One Manager: Real-World Lessons in Customer Relationship Management.* New York: Doubleday, 2001.

Porter, Michael E. *Competitive Advantage: Creating and Sustaining Superior Performance.* New York: Free Press, 1998.

Powell, Guy R. *Return on Marketing Investment: Demand More From Your Marketing and Sales Investments.* Atlanta: RPI Press, 2003.

Reichheld, Frederick F., and Thomas Teal. *The Loyalty Effect: The Hidden Force Behind Growth, Profits, and Lasting Value.* Boston: Harvard Business School Press, 2001.

Reichheld, Fred. *The Ultimate Question: Driving Good Profits and True Growth.* Boston: Harvard Business School Press, 2006.

Silverstein, Michael J., and Neil Fiske. *Trading Up: The New American Luxury.* New York: Portfolio, 2003.

Sutton, Dave, and Tom Klein *Enterprise Marketing Management: The New Science of Marketing Management.* Hoboken, NJ: John Wiley & Sons, 2003.

Williamson, David, Peter Cooke, Wyn Jenkins, and Keith Michael Moreton. *Strategic Management and Business Analysis.* Oxford: Butterworth-Heinemann, 2003.

Young, Roy, A., Allen Weiss, and Davis Stewart. *Marketing Champions: Practical Strategies for Improving Marketing's Power, Influence, and Business Impact.* Hoboken, NJ: New Jersey: John Wiley & Sons, 2006.

MAGAZINES, ARTICLES, AND WEB SITES

Abinanti, Lawson. "Messages that Matter, The 3C's of Successful Positioning – Part III: Get your channel involved in positioning. It's good for both of you." http://www.messagesthatmatter. com/columns/3Cs_of_Positioning_Part_III.pdf (accessed January 27, 2008).

Brand Finance, "Global Intangible Tracker 2006," p.12, http:// www.brandfinance.com/Uploads/pdfs/Global%20Intangible%2 0Tracker%202006. pdf (accessed December, 2007).

Brown, Pete. "Stella Artois: Reassuringly Profitable." IPA Effectiveness Awards 2000.

Bunker, Jeannie, Vice President, Marketing Execution and Customer Analytics, quoted in Scott van Camp, "Top Technology Brands are the Leading Early Adopters of MPM," *Channel Advisor,* http://www.channeladvisornews.com/story.cfm?item=18, (accessed January 27, 2008).

CII-KPMG Report. "Media penetration in India." *New York Times,* February 2007 in http://www.diehardindian.com/ntertain/media. htm (accessed January 27, 2008).

Funderstanding. "Right Brain vs. Left Brain." http://www. funderstanding.com/right_left_brain.cfm, (accessed June 24, 2007).

Halliday, Jean. "Madison+Vine: Pontiac gets major mileage out of $8 million 'Oprah' deal; Giveaway a PR victory, leads to follow-up shows." *Advertising Age,* September, 2004.

Madden, Thomas J., Frank Fehle, and Susan Fournier. "Brands Matter: An Empirical Investigation of Brand-Building Activities and the Creation of Shareholder Value." 2002, http://www. hbs.edu/research/facpubs/workingpapers/papers2/0102/ 02-098.pdf.

McCarthy, Michael. , "Miller Lite's 'Catfight' ad angers some viewers." *USA TODAY.* http://www.usatoday.com/money/advertising/2003-01-14-beer_x.htm (accessed January 15, 2003).

Nielsen Media, Glossary of Media Terms, http://www. nielsenmedia.com/glossary/terms/G/G.html (accessed January 27, 2008).

Puri, Gurdeep, and Janey Bullivant. "Kellogg's Real Fruit Winders: Unwinding the Effects of an Integrated Campaign." IPA Effectiveness Awards 2002.

Spencer, Stuart, "No Respect From CEOs, Short-Term Thinking Depress Tenure." *AdAge.com,* June 19, 2006.

Trade Ideas, http://www.trade-ideas.com/Glossary/R-Squared. html (accessed January, 2007).

CONFERENCES

Choo, Darren, StarHub, "Branding and business positioning" Paper presented at the Marketing Analytics Conference, Singapore, November, 2007.

Chung, Shirley, SmarTone-Vodafone, "Sustainable growth momentum through innovative Marketing" Paper presented at the Marketing Analytics Conference, Singapore, November, 2007.

Donnel, Bill, CMO, GE Insurance Solutions. Paper presented at the Conference on Marketing, Las Vegas, March, 2006.

Manns, Tim, SingTel Optus Australia, "Importance Of Analytics In CRM Infrastructure" Paper presented at the Marketing Analytics Conference, Singapore, November, 2007.

Or, Anna, Cathay Pacific Airways, "Online/Offline Marketing Analytics" Paper presented at the Marketing Analytics Conference, Singapore, November, 2007.

Puri, Aseem, Hindustan Unilever, "Case study: Building breakthrough brands and innovation mixes via analytics" Paper presented at the Marketing Analytics Conference, Singapore, November, 2007.

LIST OF FIGURES AND TABLES

FIGURES

TABLES